GUIDE TO
AMERICAN HISTORICAL MANUSCRIPTS
IN THE HUNTINGTON LIBRARY

GUIDE TO
AMERICAN HISTORICAL
MANUSCRIPTS
IN THE
HUNTINGTON LIBRARY

HUNTINGTON LIBRARY

1979

The preparation of this work was made possible through a grant from the Research Collections Program of the National Endowment for the Humanities

FOREWORD

The two foundations of the Huntington Library are its rare books, prints, maps, music scores, ephemera, and reference books (all together, about one million items); and its manuscripts (consisting of about five million pieces). To provide fuller access to its manuscripts, the Huntington began in 1975 a six-year project to survey its holdings, summarize groups of related manuscripts and single pieces of major significance, and then publish the results in a four-part *Guide to Manuscripts in the Huntington Library*.

The first two parts of the *Guide*, on American historical manuscripts and on literary manuscripts, are scheduled for publication in 1979. The final two parts, on British historical manuscripts and on medieval and renaissance manuscripts, will be published in 1981. When the entire project is completed, scholars around the world will have comprehensive information about one of the great repositories of research materials on British and American history and literature. We hope that these *Guides* will assist them in their scholarly investigation, whether they decide to request photocopies by mail and then work at home, or whether they choose to travel to San Marino and explore at first hand the riches of the Huntington.

The preparation of the *Guides* has been assisted generously by grants from the National Endowment for the Humanities.

DANIEL H. WOODWARD
LIBRARIAN

PREFACE

This guide provides for the first time a comprehensive description of the Huntington Library's research collections of American historical manuscripts, which number over one and one half million, date from the sixteenth to the twentieth century, and cover virtually every aspect of American society and culture, with a special concentration on Revolutionary, Civil War, and Western history. Three earlier guides, "Huntington Library Collections" (*Huntington Library Bulletin* no. 1, 1931), Norma B. Cuthbert's "American Manuscript Collections in the Huntington Library" (*Huntington Library Lists* no. 5, 1941), and John C. Parish's "California Books and Manuscripts in the Huntington Library" (*Huntington Library Bulletin*, no. 7, 1935), are selective in coverage, outdated, and long out of print. The present guide is designed to make readily available current information about the Library's holdings and to familiarize scholars with the scope of the collections.

For each collection of forty or more pieces processed before September 1975, and for selected notable individual manuscripts not attached to any specific collection, the following information is provided:

1. Name, with birth and death dates, of the originator or central figure of the collection.
2. Size of the collection; range of dates of manuscripts.
3. Biographical sketch of the central figure of the collection, with greater emphasis placed on information not readily available elsewhere. Thus a relatively obscure man will receive fuller treatment here (when possible) than a

prominent figure already covered in standard reference sources.

4. Subject matter of the collection.
5. List of all significant persons represented in the collection by five or more letters, manuscripts, or documents. "Significant" here means that the figure is included in one or more of the standard biographical dictionaries or that he is otherwise important for the study of his historical period. It should be noted that a prominent figure represented by less than five pieces in each of several collections will not appear in this guide, although the Library may hold altogether a large number of his manuscripts.
6. Brief physical description of the items in the collection, including the presence of letters, documents, manuscripts, maps, photographs, printed material, and ephemera, and the number of bound volumes, if any.
7. Provenance.
8. Bibliography of further descriptions of the collection and of works in which substantial portions of the manuscripts have been printed. No attempt has been made to list all works based on the collections.

The *Guide to American Historical Manuscripts in the Huntington Library* was compiled and edited under the supervision of Mary Robertson, Associate Curator of Manuscripts, with special help from Jean F. Preston, former Curator of Manuscripts, who planned the project. Major contributions were made by Virginia Rust, Curator of Manuscripts, and Dorothy Popp. Specialists who wrote entries include Bruce Henry, Harriet McLoone, and Valerie Franco. Further editorial assistance was provided by Edwin H. Carpenter, Jane Evans, and Betty Leigh Merrell. The index was compiled by Bruce Henry.

GUIDE TO
AMERICAN HISTORICAL MANUSCRIPTS
IN THE HUNTINGTON LIBRARY

ABBOT, GEORGE JACOB (fl. 1860–70)
373 pieces, 1780–1946

George Jacob Abbot, member of a prominent family of New England educators, and friend of Edward Everett Hale and Daniel Webster, served as American consul to Sheffield, England, after 1865 and compiled in 1856 a book of regulations for other consuls. Relatives by marriage included the four New England families of Emery, Gilman, Nicholas, and Throop, whose papers form the remainder of the collection.

Subject matter: primarily the activities of Abbot and the five interrelated families, particularly strong in the period from 1830 to 1880, when letters between Abbot, Hale, and Edward Everett provide commentaries on a wide range of current events; John Taylor Gilman (1753–1828), financier and Federalist politician who was twice governor of New Hampshire.

Significant persons: Edward Everett HALE (6)

Physical description: letters and documents, with ephemera (including newspaper clippings and a volume of printer's proofs), and some photographs.

Source: purchased from J. I. Fraser, 1959, with the exception of one letter and two photographs which were a gift of John D. Seelye, 1963.

ABERCROMBY, JAMES (1706–81)
approximately 1000 pieces, 1674–1787, mostly 1758

James Abercromby, British general, was a native of Banffshire, Scotland. He entered the army as a youth and rose to the rank of major general in 1756. In that year, through the influence of his friend the Earl of Loudoun, Abercromby was made second in command to Loudoun in North America. When Loudoun was recalled in 1758, Abercromby succeeded him. Abercromby's failure to capture Fort Ticonderoga led to his replacement in 1759 by Jeffery Amherst, the conqueror of Louisbourg.

Subject matter: the 1758 campaign of the British army in North America during the Seven Years' War, specifically: the embargo on colonial shipping, the fall of Fort William Henry, the surrender of Louisbourg, the expedition against Fort Ticonderoga, activities on the Mohawk River and at the Oneida Carrying Place, the conquest of Fort Frontenac (Cadaraqui), John Forbes's expedition against Fort Duquesne, British use of and relations with the Indians, the internal affairs of the British army, and the recall of Abercromby; also, the genealogy of Abercromby.

Significant persons: James ABERCROMBY (446), Jeffery AMHERST (9), John APPY (28), John BRADSTREET (10), James DE LANCY (28), William DENNY (18), John FORBES (25), Sir William JOHNSON (29), Charles LAWRENCE (15), William Henry LYTTELTON (10), James Gabriel MONTRESSOR (12), William PITT, 1st Earl of Chatham (20), Thomas POWNALL (36), John STANWIX (22), Pierre RIGAUD, Marquis de VAUDREUIL-CAVAGNAL (10).

Physical description: letters, documents (reports, memorials, returns, etc.); a few manuscripts (e.g., journal of Christian Frederick Post).

Source: purchased from Lathrop C. Harper, 1923.

Bibliography: letters of John Forbes are printed in *Writings of General John Forbes,* ed. Alfred P. James (Menasha, Wis.: The Collegiate Press, 1938).

ABERCROMBY, JAMES (fl. 1739–75)
An Examination of the Acts of Parliament Relative to the Trade and Government of Our American Colonies. Also the Different Constitutions of Government in the Colonies Considered (1752)
MS. volume 177 pp.

De Jure et Gubernatione Colonarium; or, An Inquiry into the Nature and Rights of Colonies, Ancient and Modern (1775)
MS. volume 216 pp.

A tract intended to refute the arguments of the American Revolutionaries.

ADAIR, DOUGLASS GREYBILL (1912–68)
approximately 10,000 pieces 1946–68

Douglass Adair, historian and editor, won his doctorate from Yale in 1943. From 1936 to 1938 he was a research assistant with the Social Security Board, which he left to join the faculty of Yale as an instructor in 1939. He went to Princeton as an instructor in 1941 and to the College of William and Mary in 1943. He was managing editor of the *William and Mary Quarterly* from 1946 to 1955, when he became professor of history at Claremont Graduate School. He specialized in early American history, particularly intellectual and constitutional history.

Subject matter: eighteenth-century American social-intellectual history; teaching; academic and professional affairs; the Claremont colleges; Adair's personal affairs to a very limited extent. Strongest for the years after 1960.

Significant persons: Douglass Greybill ADAIR (578), Julian Parks BOYD (13), Lyman Henry BUTTERFIELD (7), Lester Jesse CAPPON (10), Martin DIAMOND (8), Edmund Sears MORGAN (7), Allan NEVINS (7), John Adolph SCHUTZ (12), Clifford Kenyon SHIPTON (7).

Physical description: letters, documents, including research notes, and manuscripts.

Source: gift of Virginia Adair, 1969 and 1975.

Bibliography: Adair's most important writings are published in *Fame and the Founding Fathers. Essays by Douglass Adair,* ed. Trevor Colbourn (New York: W. W. Norton and Co., 1974).

ADAMS, PHINEHAS (1726–79)
approximately 200 pieces, 1759–1911

Phinehas Adams of Lisbon, New London county, Connecticut, married Lydia Fitch in 1751. His son Phinehas Adams, born about 1762, married Lydia Bishop and was succeeded in turn by still a third Phinehas Adams, born in 1796. In this third generation the family moved from Connecticut to Ohio, where in the course of the nineteenth century they married into the Bennett and Bingham families.

Subject matter: personal and business affairs of the Adamses and their relatives, chiefly concerning land transactions; everyday life in Ohio in the middle of the nineteenth century; genealogy.

Physical description: documents (including Connecticut and Ohio land deeds), letters, manuscripts, 1 map, 4 photographs, and several printed items.

Source: gift of Miss Fannie M. Adams, a direct descendant of the above Phinehas, June, 1939.

ADAMS & COMPANY
750 pieces, 1851<–ca.85

Adams & Company was a California branch of the eastern express firm of Adams & Company, founded in Boston in 1840. Successful throughout the state in the express and banking business, it was run by Daniel Hale Haskell and Isaiah Churchill Woods, with Adams as a special partner. The company closed down when the financial crisis of February, 1855 forced it into receivership and numerous legal problems followed.

Subject matter: chiefly the years following the failure of Adams & Co. (1855–63), especially as they affected Alfred A. Cohen, appointed first receiver of the company; Cohen's business and legal associations (1864–84) with the Central Pacific Railroad Co.; 1876 trial, Central Pacific Railroad Co. vs. Alfred A. Cohen.

Significant persons: Alfred A. COHEN (40), Augustus G. RICHARDSON (9), Isaiah Churchill WOODS (19).

Physical description: letters and documents (including 8 scrapbooks and 2 volumes of transcripts).

Source: purchased from Edwin Grabhorn, April, 1941, and January, 1945.

AGUINALDO Y FAMY, EMILIO (ca.1869–1964)
63 pieces, 1883–99

Emilio Aguinaldo y Famy was a Filipino who led the insurrection against Spain, and later the fight for independence against the U.S., until his capture in 1901 and his consequent oath of allegiance to the U.S.

Subject matter: the Philippine military campaigns against Spain and the U.S. in the fight for independence; the revolutionary government of the Philippines, mainly in the years 1898–99, with the exception of four documents for the period 1883–89.

Physical description: documents (military orders, instructions, appointments, legal papers, all in Spanish and Tagalog.

Source: acquired from Walter C. Wyman, March, 1921.

ALBERNI, PEDRO DE (1747–1802)
148 pieces, 1789–93

Pedro de Alberni, born in Spain, was a military leader in Nayarit, Mexico, from about 1774 until 1789, when he was sent as commander of the Catalonian Volunteers to the garrison at Nootka. The expedition, led by Juan Francisco de la Bodega y Quadra, was sent by the Viceroy of Mexico, Count of Revilla Gigedo, to give protection from the Russians and British to the Spanish possessions on the west coast of what is now Vancouver Island, British Columbia. Later, Alberni was appointed commandant of San Francisco from 1796–1800 and of Monterey from 1801–02.

Subject matter: the outfitting of Pedro Alberni's expedition at San Blas, Mexico, in 1789 and 1790; the occupation of his troops at Nootka, and their return to San Blas in 1792.

Significant persons: Pedro de ALBERNI (16), Juan Francisco de la BODEGA Y QUADRA (10), Manuel Antonio FLORES (8), Juan Vicente de GÜEMES PACHECO, Conde de Revilla Gigedo (63), Antonio VILLAURRUTIA Y SALCEDO (17).

Physical description: letters and documents in 1 bound volume (in Spanish).

Source: purchased from E. Eberstadt, April, 1923.

ALEXANDER, DAVID B. (1818–99?)
100 pieces, 1847–1906

David B. Alexander purchased property and settled in Los Angeles in 1884, after having visited California in 1870 and 1882. In his youth he had traveled widely, worked in the Ohio River trade, and developed business investments in Kentucky, Illinois, and Nebraska.

Subject matter: mainly Alexander's purchase, during the "boom of the eighties" in Southern California, of property in the area of Fort, Main, Fifth, and Spring Streets (where the Alexandria Hotel was built) in central Los Angeles, as well as a portion of Rancho Muscupiabe in San Bernardino County and lands in Lincoln, Nebraska (1855–94); business regarding Rancho Muscupiabe, between Alexander and his partner Samuel W. Little.

Physical description: letters (including 1 volume), documents, and 2 photographs.

Source: gift of Mrs. Richard A. Hartley, December, 1957.

ALLEN, WILLIAM HENRY (1784–1813)
92 pieces, 1800–38

William Henry Allen, U.S. naval officer and son of General William Allen, was born in Providence, Rhode Island, in 1784. He was appointed midshipman in the U.S. Navy in 1800 and served on the "George Washington," "John Adams," "Congress," and "Constitution," before joining, as a third lieutenant, the "Chesapeake" shortly before its surrender to the British ship "Leopard" in 1807. Allen was appointed first lieutenant of the "United States" in 1809, and given command of the sloop "Argus" in 1813. He was badly wounded in an action with the British brig "Pelican" later that year, and died in a British prison.

Subject matter: American naval affairs 1800–13, including the Tripolitan War and the "Chesapeake Affair"; the life and career of a junior naval officer; family life and affairs of Allen's father, sister Sarah (Allen) Rhodes, and other relatives, 1813–38; Allen's logbook for parts of the years 1807–08.

Physical description: letters, with a few documents.

Source: acquired from A. S. W. Rosenbach before 1927.

Bibliography: Allen's letters to his father and sister have been published in the *Huntington Library Quarterly*, 1, nos. 1–2 (1937–38).

AMERICAN INDIAN FILE
328 pieces, 1634–1913

This is a general file of miscellaneous pieces and four small groups of papers concerning Indians east of the Mississippi River. The transfer of land from Indians to whites (described in deeds, surveys, and treaties) is the main subject of the file, which also contains information on military and political affairs, negotiations, and Indian ethnology, primarily between 1780 and 1850. Tribes belonging to the Iroquoian language family, including the Cherokees, are the most fully represented, but tribes in the Algonquian family, especially in the Great Lakes region, are also covered. Other items include Harmen M.

van den Bogaert's "Memorial of the Principal Events that happened during a Journey to the 'Maquas' and 'Sinnikins' Indians" (1634–35) and Franz Hölzhuber's drawings of Indian clothing in *Costüm-Bilder waffen und Geräthshaften einiger Indianestaine im Nordwesten America* (1856–60).

The four small groups include 78 pieces from the files of Jasper Parrish, U.S. agent to the Six Nations, 1804–28; 26 pieces from the files of Henry Rowe Schoolcraft, ethnologist and U.S. agent to the tribes around Lake Superior, 1822–38; 18 pieces from the files of George Boyd, U.S. agent in Michigan, 1816–46; and 8 pieces from the files of Pierce Mason Butler, U.S. agent to the Cherokees, 1843–44.

Although this file is open to new acquisitions, no additions have been made in recent years.

Significant persons: Pierce Mason BUTLER (6), Thomas Loraine McKENNEY (9), Henry Rowe SCHOOLCRAFT (11).

Physical description: mostly documents, with some letters, manuscripts, and drawings.

Sources: purchased from Walter C. Wyman and others about 1920.

Bibliography: Harmen M. van den Bogaert, "Memorial of the Principal Events that happened during a Journey to the 'Maquas' and 'Sinnikins' Indians," in J. Franklin Jameson, ed., *Narratives of New Netherland, 1609–1664* (New York: Scribner and Sons, 1909), 137–62, wrongly attributed to Arendt van Corlear; John Ridge, "The Cherokee War Path. Written by John Ridge . . . as Narrated by the Cherokee Warrior of Arkansas, John Smith," ed. Carolyn T. Foreman, in *Chronicles of Oklahoma*, 9 (1931), 233–63. Ten of the treaties have been published in volume two of Charles J. Kappler, *Indian Affairs*, 2nd ed. (Washington: Government Printing Office, 1904).

ANDERSON, RICHARD CLOUGH (1788–1826)
approximately 1865 pieces, 1781–1892

Richard Clough Anderson, statesman and diplomat, was born in Louisville, Kentucky, to Richard Clough Anderson (1750–1826), a Virginia Revolutionary officer, and Elizabeth Clark, sister of George Rogers Clark. After studying law under St. George Tucker, he opened a practice in Louisville. He held a seat in the state House of Representatives from 1812 to 1816 and again from 1821 to 1823, when he chaired the Committee on Public Lands. From 1817 to 1821 he served in the U.S. Congress, where he distinguished himself as an advocate of Latin-American independence. President Monroe appointed him minister plenipotentiary to La Gran Colombia in 1823, a post he held until his death.

Subject matter: the Anderson family, particularly R. C. Anderson, Jr. and his wife Elizabeth, but also his father and brothers Charles, Robert (of Ft. Sumter fame), and Larz; the Clark and Gwathmey families; real estate transactions, legislation, and speculation in Kentucky; Louisville and Kentucky politics and some national politics; relations between Colombia and the U.S.; antislavery sentiment; the Civil War; Ohio politics and government, especially during the Civil War.

Significant persons: Richard Clough ANDERSON, father (59), Richard Clough ANDERSON, son (63), Robert ANDERSON (26), Charles ANDERSON (85), Larz ANDERSON (56), John Jordan CRITTENDEN (16), John SHERMAN (10).

Physical description: chiefly letters, with some documents.

Source: purchased from Zeitlin and Ver Brugge, 1976.

ANDERSON FAMILY COLLECTION
approximately 775 pieces, 1776–1948

Richard Clough Anderson, Sr. (1750–1826), soldier and surveyor, was born in Virginia and served as an officer in the Revolutionary War. In 1783 he was appointed surveyor general to divide western Virginia lands. The father of 6 sons, including Richard Clough Anderson, Jr. (1788–1826) (q.v.), Robert, and William Marshall, his home in Louisville, Kentucky became famous for its hospitality.

Robert Anderson (1805–71), Union soldier, was a graduate of West Point in 1825. He served in the Mexican War and the Civil War, and was in command of the defense of Fort Sumter when it was attacked by the Confederates.

William Marshall Anderson (1807–81), lawyer and adventurer, studied law with his brother, and was admitted to the Kentucky bar in 1832. In 1834, in order to regain his health, he joined the Sublette fur-trading party on a trip to the Far West. After his return home, the Anderson family was converted to Catholicism. William, converted only after a period of intense study, was afterwards often involved in religious controversy. He became interested in archaeology, especially mound builders, and in the fine arts and natural history. In 1865–66, Anderson made a trip to Mexico to search for a place for the establishment of a Confederate colony, but was unsuccessful. He returned to Ohio where he lived until his death in 1881.

Subject matter: the Anderson family, centering about William Marshall Anderson, mainly for the period 1838–1938; including the Catholic Church and its financial involvement in Ohio; bounty land grants to Virginia Revolutionary soldiers; the northwest United States in 1835; land grants, litigation, and politics in Ohio; archaeological mounds; Mexico, 1865; and civil engineering (1900–38); also William Marshall Anderson's diaries, including his trips to the Rocky Mountains (1834) and to Mexico (1865–66).

Significant persons: Robert ANDERSON (8), Lyman Copeland DRAPER (7), Don PIATT (13).

Physical description: letters (including 2 letterbooks), manuscripts (including 14 diaries, 1 commonplace book, 1 volume of reminiscences, and 1 memorandum book), documents (including 4 account books and 1 address book), 1 volume of notes and clippings, 26 photographs, and 1 photograph album.

Source: acquired by purchase and gift from various persons, 1954–66.

Bibliography: the diaries of William Marshall Anderson have been published in William Marshall Anderson, *The Rocky Mountain Journals of William Marshall Anderson,* ed. Dale L. Morgan and Eleanor T. Harris (San Marino: Huntington Library, 1967).

ANDRÉ, JOHN (1751–80)
[Journal] (1777–78)
Autograph MS. volume 117 pp.

Relates the operations of the British and American armies from June 1777 to November 1778. Contains forty-four ink and color maps. Published as the *Journal of John André,* ed. Henry Cabot Lodge (Boston: Bibliophile Society, 1903).

ANONYMOUS
Derrotero General del Mar del Sur. [atlas of maps of West Coast of the New World from Mexico to the Straits of Magel-

lan, later copied for the English by William Hack (q.v.)]
(1669)
MS. 1 volume Atlas of 149 charts

ANONYMOUS
[Diary of a German soldier in the First Ansbach Regiment in
the American Revolution] (1777–81)
Autograph MS. volume 278 pp.

Text in German. Relates a Hessian soldier's experiences in the
American Revolution from recruitment in Germany through
the surrender at Yorktown.

ANONYMOUS
[Diary of an Officer on Board the Spanish Warship "La Eu-
ropa"] (1738–42)
Autograph MS. volume 159 pp.

Text in Spanish. The ship was attached to Don Antonio Spi-
nola's squadron in the West Indies and includes an account
of the Spanish expedition against Georgia in 1742.

ANONYMOUS
A Journal from New England to Cape Breton and also during
. . . [the siege of Louisbourg] (1745)
MS. volume 96 pp.

Kept by a soldier in the fourth regiment of Massachusetts
militia between March 23 and October 6, 1745. Published in
Louis E. DeForest, ed., *Louisbourg Journals 1745* (New York:

Society of Colonial Wars in the State of New York, 1932), pp. 1–54.

ANTHONY FAMILY COLLECTION
162 pieces, 1844–1945

Various members of Susan (Brownell) Anthony's (1820–1906) family were active nineteenth- and early twentieth-century reformers, but she stood out among them. Although early involved in the temperance and anti-slavery movements, her main concern became woman suffrage. Most of her time was spent in lecturing and campaigning. She was also an officer in the National Woman Suffrage Association and the National American Woman Suffrage Association.

Subject matter: family affairs and woman suffrage activities; the Battle of Osawatamie; ideas about populism, racism, religion.

Physical description: mostly letters with some manuscripts. Includes 4 large letterbooks of Joseph Anthony, 3 loose-leaf binders of typed copies of Susan B. Anthony letters in other collections, an autograph speech of Susan B. Anthony, and a manuscript of "A Trip to the Bahama Islands" by Joseph Anthony.

Source: gift of Susan B. Anthony Memorial Committee, 1944–53.

ANTI-MASONIC PARTY IN MASSACHUSETTS
51 pieces, 1829–34

The Anti-Masonic party began in western New York in 1826–27, in Massachusetts and other neighboring states by 1828, and held a national convention in Baltimore, Maryland, in 1831, and nominated a presidential candidate for the 1832 elections. Thereafter the party quickly declined in power, and in Massachusetts was virtually dead by 1835.

Subject matter: minutes and reports of Anti-Masonic party meetings, lists of names, bills and receipts for expenses, and other miscellaneous papers.

Physical description: chiefly documents, with a few letters.

Source: purchased from the Anderson Galleries, 1919.

ANZA, JUAN BAUTISTA DE (1735–88)

Diario de la Rutta y Operaciones que Yo, el Infrascripto Capit[a]n de Cavalleria del Real Presidio de Tubac, en la Provincia de Sonora practico, en solicitud, de abrir comunicacion de d[ic]ha Provincia a la California Septemtrional, por los Rios Gila y Colorado, a cuia expedicion soy comisionado por el Ex[celentisi]mo Señor Theniente General D[o]n Antonio Maria Bucareli y Ursua, Virrey, Governador y Capittan General de la Nueba España, como consta de su Superior Orden de Diez y siete de Septiembre de mil Settecientos setenta y tres años. (January 8–May 27, 1774)
contemporary copy MS. 1 volume 56 leaves

Text in Spanish.

APPLETON-FOSTER COLLECTION
73 pieces, 1717–1897

The Appleton family of Massachusetts and the Foster family of Portsmouth, New Hampshire, were related through the marriage of Mary Appleton to John Welch Foster in 1824. Mrs.

Foster's mother, Sarah (Greenleaf) Appleton Haven (d. 1838) married, first, in 1780, Dr. Nathaniel Walker Appleton (d. 1795), a Boston physician, and second, ca.1815, Joseph Haven of Portsmouth, a first cousin of her first husband. The families were active in the Unitarian church.

Subject matter: primarily family affairs; social life and customs of New England society and family life; some references to the War of 1812 and to the activities of the Unitarian church in New England and Baltimore. Strongest for the period 1797–1849.

Physical description: chiefly letters, with ephemera.

Source: purchased from Mrs. Patricia Dykstra, 1957.

ARAM, JOSEPH (ca.1810–ca.98)
90 pieces, 1835–1912

Joseph Aram, pioneer resident of Santa Clara County, came to California with his family from Illinois in 1846. He served as a captain in the Mexican War, as a delegate to the first California Constitutional Convention, and as a member of the first state legislature. He established the first tree nursery in San Jose, where he lived from 1849 to 1898.

Subject matter: Joseph Aram; his son Eugene W. Aram, who practiced law and became state senator; his son-in-law, Peter Y. Cool, Methodist preacher in the mining country (1851–52); pioneering in California before and during the gold rush; and the Methodist Episcopal Church in California (1850–ca.1912).

Physical description: letters and manuscripts (including 1 journal).

Source: purchased from Edwin Grabhorn, January, 1945.

Bibliography: the Journal of Peter Y. Cool is published in *The Pacific Historian,* 10, no. 3 (1966): 19–42.

ARCHER, KATE RENNIE (AITKEN) (1863–1960?)
approximately 400 pieces, 1932–60

Kate Rennie (Aitken) Archer, California poet and teacher, and daughter of San Francisco artist Robert Aitken, taught poetry at the St. Rose Academy in San Rafael, California.

Subject matter: manuscripts of poetry and correspondence with persons in Western literary circles.

Physical description: letters, manuscripts, and a scrapbook of clippings.

Source: gift of Mrs. Kate Rennie Archer, 1950–60.

ARNOLD, RALPH (1875–1961)
approximately 200,000 pieces, 1836–1961

Ralph Arnold, a leading consulting geologist and petroleum engineer in the United States, came to Pasadena from Iowa with his family in 1880, and was educated at Stanford University. Arnold became a member of the U.S. Geological Survey; wrote and lectured extensively on geological subjects; engaged in numerous mining and petroleum ventures; and was active in Republican politics, especially the presidential campaigns of Herbert Hoover.

Subject matter: mining, petroleum, and seismology in the Western U.S. as well as Canada, Mexico, Cuba, South America, etc.; significant are field books, including those made at Stanford University and with the U.S. Geological Survey (1900–09); political papers from 1914 to 1956, mostly concerning the campaign of Herbert Hoover for president; family and personal papers (1836–1961) of Arnold and his father Delos Arnold, a prominent Pasadena pioneer, containing source material on local history.

Significant persons: Herbert Clark HOOVER (54).

Physical description: letters, documents (including 190,000 reports), 1200 maps, 500 photographs, and 8200 pieces of printed material.

Source: gift of Ralph Arnold, 1955–61.

ATKINSON, GEORGE HENRY (1819–89)
126 pieces, 1841–87

George H. Atkinson, Congregational minister in the Pacific Northwest, graduated from Dartmouth College in 1843, and from Andover Theological Seminary in 1846. Unable to accept an appointment to a mission in Africa because he had not yet been ordained, he sailed to Oregon by way of Hawaii with his wife, arriving in 1848. Atkinson originally settled in Oregon City. He prepared the first public school law in Oregon and helped plan for the forming of Pacific University. In 1863, he became pastor of a Portland church and also held many church offices. He was a trustee of Pacific University.

Subject matter: Atkinson's labors as a missionary, descriptions of conditions in Oregon, and his attempts to advance education.

Physical description: letters.

Source: purchased from R. W. Lull, 1926.

AZUSA-FOOTHILL CITRUS COMPANY
59 pieces, 1844–1956

The Azusa-Foothill Citrus Company was established in 1902 by James Slauson and his two sisters on property inherited from their father, Jonathan Sayre Slauson, New York banker and founder and manager of the Los Angeles Savings Bank. The land, originally part of the great Azusa Ranch owned by Henry Dalton, was purchased in 1880 and 1884 by Jonathan Sayre Slauson, who founded the town of Azusa, California and the Azusa Land and Water Co.

Subject matter: business and legal affairs of the Azusa Foothill Citrus Co., including copies of title abstracts for Ranchos Azusa, San José and Addition; minute books for the Azusa Land and Water Co., Azusa Citrus Association, and the Azusa Foothill Citrus Co.; and maps showing land and water distribution, irrigation systems, and roads for the periods 1878–1937.

Physical description: documents (including 11 volumes) and 39 maps.

Source: gift from Azusa-Foothill Citrus Co., July, 1974.

B

BACON, HENRY DOUGLAS (1817–93)
approximately 4000 pieces, ca.1766–1906

Henry Douglas Bacon was a California financier who entered the retail business in St. Louis in 1835 and later joined his wealthy father-in-law in the banking firm of Page & Bacon. In 1849 he and his partners formed Page, Bacon & Co., an express firm in San Francisco, which became primarily a banking concern. The company's failure in 1855 served as a prelude to the San Francisco crash of 1855. Bacon invested in the Ohio & Mississippi Railroad, numerous mining ventures, and the Marengo Ranch in Southern California (1871–73). He donated generously to the University of California at Berkeley.

Subject matter: banking methods in the 1850s, the failure of Page & Bacon and Page, Bacon & Co.; the financing of the Ohio & Mississippi Railroad; land transactions in Missouri and Illinois; mines and mining properties in the western states; the wine and citrus industries in Southern California; the Los Angeles and San Gabriel Valley Railroad; the purchase, boundaries, and subdivision of the Marengo Ranch (now South Pasadena, California); the construction of the Raymond Hotel in Pasadena.

Significant persons: Henry Douglas BACON (164), Julia Ann (Page) BACON (54), Samuel Latham Mitchill BARLOW (57), William Tell COLEMAN (31), Daniel Dearborn PAGE (33), Francis W. PAGE (33), Henry STARR (21), Thomas M. YERKES (100).

Physical description: letters and documents (including account books).

Source: purchased from Edwin Grabhorn, January, 1945; and Charles Yale's Bookshop (Pasadena), March, 1944 (Marengo material).

BAGG, JOHN SHERMAN (1807–70)
482 pieces, 1835–76

John Sherman Bagg, Michigan politician and editor-owner of the *Detroit Free Press*, was an ardent Democrat, active in regional politics and in close contact with most of the prominent Michigan Democrats during the 1840s and 1850s. He was appointed state printer in 1841, postmaster of the city of Detroit in 1845, and U.S. marshal in charge of the Michigan census of 1859.

Subject matter: primarily Michigan politics and the Democratic party, including material on state and national conventions and elections, boundary disputes, statehood, land speculation, tariffs, the westward movement, Indian affairs, the U.S. postal service in Michigan, and the National Census of 1860. Strongest in the period 1840–60.

Significant persons: John Stewart BARRY (16), Lewis CASS (39), Alpheus FELCH (8), Cave JOHNSON (9), Robert McCLELLAND (88), Jacob THOMPSON (6), and William WOODBRIDGE (10).

Physical description: primarily letters (a few are contemporary copies rather than originals), with some documents and printed forms, a passport for Mrs. Bagg, and an engraved portrait of John Sherman Bagg.

Source: gift of Mrs. Katherine Hastings, granddaughter of John Sherman Bagg, June, 1948.

BAKER, OBADIAH ETHELBERT (1836–1923)
350 pieces, ca.1859–ca.1923

Obadiah Ethelbert Baker, teacher, farmer, and Union soldier, was born in Eden, New York, in 1838 and moved with his family to Iowa in 1856. He taught school there until the beginning of the Civil War, when he enlisted in the 2nd Iowa Cavalry Volunteers. Baker fought chiefly in Mississippi and Tennessee, took part in the battles of Shiloh, Corinth, and Booneville, and spent several months in various army hospitals in Tennessee and Missouri. At the end of the war he resumed teaching in Mississippi and Iowa, but in 1874 moved with his family to California, where he homesteaded land in Shasta county and returned to farming. He died in Kenwood, California, in 1923.

Subject matter: Civil War; soldier's life and reminiscences, military operations, medical and hospital life.

Physical description: letters, manuscripts (including approximately 200 of Baker's poems and 20 volumes of Civil War journals and diaries), documents, photographs, newspaper clippings, and other ephemera.

Source: purchased from Argonaut Book Shop, June, 1966.

BAKER, ROBERT SYMINGTON (1825–94)
320 pieces, 1866–90

Robert S. Baker, California businessman, came to California in 1849 from his birthplace in Rhode Island. Arriving in San Diego, he went next to San Francisco, then settled in Los Angeles. He was prominently associated with Edward F. Beale in the local petroleum and wool industries and also engaged in mining, banking, and real estate. Baker married Arcadia Bandini de Stearns (widow of Abel Stearns) in 1874 and later built the Baker Block in downtown Los Angeles. He owned Ranchos San Vicente and Santa Monica and, with John Percival Jones, founded the city of Santa Monica.

Subject matter: petroleum and sheep and wool industries in California 1866–88; mining interests in California and Utah 1877–79; the city of Santa Monica 1877–79; the ranchos Jurupa, Santa Monica, San Vicente, and Temescal.

Significant persons: Robert Symington BAKER (12), Edward Fitzgerald BEALE (22), Alfred ROBINSON (8), and John Henry WISE (26).

Physical description: letters and documents.

Source: gift of Bernal F. Alfe, 1937.

BALDWIN, ANITA MAY (1876–1939)
approximately 600 pieces, 1876–1936

Anita M. Baldwin was the daughter of Elias Jackson ("Lucky") Baldwin (1828–1909), millionaire investor in Comstock mining stocks and later developer of the Santa Anita Rancho, which he bought from Harris Newmark in 1875. After Baldwin's death, Anita Baldwin inherited the ranch (including vineyards, orchards, livestock, and race horses), which she continued to run until selling several acres to the Los Angeles Turf Club in 1933 and most of the remaining acreage for subdivision in 1936.

Subject matter: business affairs of the Santa Anita Ranch (1901–04), and the Los Angeles Racing Association (1907–22); business affairs of Anita M. Baldwin and estate settlements of Elias Jackson Baldwin and his elder daughter Clara (Baldwin) Stocker, covering the period 1876–1936, including 2 volumes of Arcadia (California) city dockets on Criminal and Civil justice.

Physical description: letters, documents, and maps. Of the 600 pieces, 400 are receipts of the Los Angeles Racing Association.

Source: purchased from Anne Baldwin Purcell, May, 1965.

BALDWIN, FRANK DWIGHT (1842–1923)
approximately 5100 pieces, 1807; 1860–1923

Frank Dwight Baldwin was a career officer in the U.S. Army, who rose from lieutenant in 1861 to brigadier general in 1902. He saw service in the Civil War, in Indian campaigns in the American West, and in the Philippines, and was twice awarded the Congressional Medal of Honor.

Subject matter: Baldwin's military activities in the Civil War, especially the Battle of Peachtree Creek in 1864; Indian battles in the Southwest (mainly Texas in 1874) and with Sitting Bull and his followers in Montana after the massacre of Custer in 1876; Baldwin's tour of duty in the Philippines, 1900–03.

Significant persons: Nelson Appleton MILES (33).

Physical description: letters, manuscripts (including 7 volumes, notebooks, and account book), documents, maps, and photographs.

Source: gift of Juanita Baldwin Williams-Foote, June, 1943, and Mr. and Mrs. Baldwin Williams-Foote, May, 1970.

BALDWIN FAMILY COLLECTION
475 pieces, 1779–1886

The Baldwin Family Collection centers on the children of Michael Baldwin (1719–87) of New Haven, Connecticut, including: Abraham Baldwin (1754–1807), American statesman and founder of the University of Georgia; Henry Baldwin

(1780–1844), justice of the U.S. Supreme Court; Ruth (Baldwin) Barlow (1756–1818), wife of the poet and statesman Joel Barlow (1754–1812); and Clara (Baldwin) Bomford (1782–1856), wife of George Bomford (1782–1848), chief of the ordnance of the army. There are also papers belonging to Clara's daughter Ruth (Bomford) Paine (d. 1891).

Subject matter: Baldwin family affairs; social life and customs, particularly in Washington, D.C., descriptions of life and travel in Switzerland, Italy, and France, as reflected in letters to Clara Bomford from the American diplomat George William Erving (1769–1850). Contains relatively few references to politics or diplomacy. Strongest in the periods 1803–16, 1826–56, and 1882–86.

Significant persons: Abraham BALDWIN (25), Henry BALDWIN (8), Joel BARLOW (6), George BOMFORD (7), and George William ERVING (116).

Physical description: letters, a few documents, and 1 manuscript poem.

Source: gift of Rear Admiral M. H. Simons, Mrs. Frank O. Branch, and Mrs. R. K. Van Mater, 1956.

BANNING COMPANY
12,104 pieces, 1859–1948

The Banning Company was founded by Phineas Banning (1830–85), who came to California from Philadelphia in 1852. Banning became a partner in a freight and stage line business between San Pedro and Los Angeles, which became Banning and Company in 1858 and finally the Banning Company. In 1857 he started a settlement near San Pedro, renamed Wilmington (after his birthplace in Delaware) in 1859. The port of Wilmington served as a focal point for the Banning Company's activities in shipping, warehousing, freight and passenger service to Los Angeles and inland areas. Following his election as state senator in 1865, Banning was instrumental in the building of the Los Angeles and San Pedro Railroad, later purchased by the Southern Pacific Railroad, and in the improvement of Los Angeles Harbor. After the death of Phineas Banning, the business continued under the direction of his three sons, William, Joseph Brent, and Hancock. In 1892 the firm purchased Santa Catalina Island and developed it as a vacation resort. The island was sold to William Wrigley in 1919, and the Banning Company was dissolved in 1920 upon the death of Joseph Brent Banning.

Subject matter: Wilmington, California, and the harbor; Santa Catalina Island; the Southern Pacific Railroad and the Pacific Electric interurban lines; letterbooks (1879–1909) and account books and ledgers (1859–1924) of Banning's subsidiary firms; petroleum lease agreements; other land and business papers.

Significant persons: Phineas BANNING (20).

Physical description: letters (including 83 letterbooks), documents (including 119 account books and ledgers), and 34 maps.

Source: gift of Hancock Banning, Jr., 1962, with small addendum purchased from Green Door Books, 1972.

BARCLAY, HENRY AUGUSTUS (1849–1920<)
approximately 150 pieces, 1867–1908

Henry A. Barclay, Los Angeles lawyer, was born in Pennsylvania, engaged in surveying work as a young man, and came to California in 1874. He began his practice of law in Los Angeles in 1875 and dealt mainly in land law, including Spanish and Mexican land grants.

Subject matter: coal, gold, and silver mining in California and Mexico; the Irvington Land and Water Co.; San Bernardino; the Los Angeles Light and Water Co.; and several Southern California Ranchos (including Muscupiabe, San Bernardino, Sespe, and Tujunga).

Physical description: letters, documents, and maps.

Source: gift of George W. Beattie, May, 1935.

BARD, THOMAS ROBERT (1841–1915)
approximately 50,000 pieces, 1866–1958

Thomas Robert Bard, U.S. senator for California from 1900 to 1905 and president of the Union Oil Company, was born in Pennsylvania where he studied law. He came to California in 1865 to take charge of the large land holdings of eastern owners in Ventura County and was instrumental in the subsequent development of land and petroleum. Bard laid out the town of Hueneme, California, and was involved in many Ventura County business ventures.

Subject matter: the Union Oil Company, its subsidiaries, and other enterprises with which Bard was concerned; local and national politics from 1870 to 1915; the development of Ventura County; business papers (1909–58) of the Quimichis Colony, an American-financed agricultural company in Nayarit, Mexico, of which Richard Bard (son of Thomas R. Bard) was president.

Physical description: letters (including 9 bound volumes and 33 letterbooks) and documents (including 114 account books).

Source: gift of Richard Bard, 1941–64, and Archie Bard, 1973.

BARGRAVE, JOHN ? (fl. ca. 1623)
A Treatise Shewing Howe to Erecte a Publique and Increasing
Treasurie for Virginia (ca.1623)
MS. volume 12 leaves

Also contains a contemporary extract from Bargrave's *A Polisie to Plant and Govern Many Families in Virginia.*

BARKER, JACOB (1779–1871)
168 pieces, 1809–63

Jacob Barker, merchant, lawyer, and financier, was born to Quaker parents in Maine. Entering business in New York as a youth, he won and lost many fortunes in his career. Prior to 1812 Barker had so prospered that he was able to play a key role in financing American military efforts during the war. His involvement, however, ruined one fortune and left him with a legacy of unadjusted claims against the U.S. Government.

Subject matter: loans to the Federal Government in 1814 and Barker's claims relative thereto.

Significant persons: Jacob BARKER (36), George Washington CAMPBELL (18).

Physical description: letters and documents.

Source: purchased from C. W. Unger, 1926.

BARLOW, SAMUEL LATHAM MITCHILL (1826–89)
approximately 29,000 pieces, 1798–1905

Samuel Latham Mitchill Barlow, prominent corporation lawyer and backstage Democrat, moved from his native Massachusetts to New York in 1842, was admitted to the bar in 1849, and was cofounder of the law firm of Bowdoin, Larocque, and Barlow in 1852. He specialized in corporate law and management, particularly in railroads, mining, land, and utilities, and was a part owner of the New York *World*. Frequently retained as counsel by English investors in American business, Barlow represented the English Shareholders Association in a successful attack on the corrupt management of the Erie Railroad in 1872 and was directly responsible for the ouster of Jay Gould from the board of directors of that company. A lifelong Democrat despite his increasing disaffection after 1870, Barlow played a pivotal role in the nomination and successful presidential campaign of the Buchanan-Breckinridge ticket in 1856, served as adviser to Buchanan's administration, worked unsuccessfully to restore party unity at the Charleston Convention of 1860, and engineered the 1864 presidential candidacy of General George B. McClellan, a close personal friend. A notable collector of early Americana and early printed editions of European Renaissance literature, Barlow also played an active role in the social and cultural life of New York. He entertained lavishly at his Madison Avenue home and his Long Island estate, was cofounder of the Manhattan Club, and was a patron of the Metropolitan Museum of Art, the New York Academy of Music, and the New York Historical Society.

Subject matter: the greatest strength of this multi-faceted collection is in economic history: Barlow's business correspondence, which comprises the bulk of the papers, provides an inside view of the expansion of American capitalism between 1855 and 1889; it deals with railroad building and management (particularly the Ohio and Mississippi Railroad, the Atlantic and Great Western, and the New York, Erie, and Western, with additional papers on other eastern railroads and on the Tehuantepec route in Mexico); mining promotion and operation (particularly the Colorado Coal and Iron Co., the Elk Mountain Gold and Silver Mining Company, and the notorious Arizona diamond mine hoax); land speculation (farm lands in

Illinois, Iowa, and Ohio and urban properties in St. Louis, Missouri); and the growth of New York City in investment banking and public utilities. Barlow's correspondence is also important for a study of government and politics in the critical decades surrounding the Civil War, and particularly for the inner workings of the Democratic party at both national and state levels. The nominating campaigns and presidential conventions of 1856, 1864, and 1868 are particularly well represented, as are issues of party finance and policy. During the Civil War itself Barlow's papers contain military reports from his agents on the eastern battlefields, accounts of the Peninsular Campaign from McClellan, and political gossip about the Lincoln administration from a journalist contact in the Department of the Interior. There is relatively little personal and family correspondence, but some material survives on Barlow's cultural activities. The collection is strongest for the period from 1855 to 1889.

Significant persons: William Henry ASPINWALL (41), Henry Douglas BACON (1911), T. J. BARNETT (128), James Asheton BAYARD, Jr. (93), August BELMONT (79), Judah Philip BENJAMIN (91), Montgomery BLAIR, Sr. (79), William Montague BROWNE (101), Benjamin Franklin BUTLER (27), Roscoe CONKLING (32), George Ticknor CURTIS, Sr. (162), John Henry DILLON (59), William Maxwell EVARTS (14), Henry HARRISSE (14), Ben HOLLADAY (133), Hugh Judge JEWETT (56), Clarence KING (35), George Brinton McCLELLAN, Sr. (95), James McHENRY (8), Manton Malone MARBLE (84), Thomas Alexander SCOTT (44), Horatio SEYMOUR (18), William Davis SHIPMAN (110), John SLIDELL (60), Richard TAYLOR (133), William Henry TRESCOT (79), Morrison Remick WAITE (12), Samuel WARD (206).

Physical description: letters (including 53 letterpress copy letterbooks kept by Barlow between 1848 and 1889), documents, and manuscripts. The collection also contains miscellaneous printed matter, including mounted newspaper clippings, Confederate and other paper money and bonds, and some early photographs of public figures.

Source: purchased from Samuel L. M. Barlow (grandson) through Maury A. Bromson Associates, 1960.

Bibliography: the collection is further described by Albert V. House, "The Samuel Latham Mitchill Barlow Papers in the Huntington Library," *Huntington Library Quarterly,* 28, no. 4 (August, 1965): 341–52.

BARNEY, HIRAM (1811–95)
approximately 8300 pieces, 1772–1924

Hiram Barney, lawyer and collector of the port of New York, began practicing law in 1836 in New York City, specializing in debt collection. In 1848 he formed a partnership with Benjamin F. and William A. Butler, which lasted until 1873. A militant antislavery Democrat, Barney joined the Republicans in 1854 and earned a reputation for political acumen. In 1857 he won the confidence of Abraham Lincoln, who as president appointed him collector of the port of New York, a very powerful patronage post. Barney held the office until resigning in 1864. The remainder of his life was devoted to private business and family affairs.

Subject matter: real estate, primarily in Iowa (the "Half-Breed Tract") and New York; Keokuk, Iowa; court cases (often pertaining to debt collection) and other legal services; politics generally, but especially patronage distribution; family affairs; business transactions concerning the Erie and other canals; small railroads (largely in the Lake Plains region); Kilbourne, Leighton and Co., and White Elks Vineyard; Mexico and Mexican-American relations; the Civil War; U.S. Customs Service. Strongest for the period 1840–90.

Significant persons: Hiram BARNEY (ca.1050), William Cullen BRYANT (41), William Allen BUTLER (141), Salmon

Portland CHASE (97), Erastus CORNING (27), Edward Cornelius DELAVAN (145), John JAY [1817–94] (28), David Wells KILBOURNE (94), Eugene KOZLAY (33), Edward Lillie PIERCE (31), Matías ROMERO (314), Horatio SEYMOUR (141), William Tecumseh SHERMAN (137), Brcese Jacob STEVENS (143), Lewis TAPPAN (27), William D. WATERMAN (31).

Physical description: letters, documents, and photographs.

Source: purchased from Walter T. Shatford, 1962.

BARTLETT, JULIA S. (fl. 1890s)
109 pieces, 1889–98

Julia S. Bartlett, Christian Science teacher and practitioner, was the principal of the New England Academy of Christian Science in Boston.

Subject matter: Boston life and the Christian Science church in Massachusetts, as seen in the correspondence of the Bartlett family.

Physical description: letters.

Source: purchased from Robert K. Black, May, 1960.

BARTON, CLARA HARLOWE (1821–1912)
44 pieces, 1850–90

Clara Harlowe Barton, organizer of the American Red Cross, began her humanitarian career by organizing a relief agency for wounded soldiers while working in the Patent Office in Washington, D.C. in 1861, and served in the later years of the Civil War as a superintendent of nurses with the Army of the James. After travel in Europe from 1869 to 1873, during part of which time she was active in the International Red Cross in Geneva, she returned to the United States and revived an earlier movement to establish an American chapter of the organization. The National Society of the Red Cross was founded in 1881; Miss Barton served as president from its inception until 1904.

Subject matter: Civil War and wartime medical conditions, Clara Barton and the Barton family.

Physical description: letters with 1 manuscript poem and ephemera.

Source: acquired from Carlton B. Swift, 1945, with 1 additional piece from Robert K. Black, 1960.

BEATTIE, GEORGE WILLIAM (1849–1949) and HELEN (PRUITT) BEATTIE
approximately 4065 pieces, 1895–1944

George W. Beattie, historian and teacher, came to California in 1874. He was a leading educator in Redlands, California, and later taught at the University of California at Berkeley and in the Philippines where he served as a superintendent of schools and helped organize the University of the Philippines in Manila. In San Bernardino, California, he was active in community service and historical research. With his wife, Helen (Pruitt) Beattie, he wrote *Heritage of the Valley* and other publications.

Subject matter: California history, especially that of the San Bernardino County region and Mormon pioneers in the San Bernardino Valley; education in the Philippine Islands. Chiefly secondary source material.

Physical description: letters, documents, and manuscripts, with maps, clippings, and photographs.

33

Source: gift of Mrs. George W. Beattie, October, 1949, to April, 1954.

BEHYMER, LYNDEN ELLSWORTH (1862–1947)
approximately 3990 pieces, 1881–1948

Lynden E. Behymer, California impresario, was a leader in the musical development of the Southwest. He came to Los Angeles in 1886 and soon afterwards brought the first important operatic organization to Los Angeles. In 1898 Behymer founded, and then managed, the Los Angeles Symphony for twenty years, and in 1918 formed the Los Angeles Philharmonic Symphony for William Andrews Clark, Jr.

Subject matter: California musical and theatrical organizations from 1914 to 1947; plays, promptbooks, and music.

Physical description: letters, documents (including 32 volumes of accounts, agreements, and box office receipts), manuscripts, and photographs. In addition, the Library's Rare Book Department contains a large collection of programs, playbills, and printed material gathered by Behymer relating to the history of the theater and music in Southern California from 1875 to 1947.

Source: gift of Mrs. Lynden E. Behymer, December, 1948.

BELL, HORACE (1830–1918)
71 pieces, 1829–90

Horace Bell, pioneer Los Angeles resident, came to California in 1850 to engage in mining and settled in Los Angeles in 1852. Bell joined the Rangers, a local group formed to provide law and order, and later wrote *Reminicences of a Ranger,* describing his experiences in early Los Angeles. He saw military service in 1856 with General William Walker in Nicaragua, in 1859 with Benito Juárez in Mexico, and in the Civil War. Bell returned to Los Angeles, where he practiced law and published a weekly newspaper, *The Porcupine.*

Subject matter: Bell's published works, including *On the Old West Coast* and twelve other stories; family matters, as represented in letters to his sister Caroline (Bell) Rush; early California, as seen in material collected by Bell.

Physical description: letters and manuscripts.

Source: gift of Mrs. J. R. Phillips, November, 1936; and E. H. Yocam, August, 1973.

BELL, JAMES ALVIN (ca.1834–63)
approximately 475 pieces, 1854–83

James Alvin Bell was a farmer in Kaneville, Illinois, until the outbreak of the Civil War, and was long engaged to (but never married) Augusta Anna (Hallock) Elliott, a schoolteacher from rural New York. Bell enlisted in the 8th Illinois Cavalry in May, 1861, and died at the Stanton Army Hospital in Washington, D.C., in October, 1863.

Subject matter: chiefly Bell and his fiancée, concerned only with their private life; a few letters written by others to Augusta after Bell's death, depicting the hardships of a soldier's life.

Physical description: letters, a few manuscript poems, 7 photographs, and some fragments.

Source: purchased from G. E. Woodley, July, 1964.

BENEDICT (RUSSELL) COLLECTION
188 pieces, 1638–1793

Russell Benedict, lawyer and collector, was a justice of the Supreme Court of New York (1911–1925). He was active in civic affairs in Brooklyn and was a member of various patriotic organizations.

Subject matter: routine business of New York provincial and state governments, with a little on New York City government, the Seven Years' War, and the Revolution.

Significant persons: William BURNET (9), George CLARKE (8), George CLINTON (11), James DE LANCY (9), Abraham DE PEYSTER (7), Robert HUNTER (13), Edward HYDE (14), Francis LOVELACE (6), William TRYON (9).

Physical description: predominantly documents (some in French and Dutch), including deeds, civil and military appointments, licenses, maps, proclamations, and letters.

Source: purchased from Russell Benedict, 1917.

BIDAMON, LEWIS CRUM (1807–91)
276 pieces, 1837–1962

Lewis C. Bidamon, major in the Illinois Militia, moved to Nauvoo, Illinois, at the time the Mormons were being driven out in 1846. There, in 1847, he married Emma (Hale) Smith, widow of the Mormon prophet Joseph Smith (1805–44). Bidamon was involved in various business ventures and land transactions in Nauvoo, including operation of the Nauvoo House, a hotel whose construction was begun by Joseph Smith and completed by Bidamon and his wife.

Subject matter: business and legal papers of Bidamon, his brother, and his son from 1837 to 1892, including Bidamon's correspondence with members of the Mormon Church pertaining to the sale of Nauvoo House. Of special interest: information about the prophet Joseph Smith, the papers of Emma (Hale) Smith Bidamon and her son Joseph Smith (1832–1914), founder and lifelong president of the Reorganized Church of Jesus Christ of Latter Day Saints.

Physical description: letters and documents.

Source: purchased from Stanley B. Kimball, July, 1966.

BILL, ANNIE CECILIA (BULMER) (1861–1936)
approximately 4000 pieces, 1893–1944

Annie C. Bill, religious leader and author, was an English adherent of Christian Science. In 1909 she broke with the main Christian Science organization over church government. Seeing herself as Mary Baker Eddy's rightful successor, she labored for years to reform the movement but failed to make much headway. In 1928, Bill severed all ties with Christian Science and transformed her reform movement into a new denomination, the Church of the Universal Design, which taught her version of Christian Science. This church, never large, disappeared after the death of Bill and other leaders in the 1930s.

Subject matter: Christian Science; scientific concepts of the painter Walter Russell (1871–1963).

Significant persons: Annie C. BILL (ca.800), John V. DITTEMORE (ca.500), Walter RUSSELL (22).

Physical description: letters, documents, manuscripts, a few photographs, and printed matter.

Source: purchased from Edward Morrill & Sons, 1959–61.

BISHOP, FRANCIS AUGUSTUS (1829–98?)
approximately 1400 pieces, 1851–1913

Francis A. Bishop was an engineer for the Western portion of the Lander Wagon Road in 1857 and afterward became chief engineer of the Placerville and Sacramento Valley Railroad and hydraulic engineer for the El Dorado Water and Deep Gravel Mining Co., then worked on inventions for hydraulic machinery. After his years in California he moved to Sydney, Australia, for five years, then spent the remainder of his life in Connecticut.

Subject matter: the Placerville and Sacramento Railroad from 1865 to 1877; the California and Nevada Railroad in 1881–82; and various water and hydraulic mining companies in the Placerville, California, area between 1853 and 1855. Two documents deal with the Lander Wagon Road Survey of 1857.

Physical description: letters, manuscripts, and documents, including 50 volumes (27 diaries, 3 letterbooks, and various account books), and 2 maps.

Source: purchased from William F. Dashiell, August, 1971.

BISSELL, MARY ELEANOR (ca.1870–ca.1962)
approximately 160 pieces, 1738–1958

Mary Eleanor Bissell was born about 1870 in Windsor, Connecticut, where her father, Thomas H. Bissell, was a banker and landowner and where her ancestors in the Miles and Bissell families had lived since at least the early eighteenth century. Miss Bissell moved to Pasadena, California, about 1924 and was active there in prominent social organizations until her death about 1962.

Subject matter: the Bissell and Miles families from 1738 to 1848; a few later items related to Miss Bissell's lifetime, including a diary from her Smith College days (1893–95) and a guest book and photographs of her home in Pasadena.

Physical description: letters, documents, 21 photographs, and slides.

Source: gift of the estate of Eleanor Bissell through the agency of the Pasadena Art Museum, August 2, 1963.

BLASDEL, HENRY GOODE (1825–1900)
155 pieces, 1864–70

Henry G. Blasdel was the first governor of the state of Nevada. Born in Indiana, he engaged in farming, merchandising, and riverboating before coming to California in 1852. Blasdel, after living in San Francisco, moved to Virginia City, where he became a mining superintendent. Following service in the Civil War, he was elected governor of Nevada and served from 1864 to 1871.

Subject matter: Henry Blasdel's term as governor of Nevada, mainly communications from Washington officials concerning education land grants, immigration, etc.; Indian disturbances in Humboldt and Lander Counties; the organization of the Nevada Militia.

Physical description: letters.

Source: purchased from Edwin Grabhorn, January, 1945.

BLATHWAYT, WILLIAM (1649–1717)
461 pieces, 1657–1770

William Blathwayt, English politician and colonial administrator, was a distinguished civil servant. Through the influence of his uncles Thomas and Richard Povey, he secured a position in the Plantation Office in 1675 as a minor clerk. Advancement came rapidly, and among the offices he held were: clerk of the Privy Council, 1675; secretary to the Lords of Trade, 1679; auditor general of plantation revenues, 1680; secretary at war, 1683; acting secretary of state with William III in Flanders, 1692; member of the Board of Trade, 1696. In 1712 he retired from public life.

Subject matter: administrative operations, taxation, defense, slavery, piracy, trade and shipping, Anglo-French rivalry, Indian affairs, tobacco and politics in the West Indies and North America. Strongest for the period 1680–1709.

Significant persons: Sir William BERKELEY (14), William BLATHWAYT (32), Philip CALVERT (7), George CLARK (8), Edward D'OYLEY (6), Joseph DUDLEY (9), Edward HYDE 3rd Earl of Clarendon (7), William LOWNDES (9), John NANFAN (16), Samuel PENHALLOW (6), John POVEY (8), Edward RANDOLPH (10).

Physical description: letters and documents.

Source: purchased from A. S. W. Rosenbach, 1924.

Bibliography: about forty pieces summarized in the HMSO *Calendar of State Papers: America and the West Indies.*

BODEGA Y QUADRA, JUAN FRANCISCO DE LA (1743–94)

Viaje a la Costa N[or] O[este] De la America Septentrional por D[on] Juan Fran[cis]co de la Bodega y Quadra, Del Orden de Santiago, Cap[ita]n de Navio de la R[eal] Armada y Comandante del Departmento de San Blas en las Fragatas de su mando S[an]ta Gertrudis, Aranzazu, Princesa y Goleta Activa. (February 29, 1792–February 2, 1793)
Contemporary copy MS. 1 volume 188 pp.

Text in Spanish. Annexed: Table of ship's course. 2 leaves.

BOGAERT, HARMEN MEYNSERTSEN VAN DEN (fl. 1634–35)
[Memorial of the Principal Events that Happened During a Journey to the "Maques" and "Sinnikins" Indians] (1634–35)
MS. volume 32 pp.

Text in Dutch. This journal was once attributed to Arendt Van Corlear. Published in J. Franklin Jameson, ed., *Narratives of New Netherland, 1609–1664* (New York: Charles Scribner's Sons, 1909).

BOREMAN, JACOB SMITH (1831–1913)
63 pieces, 1857–1912

Jacob S. Boreman was the judge in the trial of John Doyle Lee (q.v.), defendant in the Mountain Meadows (Utah) Massacre. Boreman received his law degree from the University of Virginia in 1855 and in 1858 moved to Missouri, where he practiced law, served in the state legislature, and was editor of the *Kansas City Evening Bulletin*. He later served as judge and practiced law in Utah.

Subject matter: the complete typed and shorthand records of the Mountain Meadows Massacre trial, held in Beaver, Utah, 1875–77; Boreman's personal correspondence; records of the 2nd Judicial District Court of Utah (1857–77); Boreman's reminiscences of early Utah life and legislation.

Physical description: letters, documents, and manuscripts.

Source: purchased from G. F. Boreman, September, 1934.

Bibliography: material from the collection has been published in Leonard J. Arrington, ed., "Crusade Against Theocracy: the

Reminiscences of Judge Jacob Smith Boreman of Utah, 1872–77," *Huntington Library Quarterly*, 24 (1960): 1–45.

BOUVIER, JOHN (1787–1851)
347 pieces, ca.1762–1895

John Bouvier, printer and lawyer, opened his first printing shop in Philadelphia in 1808. Two years later he married Elizabeth Widdifield, daughter of a prominent Philadelphia Quaker family. The Bouviers had one child, Hannah Mary Peterson (1811–70), who became an accomplished astronomer. Bouvier also began to publish newspapers, including the *American Telegraph* (from 1814) and the *Genius of American Liberty,* which he established in 1818. That same year he was admitted to the bar. He published several law books, the most famous being his *Law Dictionary* (1839). Though he followed closely the course of Democratic-Republican politics in Pennsylvania, the only offices he himself held were city recorder of Philadelphia and associate judge of the Court of Criminal Sessions (1838).

Subject matter: family history; personal affairs of John Bouvier; charges of corruption against Pennsylvania Governor William Findlay (1817–1820); Democratic-Republican politics in Pennsylvania (1820–1824); business affairs of Robert Evans Peterson, including matters concerning the American Life Insurance Co.; business affairs of George William Childs; the astronomy text of Hannah Peterson.

Significant persons: John BOUVIER (29).

Physical description: letters, documents, and photographs.

Sources: acquired from David Blankenhorn, 1956 and Maurice Wells, 1973.

BOVEE, MARVIN H. (fl. 1860–80)
100 pieces, 1850–87

Marvin H. Bovee was a Wisconsin Democrat and member of the state senate who was active in state politics during the post-Civil War period.

Subject matter: state and national politics, primarily as reflected in Bovee's personal correspondence; some material on the abolition of capital punishment.

Significant persons: Horace GREELEY (14), Horatio SEYMOUR (7), and Gerrit SMITH (11).

Physical description: letters.

Source: purchased from H. B. Halverson, 1956.

BOWEN, EDWIN A. (1831–1900)
119 pieces, 1848–95

Edwin A. Bowen, prospector and Union officer, was born and educated in Illinois, where he helped establish the First National Bank of Mendota, Illinois. In 1859 he prospected for gold at Pike's Peak, Colorado, and served during the Civil War in the 52nd Illinois Infantry, rising to the rank of lieutenant colonel.

Subject matter: Bowen's wartime service; Sherman's Georgia campaigns; routine military matters of ordnance and orders; a journal of Bowen's trip to Pike's Peak.

Physical description: letters, documents (including 1 volume of General and Special Orders, manuscripts (including 5 journals), and some printed forms.

Source: purchased from Mr. and Mrs. Ramsdell S. Lasher, 1962.

BOWER (LAWRENCE F.) COLLECTION
63 pieces, 1802–1904

Lawrence F. Bower, of whom little is known, began about 1889 an autograph collection specializing in naval and military officers of the War of 1812 and the Civil War. He wrote personally to many of the officers still living in the 1890s, at which time Bower was apparently still a young boy.

Subject matter: unrelated letters collected for their autographs.

Physical description: letters and a few documents.

Source: purchased from the American Art Association, 1923.

BOWRON, FLETCHER (1887–1968)
approximately 20,000 pieces, 1934–70

Fletcher Bowron, mayor of Los Angeles from 1938 to 1953, came into office as a reform candidate in a recall election and served during a period of unusual growth and problems. Bowron had been a newspaper reporter, practiced law, and spent six years as a judge of the Superior Court of Los Angeles County. Following his term as mayor, Bowron was reelected judge of the Superior Court. After retirement he became interested in the study of Los Angeles history and initiated the Metropolitan Los Angeles History Project, which produced the bibliographical work, *Los Angeles and Its Environs in the Twentieth Century.*

Subject matter: official correspondence kept during Fletcher Bowron's term as mayor of Los Angeles; reports; information on his election campaigns; source material gathered for his Metropolitan Los Angeles History Project, particularly in the fields of public housing, city planning, and transportation.

Physical description: letters, documents, manuscripts, photographs, and ephemera.

Source: gift of Mrs. Fletcher Bowron, 1974 and 1976.

BRANNER, JOHN CASPER (1850–1922)
approximately 100 pieces, 1881–1925

John C. Branner, American geologist, was the second president of Stanford University (1913–15). His career featured scientific expeditions to Brazil, where he went as geologist and botanist; U.S. government geological posts; and academic positions, including that of professor of geology when Stanford University was established.

Subject matter: Branner's life and work; Brazil.

Physical description: letters (including 1 volume letterbook) and manuscripts (including 7 volumes of diaries for the period 1881–1913).

Source: gift of Mrs. Elsie Branner Fowler, June, 1954.

BRENT, JOSEPH LANCASTER (1826–1905)
460 pieces, 1850–1939

Joseph L. Brent, lawyer and Confederate officer, was born in Maryland. In 1850 he settled in Los Angeles, where he held various public offices between 1851 and 1854. He also served as a lawyer before the Land Commission for the Verdugo Rancho and for the City of Los Angeles and was prominent in the Lugo trial (1851). From 1856 to 1860 he was a state legislator. At the outbreak of the Civil War he joined the Confederacy, serving first under John B. Magruder and then under Richard Taylor as chief of ordnance and artillery. His notable military feat was leading the expedition that captured the Union ironclad "Indianola" in 1863. Following the war Brent traveled in Europe, managed a sugar plantation in Louisiana, practiced law in Baltimore, and wrote on national issues.

Subject matter: the capture of the "Indianola"; Brent's military promotions; various peripheral matters pertaining to the Confederate war effort; Brent's social and business affairs in California, Louisiana, and Maryland after the war; his ideas about U.S. foreign relations, national defense, and the economy; his experiences in California from 1850 to 1861.

Significant persons: Joseph Lancaster BRENT (82), Winfield Scott HANCOCK (12), Ignacio del VALLE (8), Benjamin Davis WILSON (11).

Physical description: letters, documents, and manuscripts of articles and speeches.

Source: gift of Duncan K. Brent, 1966 and 1974.

Bibliography: Brent's "Life in California" appeared in his *Memoirs of the War between the States* (New Orleans: Fontana Printing Co., 1940). Also published were the *Capture of the Ironclad Indianola* with *The Lugo Case, A Personal Experience* (New Orleans: Searcy & Pfaff, 1926).

BROCK, ROBERT ALONZO (1839–1914)
approximately 50,000 pieces, 1582–1914

Robert Alonzo Brock, historian, antiquarian, and collector, was born in Richmond, Virginia, in 1839. He left school at the age of thirteen to enter his uncle's business, but at the outbreak of the Civil War enlisted in the 21st Virginia Regiment, transferring later to a hospital unit with which he remained for the duration of the war. Brock later served as associate editor of the *Richmond Standard* (1879–83), as corresponding secretary of the Virginia Historical Society (1875–93), and as secretary of the Southern Historical Society (1887–1914). He edited numerous volumes of source materials for Virginia history and was an avid private collector, accumulating nearly 35,000 manuscripts relating to Virginia and the history of the South, in addition to some 15,000 letters as secretary of the two historical societies.

Subject matter: this multi-faceted collection provides substantial information about the political, military, economic, religious, social, and genealogical history of the state of Virginia. It is strongest for the period after 1800 but also contains approximately 2000 pieces relevant to the colonial and revolutionary periods. Among the letters, diaries, journals, account books, wills, maps, genealogies, and official records and documents are groups of papers relating to: *prominent Virginia families* (Alfriend, Blair, Branch, Brown, Cabell, Chevallie, Daniel, Fairfax, Garland, Harrison, Johnston, Lee, Lipscomb, Lyons, Maury, Minor, Nelson, Pegram, Perkins, Plesants, Randolph, Ruffin, Tinsley, and Tucker); *Virginia business firms and businessmen* (Joseph Reid Anderson and Co., Bacon and Baskerville, George I. Bigod and Co., James Brown, Micajah Crew, William Cunninghame and Co., John Cunliffe, Freeland and Gillies, Lewis Hill, Thomas Muldrup Logan, Mitchell and Tyler, Mutual Assurance Society of Virginia, Norton-Savage Co., Benjamin Oliver, Piedmont and Arlington Life Insurance Co., Jacquelin P. Taylor and Co., Shapard and Webb, Webb Brooker and Hamilton, Lewis Webb and Co., West, Johnston and Co., Woodhouse and Parham, and numerous Virginia railroads, banks, and newspapers); *religious and fraternal organizations* (American Tract Society, Grand Lodge of Virginia Freemasons, Georgia State Sunday-School Association, Presbyterian Committee of Publication, the Society of Friends) and individual clergymen of several denominations; *government offices and departments* (U.S. Treasury Depart-

ment, U.S. Circuit and District Courts for Virginia, Virginia
General Assembly, Virginia Board of Immigration, the Virginia
County Courts, Virginia Supreme Court of Appeals, Virginia
Superior Courts of Chancery, Virginia Land Office, Richmond
Custom House and other municipal records, and the Washing-
ton National Monument Society); *Virginia politicians, states-*
men, and administrators (Joseph Christian, William Wood
Crump, William Green, Benjamin Harrison, James Lawson
Kemper, Fitzhugh Lee, Lunsford Lomax Lewis, Philip Wat-
kins McKinney, Hunter Holmes Marshall, Arthur A. Morrison,
Charles Triplett O'Ferrall, Francis Harrison Pierpoint, Wind-
ham Robertson, Joseph Scott, Joseph M. Stevens, Henry Alex-
ander Wise, and James Hoge Tyler); *and other Virginia*
citizens (Joseph Reid Anderson, E. T. Baird, James Allen
Bates, John Durbarrow Blair, John George Blair, Herman
Boye, William and Elizabeth Brown, Henry Gibbon Cannon,
Allen Caperton, Herbert A. Claiborne, George Evans, William
Staunton Field, William Green, Gerard Hallock, Daniel J. Hart-
sook, Meade Haskins, Robert Hill, William Hill, Edward
Johnson, Robert Means, Samuel Miller, Arthur Morson, Wil-
liam H. Richardson, John B. and Rebecca Roy, J. D. K. Sleight,
Benjamin H. Smith, John H. Steger, Joseph C. Stiles, John E.
Swift, John Curtis Underwood, George C. Wedderburn, and
Thomas Hicks Wynne).

Among the important items of the colonial and Revolutionary
War periods are: 66 quit-rent rolls for 14 counties in the
Northern Neck Proprietary; Virginia Proprietor's Office and
Virginia Land Office papers, including warrants for surveys
(some of which are addressed to George Washington); soldiers' certificates of military service and other records during
the colonial and Revolutionary Wars; Treasury Office expense
accounts for the repair and maintenance of public buildings
in Williamsburg, Virginia; correspondence between Governor
Thomas Jefferson and the Virginia Boards of Trade and War;
War Office communications concerning the collection of the

Specific Tax for supplying Virginia armed forces (1780–82); and legal records of the Virginia General Court (from 1688), the High Court of Chancery (1780), the Court of Admiralty (1786), and various county courts (from 1687).

Manuscripts relating to the Civil War include: state papers of the Virginia General Assembly (1861–65) and legal records of the C.S.A. District Court, Eastern Virginia District (1861–65); military records of the 1st (or 21st) Virginia Infantry Regiment (1859–1901), the 4th Virginia Cavalry Regiment (1862–65), the North Carolina 13th Regiment (1861–64), and the 2nd South Carolina Brigade and Leonidas William Spratt (1862–63); papers of the U.S. Army's Assistant Quartermaster at the Washington D.C. depot (1863–67); papers of the U.S. Army's Department of Virginia and its successor, the First Military District (1865–69); papers of James Allen Bates, a Union officer serving in Maryland and, after August 1865, in the Bureau of Refugees, Freedmen, and Abandoned Lands in Richmond, Virginia (1864–68); and postwar records of the United Confederate Veterans (1875–1909) and the Lee Camp Confederate Soldiers' Home (1885–94).

In addition to related groups of manuscripts, the collection contains many individual items of note, a representative sample of which includes the following: William Byrd's notebook (1697–1702) and shorthand journal (1709–12), Richard Henry Lee's memoranda book (1776–94), parish register of St. John's Church of Richmond, Virginia (transcript in Brock's hand, 1785–1870), General Anthony Wayne's orderly book (1778), Harry Toulmin's "Journal of a Voyage to North America" (copy, 1793–94), Assessment of Houses and Lots in the city of Richmond, Virginia, by the City Assessor (1799), George Evans' account of the weather kept at Oakland (1801–08), lecture by Elias Boudinot (1806), Proceedings of the Trustees of the Academy for Female Education in the City of Richmond (1807–08), Proceedings of the Society for promoting the success of the War against Great Britain (1812–14), Medical records of the case of "Mrs. M." (1819), Account of the Devotional Services of the Jewish Liturgy for the observance of the Sabbath (ca.1825), John Esten Cooke's manuscript novel "Old Virginia; or, the Fortunes of Henry St. John" (1856), Proceedings of the Virginia Medical Society (1833–42), William Galt's Plantation books (1839–51), William Buell's treatises on Siamese life and language (ca.1844), Philip Slaughter's history of Bristol Parish (1846), Journal of a trip up the Parana River, Argentina (1846), Confederate States of America, Senate Journal of Secret Sessions, Pinkerton Agency's report of an investigation into a railroad strike at Paris, Kentucky (1887).

The collection also contains Brock's own voluminous correspondence and many of the private and official papers of the Virginia Historical Society and the Southern Historical Society, the latter groups involving such topics as other historical and antiquarian societies, libraries, colleges and universities, historians, antiquarians, genealogists, and scholarly publishing.

Physical description: letters, manuscripts, documents (including 200 bound volumes), and approximately 100 maps and surveys.

Source: purchased from the daughters of Robert Alonzo Brock, 1922.

BROOKHAVEN (N.Y.) COMMITTEE OF SAFETY

Record of the Proceedings of the Committee, kept by Ebenezer Dayton, Clerk. (1776)

Autograph MS. volume 22 leaves

Covers the period from April 16 to June 25, 1776.

BROPHY-BEESON COLLECTION
240 pieces, 1827–1900

John Brophy (? –1866) came to California in 1849, engaged in mining, and purchased land in Yuba County from early pioneer John Rose before bringing his family to settle in the west. He participated in Democratic politics and prospered in ranching until about 1857, when he suffered reverses, and subsequently moved to a farm in Oregon in 1865. John Beeson (1803–89) brought his family from Illinois to Oregon in 1853 and took up farming. Beeson's distress with the cruel treatment of the Indians caused him to go east to write and lecture on their behalf in 1856. John Beeson's son, Welborn Beeson, married John Brophy's daughter and continued the management of the family farm and served in the Oregon Militia.

Subject matter: gold mining and ranching in Yuba County in the 1850s; disputed California land titles; California and national politics (1856–61); rural life in Lasalle County, Illinois (1856–64) and in Oregon (1860–85); life of the Oregon Militia (1863–66); and aid to Indians. Strongest in the years 1849–90.

Significant persons: John BROPHY (11) and John ROSE (11).

Physical description: letters and documents (including 1 account book).

Source: purchased from Edwin Grabhorn, January, 1945.

BROWN, ANDREW (1829–1909)
approximately 2756 pieces, 1856–96

Andrew Brown was a pioneer businessman and prominent citizen of Kern County, California. He went from San Francisco to Kernville about 1873, where he was active in several business enterprises and served as postmaster and agent for Wells, Fargo Express Co. until his retirement to Los Angeles in 1904.

Subject matter: Brown's general store in Kernville, his jobs as postmaster and agent for Wells, Fargo Express Co., and his other business interests.

Physical description: letters and documents (including about 100 volumes of day books, invoices, and account books).

Source: gift of Mr. and Mrs. P. Sumner Brown, August, 1935.

BROWN, WILLIAM A. (1828?–53)
58 pieces, 1849–55

William A. Brown came to California from Cleveland to seek gold but instead became the founder of one of the early express services (1850–53) from San Francisco and Stockton to the mining regions of Murphy's Camp and Sonora.

Subject matter: Brown's family from 1849 to 1855, Brown's trip to San Francisco via the Isthmus of Panama, his brief mining ventures, and the establishment of a mail and express service.

Physical description: letters and documents.

Source: purchased from John Howell, 1962.

BRUFF, JOSEPH GOLDSBOROUGH (1804–89)
267 pieces, 1849–53

Joseph G. Bruff attended West Point, but left to sail, as a cabin boy, to Europe and South America in 1822. After working as a draftsman for the navy and the Bureau of Topographical Engineers, he went to California to seek gold. He was leader of the Washington City and California Mining Association wagon train which crossed the plains in 1849. Bruff later returned to Washington, D.C. where he was employed in the Office of Supervising Architect of the Treasury Department until his death in 1889.

Subject matter: overland journey to California by way of Lassen Trail in 1849–50 (two portions of the original journal, August 28–November 5, 1849 and March 17–October 9, 1850, and Bruff's revised version of the complete journey with 264 drawings, many in color, which he prepared hoping for publication).

Physical description: manuscripts (including 2 volumes), and 264 drawings.

Source: purchased in 1919.

Bibliography: much of the material is published in *Gold Rush: The Journals, Drawings, and Other Papers of J. Goldsborough Bruff,* ed. Georgia W. Read and Ruth Gaines, 2 vols., (New York: Columbia University Press, 1944).

BUCKNER, SIMON BOLIVAR (1823–1914)
1177 pieces, 1828–1913

Simon Bolivar Buckner, Confederate general, businessman, editor of the Louisville *Courier,* and governor of Kentucky (1887–91), was born in 1823 near Nunfordville, Kentucky, graduated from West Point in 1844, served in the Mexican War beginning that year, and remained on active duty until his resignation in 1855 to enter a business career. Despite strenuous efforts to preserve both his own neutrality and Kentucky's as the Civil War approached, Buckner was instrumental in organizing the state's militia and subsequently accepted a Confederate commission as brigadier general. He served until the end of the war, during which time he was promoted to lieutenant general, and then lived in New Orleans for three years before returning to Kentucky in 1868 to serve as editor of the Louisville *Courier* and to enter the insurance business. After much litigation involved in the recovery of his confiscated Northern properties, Buckner entered politics himself, served as governor of Kentucky, was active in the state constitutional convention of 1891, and was the vice-presidential candidate of the National Democratic Party in the 1896 campaign. His later years were spent at "Glen Lily," his country estate near Nunfordville, where he died in 1914.

Subject matter: the military history of the Civil War (particularly the Chickamauga campaign); the Confederate army; the Reconstruction period; Kentucky government and politics (particularly the prison system and the Sinking Fund Commission); the national presidential election of 1896; the insurance business (particularly the Globe Mutual Life Insurance Co.); land litigation in Chicago and Kentucky; also includes the papers of Buckner's father, Aylett Hartswell Buckner, a farmer and iron manufacturer, and of Major Joseph Walker Taylor, the nephew of President Zachary Taylor, who was a scout for Buckner during the war.

Significant persons: Braxton BRAGG (6), George William BRENT (21).

Physical description: chiefly letters (including 3 letterbooks), with documents, manuscripts, 38 Civil War maps, 9 photographs, newspaper clippings, and other ephemera.

Source: gift of Mrs. Simon Bolivar Buckner, Jr., 1956.

BULLOCK, RUFUS BROWN (1834–1907)
41 pieces, 1851–95

Rufus Brown Bullock, although born in New York, moved to Georgia before the Civil War and was active in the newly invented telegraph business while working for Adams Express Company (later Southern Express Company). After service for the Confederacy during the war, he helped frame the Georgia constitution of 1868 and was elected governor of the state in that year. In November 1871, amid charges of corruption and carpetbagging, Bullock resigned and returned to New York, where extradition orders for his return failed. He was tried and acquitted of all charges in 1878 and thereafter divided his time between Georgia, New York, and a new home in Rhode Island. Bullock retained an interest in politics until his death in 1907.

Subject matter: Georgia politics and administration; Bullock's personal life; the Republican party.

Physical description: letters, documents, and 1 manuscript poem, with numerous relevant newspaper clippings and other ephemera.

Source: purchased from N. Kovach, September 16, 1946.

BURDETTE, CLARA (BRADLEY) (1855–1954)
approximately 50,000 pieces, 1843–1954

Clara (Bradley) Burdette, Southern California social, business, and philanthropic leader, was born in New York and attended Syracuse University, where she was a founder of Alpha Phi Sorority in 1872. After graduation, she married Nathaniel Milman Wheeler, who became a teacher at Lawrence College in Appleton, Wisconsin, but moved in 1885 to California to recover his health. He began teaching at the University of Southern California but died the following year, leaving Clara to care for their young son Roy Bradley Wheeler. Clara was then married for a short time to Col. Presley C. Baker, a wealthy man many years her senior, who died in 1893. She is best known, however, as the wife of Robert Jones

55

Burdette (1844–1914), humorist and lecturer, who was associate editor of the *Burlington* (Iowa) *Hawkeye* and a friend of James Whitcomb Riley, Melville Delancy Landon ("Eli Perkins"), and other midwestern writers. After their marriage in 1899, Burdette moved from lecturing on the Chautauqua circuit to the ministry. He founded the Trinity Baptist Church in Los Angeles and preached to record crowds. Clara became a leader of women's societies and was founder and first president of the California Federation of Women's Clubs in 1900, chairman of the board of trustees of the General Federation of Women's Clubs, trustee of Syracuse University, Mills College, California College in China, Pasadena Hospital, and the Southwest Museum. She was director of food conservation for California during World War I and active in Republican politics, particularly in Herbert Hoover's campaign for the presidency.

Subject matter: Clara (Bradley) Burdette's life and family; women's clubs and societies (especially the General Federation of Women's Clubs, California Federation of Women's Clubs, and Alpha Phi Sorority); Mills College, Syracuse University, California College in China, the Southwest Museum, Trinity Baptist Church in Los Angeles (including manuscripts of sermons by Robert Burdette); Republican Party activities.

Significant persons: Susan (Brownell) ANTHONY (5), Carrie (Jacobs) BOND (23), Clara (Bradley) BURDETTE (1254), Robert Jones BURDETTE (948), Harry CHANDLER (16), Herbert Clark HOOVER (37), Lou (Henry) HOOVER (18), Melville Delancy LANDON (5), Charles Fletcher LUMMIS (65), John Steven McGROARTY (10), Ralph Palmer MERRITT (77), Harrison Gray OTIS (25), Aurelia (Henry) REINHARDT (96), James Whitcomb RILEY (23), Caroline M. (Seymour) SEVERANCE (11).

Physical description: letters, manuscripts (including diaries), documents, scrapbooks, and photographs.

Source: gift of Florence A. Walker, 1955 and 1962.

BURNETT, WELLINGTON CLEVELAND (1828–1907)
869 pieces, 1830–1935

Wellington C. Burnett was born in Connecticut of colonial ancestry. He left home at the age of seventeen, joined the U.S. Army, and received a commission after service in the Mexican War (1846–48). Burnett then attended Harvard Law School, practiced in Chicago, and in 1852 came to California, where he served as state senator for Yuba and Yolo Counties from 1855 to 1857. In 1859 he began the practice of law in San Francisco and was elected city and county attorney of San Francisco in 1869.

Subject matter: Burnett and his family (1843–1917), articles about early California, and a journal containing an account of Burnett's experiences as a soldier during the Mexican War.

Physical description: letters, documents, and manuscripts.

Source: purchased from Argonaut Book Shop, January, 1956, and from Laurence Lingle, August, 1972.

BURR, AARON (1756–1836)
[Diary] (1808–12)
Autograph MS. volumes 1257 pp.

Concerns mundane matters of Burr's life while he sojourned in Europe. Published in *The Private Journal of Aaron Burr,* ed. William K. Bixby (Rochester, N.Y.: The Post Express Printing Co., 1903, reprinted in 1976 by AMS Press.)

BURR-LEGUEN COLLECTION
73 pieces, 1797–1826

Aaron Burr (1756–1836), soldier, lawyer, politician, and con-
spirator, was U.S. senator (1791–97), member of the New
York state legislature (1797–99), and vice-president of the
United States (1801–04). After several abortive attempts to
free Spanish colonies in North America, Burr returned in 1812
to his legal practice in New York. He also returned to a lawsuit brought against him for the recovery of extensive debts
owed to Louis Leguen, a former client whom Burr and Alexander Hamilton had represented in litigation involving the
mercantile firm of Gouveneur and Kemble.

Subject matter: primarily the lawsuit, as reflected in correspondence between Burr and Leguen and their respective
lawyers.

Physical description: letters and documents (a few in French).

Source: gift of Mrs. Edward L. Doheny, 1952.

BURRIEL, ANDRÉS MARCOS (1719–62)
[Noticia de la California y de su Conquista Temporal y
Espiritual . . .] (Draft of portions of 2 volumes) (ca.1750)
Autograph MS. 2 volumes. Volume I contains map of upper
portion of Gulf of California as explored by Father Francisco
Eusebio Kino from 1698 to 1701.

Text in Spanish.
There are also extracts of reports covering missions in Lower
California and Pimería Alta.

BUSINESS WOMEN'S LEGISLATIVE COUNCIL OF CALIFORNIA
approximately 150 pieces, 1927–43

The Business Women's Legislative Council of California was organized to bring about and maintain, under the law, equal business opportunities for men and women.

Subject matter: organization and activities of the Business Women's Legislative Council.

Physical description: letters and documents.

Source: gift of Mrs. Marjorie Longwell, July, 1947.

C

CALIFORNIA FILE
approximately 1500 pieces, 1625–1964

This is a general file of miscellaneous, unrelated individual items and small groups of manuscripts dealing with California and the Trans-Mississippi West. The papers touch upon virtually every aspect of Western American history, ranging from a document signed by the founder of New Mexico, Juan de Oñate, written from Spain in 1625 and a contemporary copy of the report of Andrés Suárez complaining of the treatment of the Indians in New Mexico in 1647, through the period of exploration of California, the missions, the ranchos, the change to American political control, the gold rush and subsequent land boom, up to the latest letter containing a description of the Alaskan earthquake at Resurrection Bay in 1964.

The California File is a constantly growing collection to which new pieces are being added as they are received.

Significant persons: José Darío ARGÜELLO (7), Horace BELL (6), Diego de BORICA (9), José CASTRO (5), John Charles FRÉMONT (8), José de GÁLVEZ, Marqués de Sonora (5), Edward Meyer KERN (7), Charles Fletcher LUMMIS (6), Felipe de NEVE (5), James Hervey SIMPSON (5).

Physical description: letters, documents, and manuscripts (in English and Spanish).

Source: acquired from various sources throughout the years.

CALIFORNIA HISTORICAL DOCUMENTS COLLECTION
162 pieces, 1812–1912

The collection contains letters and documents by early Californians (including Pío Pico and José Castro) relating to politics and government, business, and mission affairs, especially that of Mission Santa Cruz. There are papers concerning the life and times of Abel Stearns, the activities of John Rowland in New Mexico and California (1835–65), the agitation of Alta Californians demanding self-government, the war between Mexico and the United States, and the events leading to California statehood. Included are final drafts of certain articles of the 1849 California Constitution and indexes and lists of civil and criminal cases in the courts of Los Angeles for the years 1830 to 1850.

Significant persons: Abel STEARNS (19).

Physical description: letters and documents, mainly from 1830–52 (in English and Spanish).

Source: gift of the Historical Society of Southern California, September, 1974.

CALLENDER, GUY STEVENS (1865–1915)
1315 pieces, ca.1897–ca.1914

Guy Stevens Callender, historian and economist, was born in Ohio in 1865, graduated from Oberlin College in 1891, and entered the senior class at Harvard in 1892, receiving his Ph.D. there in political science in 1897 and remaining as an instructor until 1900. From 1903 until his death in 1915 he occupied the Chair of Political Economy at the Sheffield Scientific School at Yale University. A recognized authority in the field of American economic history, Callender published his *Selections from the Economic History of the United States* in 1909.

Subject matter: Callender's research in the field of American economic history since the Civil War: economic aspects of the Civil War, Emancipation, Reconstruction, Negro suffrage, the condition and prospects of the Negro, capital development, industrial diversification, tariff policy, the laboring class and labor problems, immigration, agriculture, cotton and southern industry, transportation, monopolies, foreign trade, labor-saving machinery, and Ohio economics.

Physical description: manuscripts (carbon copies).

Source: gift of Max Farrand, June 3, 1942.

CANBY, WILLIAM J. (1825–90)
110 pieces, 1870–1974

William J. Canby, grandson of the seamstress Betsy Ross, read a paper in March, 1870, to the Pennsylvania Historical Society relating for the first time in public his family's tradition that Betsy Ross (Elizabeth Claypoole) made the first U.S. flag. He also spoke of his fruitless search for corroborative evidence. Upon Canby's death his brother George continued research on the story, and his findings were published in *The Evolution of the American Flag* (1909).

Subject matter: Betsy Ross and the American flag.

Physical description: mostly documents, with some letters, manuscripts, photographs, and printed matter.

Source: gift of Marion Balderston, 1974–75.

Bibliography: many of the significant pieces of this collection may be found in George Canby and Lloyd Balderston, *The Evolution of the American Flag* (Philadelphia: Ferris and Leach, 1909).

CAPLINGER, LEONARD J. (fl. 1862–68)
83 pieces, 1835–97

Leonard J. Caplinger was an Illinois farmer who served during the Civil War as a private in the Union Army.

Subject matter: the Civil War, particularly the siege of Vicksburg, medical and hospital care, and attitudes towards the war and Negroes, as reflected in letters exchanged between Caplinger and his wife Mary during 1862 and 1863.

Physical description: letters, documents, and 1 manuscript (pocket day-book).

Source: gift of Glen Joseph Goddard, September, 1965.

CARMICHAEL, JOHN F. (fl. 1795)
[Diary of a Surgeon in the Fourth Sub-Legion Under the Command of Maj. Gen. Anthony Wayne] (1795)
Autograph MS. 62 leaves

Covers the period from June 16 to December 3, 1795 and concerns the negotiations with the Indians in the Northwest Territory leading to the Treaty of Greenville, August 3, 1795.

CARR, JEANNE CAROLINE (SMITH) (1823–1903)
192 pieces, 1842–>1903

Jeanne C. Carr is best known for her influence in the lives of John Muir (q.v.), Helen Hunt Jackson, Charles Warren Stoddard, and others. She was born in Vermont and married Ezra Slocum Carr (1819–94), a physician and professor, who taught in eastern colleges and at the University of Wisconsin, and who also held government geological positions. In 1869 the Carrs came to California, where Ezra became professor at the University of California, and in 1873 together they organized the State Grange. In 1875 Ezra Carr was elected state superintendent of public instruction, and his wife was made assistant superintendent. The Carrs settled in Pasadena in 1880, where Jeanne Carr's long interest in botany inspired the development of their home "Carmelita," a garden showplace and center of cultural influence.

Subject matter: the history and description of California (especially early Pasadena), botany, agriculture, and education.

Significant persons: Ezra Slocum CARR (7), Jeanne Caroline (Smith) CARR (47), Asa GRAY (7), Helen Maria (Fiske) Hunt JACKSON (9), Helena (Opid) MODJESKA (6), John MUIR (1), and Charles Warren STODDARD (9).

Physical description: letters and manuscripts.

Source: purchased from Albert L. Carr, 1931 and 1936.

Bibliography: the collection is summarized in John C. Parish, *Huntington Library Bulletin,* no. 7 (April, 1935): 556.

CATLIN, AMOS PARMALEE (1823–1900)
approximately 2760 pieces, 1849–71

Amos P. Catlin was a lawyer from New York State who came to California in 1849, engaged in mining operations in the Mormon Island area, and later formed the American River Water and Mining Co. and the Natoma Water and Mining Co. During the 1860s he was associated with the assay and banking firm of Charles T. H. Palmer and Roger S. Day. Catlin, a member of the California bar for many years, was influential in establishing the state capital at Sacramento. He was elected to the state senate in 1852 and judge of the Superior Court at Sacramento in 1890.

Subject matter: mining in the Mormon Island area, activities of the American River Water and Mining Co. and the Natoma Water and Mining Co., and operations of the assay and banking firm of Palmer and Day.

Significant persons: John CURREY (7)

Physical description: letters and documents.

Source: purchased from Frank A. Guernsey, June, 1947.

CATLIN, GEORGE (1796–1872)
239 pieces, ca.1868–70; 1892

George Catlin, artist and author, was known especially for his paintings of Indians. Born in Wilkes-Barre, he studied law and practiced in Pennsylvania until his talent for painting led him to sell his law library and join a group of artists in Philadelphia in 1823. Catlin concentrated on portrait painting in Washington, D.C., until 1829, when he saw a dignified-looking delegation of visiting American Indians in Philadelphia. He then resolved to devote his life to preserving the appearance and character of the vanishing Indians and for forty-two years traveled extensively in the West and lived among the tribes. Catlin wrote many books and articles related to his experiences.

Subject matter: mainly Indians of North America: 1 unpublished, bound manuscript entitled *The North Americans in the Middle of the Nineteenth Century,* with separate pencil drawings, paintings, counterproofs, and engravings of paintings by Catlin, the majority of which are intended to illustrate the volume. Also includes a report written in 1892 by J. Garland Pollard containing a list of illustrations and letters concerning the acquisition and contents of this collection.

Physical description: letters and documents (in 1 bound volume), 1 manuscript volume, 203 manuscript drawings, and engravings and maps.

Source: purchased from Frank Glenn, November, 1954.

CAWSTON OSTRICH FARM
approximately 600 pieces, 1898–1952

The Cawston Ostrich Farm was established in South Pasadena, California, in 1898 by Edwin Cawston. The farm, developed as a source for the ostrich feather industry, sold its product all over the world and was awarded prizes at world expositions. The picturesque, semitropical park became a popular tourist attraction in the early 1900s.

Subject matter: business records of the Cawston Ostrich Farm, information about ostriches, and the personal and business affairs of Herbert James Vatcher, Jr., who was vice-president and manager of the firm.

Physical description: letters and documents.

Source: gift of the South Pasadena Public Library, December, 1968, and April, 1975.

CENTER, JOHN (1817–1908)
362 pieces, 1849–84

John Center came from Wisconsin to California in 1849 to seek his fortune in gold, but instead settled in San Francisco, becoming involved in many enterprises, including the nursery business, real estate, and mining speculation. Center promoted the expansion and civic improvement of San Francisco, especially in the Mission District. In 1863 he established a mining company in the Owens Valley.

Subject matter: gardening business, real estate and mining transactions, and civic enterprises in San Francisco from 1849 to 1884; papers regarding The Center Company, dealing with mining and water in the Owens Valley in 1863.

Physical description: letters, documents, and 1 map.

Source: purchased from Albert Dressler, April, 1926.

CHAMBERLIN, LEWIS H. (1843–1923)
152 pieces, 1862–65

Lewis H. Chamberlin, Union soldier, joined the 24th Michigan Infantry as a sergeant on June 12, 1862, and advanced to the rank of adjutant in 1864, mustering out on June 30, 1865.

Subject matter: the personnel of the 24th Michigan Infantry and the supplies and equipment used; the victory march of the Army of the Potomac in 1865.

Physical description: letters and documents, with 4 photographs of Chamberlin in the early 1900s.

Source: purchased from Dawson's Book Shop, 1958.

CHAPMAN, SOLON MAXLEY (1834–1927?)
approximately 600 pieces, 1859–1928

Solon M. Chapman, born in Connecticut, came to California before 1862. He was affiliated with the Bank of Napa from 1890 to 1920 and was president for many years.

Subject matter: banking and the daily life of a businessman in the Napa Valley, California (1862–1926).

Physical description: letters, manuscripts (including 85 volumes of diaries and a volume of reminiscences), and documents (including 2 volumes of account books).

Source: gift of Goldie Starr, August, 1939; and George M. Chapman, June, 1940.

CHIPMAN–DWINELLE COLLECTION
approximately 435 pieces, 1845–1943

William Worthington Chipman (1820?–66<), an attorney, with Gideon Aughinbaugh as partner, laid out the city of Alameda, California. The partners had first subleased the land from two Frenchmen in 1850, then purchased the entire Rancho Encinal San Antonio from its original owner, Luis María Peralta, in 1851. Following the death of William W. Chipman, his widow, Caroline E. Chipman, married John Whipple Dwinelle (1816–81), San Francisco lawyer and historian, who practiced law in San Francisco for thirty years and was one of the organizers of the San Francisco Bar Association. Dwinelle lived in Oakland and represented Alameda County in the state assembly.

Subject matter: the defense of titles in the Encinal San Antonio-Alameda City land transactions; the law practice of John Dwinelle; the law suits regarding the will of Josephine A. Phelps; the papers of Fanny J. Chipman, daughter of William Worthington Chipman; also a few mining papers (1862–67).

Significant persons: John Whipple DWINELLE (12).

Physical description: letters, documents, and maps.

Source: purchased from Grahame H. Hardy, December, 1949.

CHITTENDEN, LUCIUS EUGENE (1824–1900)
[Commonplace Book and Journal] (1869)
Autograph MS. volume 85 pp.

Contains short essays on political subjects and notes taken on a trip to Europe.

Memoranda (1869<)
Autograph MS. volume 121 pp.

A commonplace book containing quotes, short essays on various subjects, a genealogy of the Hatch family, and a list of "Vermont editions."

President Lincoln and His Administration at the Commencement of the War (1867)
Autograph MS. volume 48 pp.

CIVIL WAR COLLECTION
546 pieces, 1781–1915

The collection consists primarily of letters written by famous military figures during the Civil War. The principal topics covered are military maneuvers and battles, ordnance and other supplies, promotions and resignations, and military organization and personal affairs. The collection is strongest for the period 1861–65.

Significant persons: Pierre Gustave Toutant BEAUREGARD (20), Braxton BRAGG (5), Benjamin Franklin BUTLER (7), Jefferson DAVIS (5), David Glasgow FARRAGUT (7), Samuel Gibbs FRENCH (5), Ulysses Simpson GRANT (14), Henry Wager HALLECK (8), Edward HATCH (13), John Bell HOOD (7), Joseph HOOKER (5), Joseph Eggleston JOHNSTON (11), Philip KEARNY (5), Robert Edward

LEE (7), Abraham LINCOLN (6), James LONGSTREET (7), Nathaniel LYON (5), George Brinton McCLELLAN (5), Irvin McDOWELL (5), George Gordon MEADE (5), Francis Wilkinson PICKENS (15), David Dixon PORTER (5), Israel Bush RICHARDSON (7), Roswell Sabine RIPLEY (6), Philip Henry SHERIDAN (5), William Tecumseh SHERMAN (21), Henry Warner SLOCUM (6), George Henry THOMAS (19), Joseph WHEELER (2).

Physical description: primarily letters, with some documents and manuscripts (including 1 diary, maps, and battle plans).

Source: the collection is formed from manuscripts removed from the extra-illustrated book, *Battles and Leaders of the Civil War,* 4 vols. (The Century Company, [1887–88]), purchased from George T. Keating, 1955.

CLARK, FRANCIS (fl. 1850s)
46 pieces, 1856–59

Francis Clark was a resident of Folsom, California, in the eighteen-fifties. He engaged in businesses related to gold mining and was a partner in the firm of Brooks, Clark and Co. and in the American River Water and Mining Co.

Subject matter: gold mining property and finance in Placer and El Dorado Counties in California.

Physical description: letters and documents.

Source: purchased from Edwin Grabhorn, January, 1945.

CLARK, LINCOLN (1800–86)
690 pieces, 1758–1942

Lincoln Clark, lawyer and judge, was born in Conway, Massachusetts, in 1800, studied law in North Carolina after graduating from Amherst College in 1825, was admitted to the bar, and in 1837 moved with his wife (the former Julia Annah

Smith) to Tuscaloosa, Alabama, where he opened a law practice, served for a time in the state legislature and as state attorney general, and was raised to the circuit court bench. Clark's increasing opposition to slavery, however, led the family to free their own slaves and move, in 1847, to Dubuque, Iowa, where the judge was elected (as a Democrat) to the 32nd Congress and, aside from two years in Washington, continued to practice law. After the depression of 1857 (in which Clark suffered serious financial losses) and the outbreak of the Civil War (in the later years of which Mrs. Clark and her daughter served on the U.S. Sanitary Commission in the South), the family moved again, this time to Chicago, where Clark continued to practice law until retiring, six years before his death, to Conway.

Subject matter: Massachusetts social life and customs, the practice of law in Alabama and Iowa, government and Washington politics, the depression of 1857, and the U.S. Sanitary Commission. Primarily correspondence between Judge Clark and his wife in the 1840s and 1850s, and between Mrs. Clark and her friends and relatives in the 1870s and 1880s; a few papers from earlier generations of the families, and some correspondence concerning Mrs. Clark's work on the Sanitary Commission. Strongest in the decade of the 1850s.

Physical description: primarily letters, with a few documents, and 1 typescript narrative history of the Clark family, written in 1942 by a granddaughter, Mrs. Julia Lincoln (Ray) Andrews.

Source: gift of Judge Clark's grandchildren, 1943–47.

CLARKSON, DAVID (1726–82)
Copy Book of Letters 1765 (1765–86)
MS. volume 161 pp.

Also contains entries by Mathew Clarkson. Both men were New York City merchants.

CLAY, HENRY (1777–1852)
approximately 425 pieces, 1825–29

Henry Clay, statesman and politician, was raised in Virginia and, after studying law, entered politics in 1798. Thereafter he served his adopted state of Kentucky as both state and federal legislator for over fifty years. He was thrice defeated for the presidency and served from 1825 to 1829 in the administration of John Quincy Adams (for whose election in the House of Representatives Clay had voted despite contrary instructions from the Kentucky legislature) as secretary of state.

Subject matter: Clay's activities as secretary of state; international trade and commerce (particularly the Convention of 1822, the Colombian Convention, and the St. Petersburg Convention); the foreign relations of the United States (particularly with Great Britain, concerning such issues as the U.S.–Canadian boundary, the West Indian trade, and impressed American seamen; Brazilian and Colombian independence; the Panama Congress of 1826; American activity in Texas; the possibility of a Nicaraguan canal); routine State Department matters (instructions to U.S. diplomats, meetings with foreign representatives, and the behavior of both private citizens and diplomats). Letters by Clay to resident representatives of: Great Britain (120 letters), Russia (38), France (34), Brazil (30), Colombia (30), Spain (28), Sweden and Norway (21), Denmark (16), Mexico (16), the Netherlands (13), Sicily and the Papal States (13), Portugal (9), Prussia (9), Austria (6), Central America and Guatemala (6), and Saxony (6).

Physical description: letters (entirely Clay's out-letters, some of which are first or successive drafts, many of which bear corrections and additions, and many of which are in the handwriting of Clay's chief clerk, Daniel Brent).

Source: purchased from the Washington Cathedral through the agency of Thomas M. Spaulding, 1937.

CLELAND, ROBERT GLASS (1885–1957)
approximately 3000 pieces, 1809–1950

Robert G. Cleland, educator and historian, was born in Kentucky but came to California with his family at an early age. He lived in Duarte and Azusa, where his father was a Presbyterian minister. He received his B.A. and Ph.D. degrees from Occidental College and Princeton University. Subsequently he became an authority on California history and author of many books, and served as professor of history, dean of the faculty, and vice-president of Occidental College. After his retirement he was made a full-time member of the research staff of the Huntington Library.

Subject matter: research on Mexico compiled for the Doheny Foundation; source material on the fur trade; speeches; drafts and notes for books on California and the Southwest written by Cleland.

Physical description: documents and manuscripts.

Source: acquired from office files of Robert G. Cleland, September, 1964.

CLENDENEN, CLEMENS L. (fl. 1860s)
61 pieces, 1855–69

Clemens L. Clendenen, Union soldier, was a cook and barber for the 4th West Virginia Cavalry at Clarksburg and New Creek during the Civil War.

Subject matter: personal and family matters, sentiments about the war, and information about the life of the common soldier, as seen primarily in letters from Clendenen to his wife in Beverly, Ohio.

Physical description: letters.

Source: gift of Colonel C. C. Clendenen, 1948.

CLOUGH, STEPHEN (fl. 1800–01)
Journal Kept on Board the United States Frigate "Boston" of
32 Guns, George Little Esq. Commander (1800–01)
Autograph MS.S. volume 50 leaves

Covers the period from September 7, 1800 to July 4, 1801.
Concerns West Indian convoy duty.

CLYMAN, JAMES (1792–1881)
52 pieces, 1827–81

James Clyman, frontiersman and trapper, who was born in
Virginia and lived in Pennsylvania and Ohio, participated in
early pioneering exploits, such as the ascension of the Missouri
River, the discovery of South Pass in 1824, and the circum-
navigation of the Great Salt Lake in 1826. In partnership with
Goulding Arnett, Clyman engaged in a general store proprie-
torship and a sawmill business in Danville, Illinois, and later
saw service as a mounted ranger in the Black Hawk War. In
1844 Clyman traveled with a party of emigrants from Independence, Missouri, to Oregon, then led the McMahon-Cly-
man party from Oregon to California in 1845. He returned to
Independence in 1846, and in 1848 brought another group of
emigrants to California. Clyman settled in Napa, California,
married in 1849, and established his own ranch in 1850.

Subject matter: the Black Hawk War (1832–35); the business
papers of Clyman and Arnett (1832–40); Clyman's experiences during his overland journey to the West (1844–46).

Physical description: letters, manuscripts (including 10 diaries and 1 volume of verse), and documents.

Source: purchased from Charles L. Camp, October, 1925, and gift of Wilber Lamar Tallman, March, 1932.

Bibliography: Manuscripts of James Clyman have been published in *James Clyman, American Frontiersman,* ed. Charles L. Camp (San Francisco: California Historical Society, 1928).

COLBY, CLARA (BEWICK) (1846–1916)
237 pieces, 1882–1914

Clara (Bewick) Colby was an early and active member of the woman suffrage movement. While married to Leonard Wright Colby, a Nebraska lawyer and state senator who later served as a deputy attorney general in the Harrison administration (they were divorced by 1904), she served as president of the Nebraska Woman Suffrage Association and edited the influential feminist newspaper *Woman's Tribune.* In later years, although overshadowed by a younger generation of less militant suffragists, she was active in the international suffrage movement and as a lecturer.

Subject matter: the activities of the National American Woman Suffrage Association, the attempt to pass a constitutional amendment legalizing woman suffrage, and the general philosophy of the suffragist movement; comments on populism, racism, and civil violence.

Significant persons: Susan (Brownell) ANTHONY (117), Olympia BROWN (7), James Gowdy CLARK (25), Isabella (Beecher) HOOKER (14), and Elizabeth (Cady) STANTON (6).

Physical description: primarily letters, with a few documents, and one 333-page scrapbook containing clippings from the *Woman's Tribune* during the period 1883–91.

75

Source: gift of the Susan B. Anthony Memorial Committee of California, 1956.

COLDEN, CADWALLADER (1722–97)
The Journal of Cadwallader Colden, Esq., during the Revolutionary War (1776–79)
Autograph MS. 196 pp.

A Loyalist journal.

COLORADO RIVER RELOCATION CENTER
approximately 400 pieces, 1942–45

The Colorado River Relocation Center was established in May, 1942, at Poston, Arizona, to confine those Americans of Japanese descent who were required to leave the Pacific Coast during World War II. Edythe N. Backus, author of *Catalogue of Music in The Huntington Library Printed Before 1801,* volunteered to go to Poston as a teacher. Feeling the historic importance of the period, she collected materials relating to the life in the Relocation Center.

Subject matter: life at the Colorado River Relocation Center; included are the January 6 to June 27, 1945 issues of the camp newspaper, the *Poston Chronicle,* copies of the high school and junior high school newspapers from 1943 to 1945, and mimeographed bulletins and memoranda.

Physical description: letters, photographs, watercolor drawings, and printed material.

Source: gift of Edythe N. Backus, June, 1948.

COLTON, SHELDON (1835– ?)
106 pieces, 1823–1903

Sheldon Colton, businessman, Union soldier, and sometime poet, worked in Milan, Ohio, until the outbreak of the Civil War, when he left to serve with the 67th Ohio Infantry. In October 1864 he married Mary Whiting, and at the end of the war settled in Columbus, Ohio, where he worked at one time for the Lock Run Coal Co.

Subject matter: everyday life and family affairs in Ohio in the 1850s and 1860s; Civil War and a soldier's life; a few early letters from George B. Whiting relating to the activities of American missionaries in Lebanon in the 1830s. Strongest for the period 1851 to 1866.

Physical description: chiefly letters and manuscripts (including 2 volumes of poetry), with documents, 1 photograph, and ephemera.

Source: gift of Paul J. Appell, through Anne Huff Skousen, 1965.

COLYER, HENRY ISAAC (fl. 1860s)
146 pieces, 1862–65

Henry Isaac Colyer, Union soldier, enlisted in the 157th New York Volunteers in 1862 but was hospitalized for a heart condition from December of that year until August 1863. For the remainder of the war he served in the Veteran Reserve Corps, doing guard duty at a Connecticut conscript camp and in and around Washington.

Subject matter: primarily letters from Colyer to his family, in particular his mother and sisters, dealing with a soldier's everyday life of barracks, rations, finances, hospitals, conscripts, substitutes, desertions, drinking, courts martial, prisons, hospitals, and demobilization.

Physical description: letters.

Source: purchased from Clifford Couch Colyer (son), 1966.

CONSAG, FERNANDO (1703–59)
Derrotero del Viage que en descubrimiento de la Costa Oriental de Californias hastta el Rio Colorado, en donde seacaba su estrecho, hizo el P[adr]e Fernando Consag de la Compania de Jesus y Misionero de Californias, por Orden del P[adr]e Christoval de Escobar y Llamas Provincial de Nueva España de la Comp[añí]a de Jesus. (June 9, 1746–July 25, 1746)
MS.S. volume 36 pp. with MS. map of upper portion of Gulf of California

Text in Spanish.

CONSOLIDATED VIRGINIA MINING COMPANY
approximately 1300 pieces, 1876–1955

The Consolidated Virginia Mining Company, on the Comstock Lode at Virginia City, Nevada, was organized in 1867, but the lode was difficult to find, work stopped, and the stock fell considerably in 1870. In 1871 James Flood began to buy stock in Consolidated Virginia and, joined by John Mackay, James Fair, and William O'Brien, formed the Bonanza Firm. They then bought the land owned by the Consolidated Virginia Company and in 1873 struck the "Big Bonanza," which produced over $100,000,000 from 1873 to 1882. The firm bought control of the adjoining Ophir and Mexican mines in 1877. Although the Bonanza Firm dominated the Comstock from 1875 until 1895, when Mackay sold the interests to San Francisco stockbrokers, the last dividend was paid in 1880. The Consolidated Virginia Mine was the most successful mine on the Comstock and one of the few to pay more in dividends than it levied in assessments. In the 1930s the Consolidated Virginia Mining Company was reactivated to mine and mill the remaining ore. Some high-grade veins were found, and production continued until 1942 when mining was curtailed because of wartime restrictions, and continued only sporadically thereafter.

Subject matter: the business affairs of the Consolidated Virginia Mining Company in the period 1919–55 as seen in its correspondence, account books, and other records; a collection of 112 maps (both historic maps gathered by the firm in the 1930s and detailed new maps made to show the older workings of the mine, level by level); maps of Consolidated Virginia and Ophir mines; general maps of the district (including one made about 1879 and signed by Charles Frederick Hoffmann); maps of various other mines along the Comstock Lode.

Physical description: letters and documents (including 16 volumes) with maps.

Source: purchased from Neil Weinstein, May 9, 1975.

COOPER, SAMUEL (1725–83)
270 pieces, 1718–98

Samuel Cooper, scholar and Congregational minister, was born in Boston, educated at Harvard, and in 1743 appointed assistant pastor at Boston's Brattle Street Church. Four years later he became the sole incumbent and continued in the post for the remainder of his life. An ardent patriot and orator, Cooper numbered Franklin, John Adams, and other revolutionary leaders among his friends and was well known to many foreigners (particularly Frenchmen) visiting in New England.

Subject matter: primarily Cooper's sermons (strongest for the period 1740–59) and correspondence (particularly after 1771), covering such subjects as Congregationalism in New England, English America in international politics (from 1769 to 1783), French naval officers in North America (1778–83), and family affairs (1759–98); also includes a description of the campaign of 1778 and a biography of Cooper.

Significant persons: William COOPER (43), Benjamin FRANKLIN (5), and Anne-CÉSAR, Chevalier de LA LUZERNE (6).

Physical description: letters, manuscripts (including 195 sermons, 3 diaries, and 1 poem), and documents. Some of the pieces are in French.

Source: purchased from Marvin C. Taylor, 1926.

CORNELIUS, THOMAS R. (1827–99)
445 pieces, 1831–1925

Thomas R. Cornelius, author and soldier, was born in Mississippi and emigrated to Oregon with his family in 1845 as a member of the Meek party. He participated in the Cayuse War of 1847–48 and the Yakima War of 1855–56 and served in the Oregon State Legislature for twenty years. In 1861 Cornelius was made a colonel by the U.S. War Department and ordered to raise a volunteer regiment, the Oregon First Cavalry, which he commanded at Ft. Walla Walla until his resignation the next year.

Subject matter: the military protection of the Oregon area during the Civil War period and the development of the Oregon Central Railroad, 1867–70.

Significant persons: John T. APPERSON (67).

Physical description: letters (including 2 volumes of letterbooks) and documents (including account books).

Source: purchased from Fred Lockley, Jr., 1924.

COTTON, ROBERT CHRISTIE (1885–1940 <)
160 pieces, 1903–40

Robert Christie Cotton, career army officer and historian, graduated from the U.S. Military Academy at West Point in 1908 and was commissioned a second lieutenant in the 2nd Infantry. He served in the Philippine Islands (1909–11, 1915), along the Mexican-American border (1913–15), in the Hawaiian Islands (1917), and with the American Expeditionary Forces in France in 1918. By 1919 he was attached to the General Staff with the rank of major, and served as executive officer of the Historical Branch of the War Plans Division of the General Staff from 1919 to 1921. Cotton edited the *U.S. Infantry Journal,* wrote a doctoral thesis in history at Georgetown University in 1931, taught military science, contributed articles on military and diplomatic history to several journals, and was joint translator (with John N. Greeley) of Charles Ardant du Picq's *Battle Studies.* Promoted to the rank of colonel in the 1930s, Cotton retired from the service in 1940 because of continued ill health and settled in Los Angeles.

Subject matter: army life and military affairs; military and diplomatic history, including Cotton's papers about George Washington; the Philippine insurrection, Cuba, Puerto Rico, and the Spanish-American War; Mexican-American relations and military affairs from 1909 to 1912; the Far East in 1917; the St. Mihiel Offensive of 1918 and the Neuilly Treaty with Bulgaria in 1919; the economic condition of Italy in 1929; U.S. foreign relations.

Physical description: letters, manuscripts (many typewritten), documents, and some newspaper clippings.

Source: acquired from Mrs. Sally Cotton, 1953.

COUTS, CAVE JOHNSON (1821–74)
approximately 16,000 pieces, 1832–1951

Cave J. Couts, an army officer sent to California in 1848, married the daughter of Juan Bandini and became the owner of the large Guajome Rancho in San Diego County. Couts attended the U.S. Military Academy from 1838 to 1843, was ordered to Monterrey, Mexico, with the First Dragoons and then to California. In 1849 he led the escort for the U.S. Boundary Commission mapping the border from San Diego to the Colorado River. After his marriage in 1851, he engaged in the cattle business on his extensive rancho. His son, Cave J. Couts, Jr. (1856–1943), became a civil engineer and worked in Central America and as deputy surveyor for San Diego County in 1884. Thereafter he managed the Guajome Ranch and engaged in various business ventures.

Subject matter: the history of San Diego County, particularly Indians (including the uprising led by Antonio Garra in 1851); ranchos and cities (with survey maps and land papers); Mission San Luis Rey; the cattle industry; politics; there is also some material on the Civil War and the army papers (306 pieces, 1852–61) of Aaron B. Hardcastle.

Significant persons: John FORSTER (188), John Strother GRIFFIN (34), Benjamin Ignatius HAYES (44), Charles Robinson JOHNSON (265), Ephraim W. MORSE (84), George Allan PENDLETON (59), Alfred ROBINSON (22), Abel STEARNS (120), and Jonathan Trumbull WARNER (6).
Physical description: letters, documents, maps, and photographs.

Source: purchased from Mrs. Ida Richardson, 1958.

Bibliography: the diary of the journey of Cave J. Couts, Sr. from Monterrey, Mexico to Los Angeles, California in 1848–49, has been published: *Hepah, California!, The Journal of Cave Johnson Couts* (Tucson: Arizona Pioneers' Historical Society, 1961).

CRAIGHEAD, JACOB DITZLER (1873–1958<)
approximately 1800 pieces, 1850–1959

J. D. Craighead, Colorado rancher, graduated from college in South Carolina in 1893. He brought his ailing wife to Springer, New Mexico, from Ohio in 1900. In 1905 he started a cattle ranch in La Junta, Colorado, which was the beginning of the Hereford industry in that area.

Subject matter: the Craighead family, the Craigland Ranch, and irrigation projects (the Catlin Canal, the La Junta Canal and Reservoir, and the Otero Irrigation District).

Physical description: letters, manuscripts (including diaries), documents, maps, and photographs.

Source: gift of Margaret Craighead, February, 1964.

CRANK, JAMES FILMORE (1842–1928<)
450 pieces, 1880–1902

James F. Crank came to California from New York in 1874 and bought the Fair Oaks Ranch in Pasadena from Benjamin S. Eaton in 1877. Crank was active in Los Angeles, where he organized the First National Bank, became an owner of the Los Angeles *Times*, helped secure Westlake Park for the city, and gave land for the Raymond Hotel in Pasadena. He was instrumental in the founding of the Los Angeles and San Gabriel Valley Railroad, which began operation in 1885 and was sold to the Santa Fe Railroad in 1887. He built the first cable street railway in the West in Los Angeles in 1889 and helped found the city of Monrovia, California, in 1886.

Subject matter: the development of Los Angeles County, particularly city and interurban railways (Los Angeles Cable Railway Co., Pacific Railway Co., Los Angeles and San Gabriel Valley Railroad Co., Los Angeles Development Co.); the wine industry (Sierra Madre Vintage Co., Lamanda Park, California); the Fair Oaks Ranch, Pasadena; the Azusa Land and Water Co.; education in California private schools during the late nineteenth century.

Physical description: letters, manuscripts, documents (including 10 bound volumes), and 32 maps.

Source: purchased from Mrs. Mildred M. Crank, May, 1935, and March, 1936.

CUCAMONGA CITRUS FRUIT GROWERS' ASSOCIATION
350 pieces, 1896–1927

The Cucamonga Citrus Fruit Growers' Association was a San Bernardino County, California, organization formed to facilitate the packing and distribution of citrus fruit through a central exchange.

Subject matter: the operation of the Cucamonga Citrus Fruit Growers' Association from 1896 to 1927.

Physical description: documents.

Source: gift of California Fruit Growers' Association, August, 1937.

CUNNINGHAM, EUGENE LAFAYETTE (1896–1957)
approximately 6000 pieces, 1915–58

Eugene Cunningham, author of Western fiction and other works, grew up in Texas, served in the Navy during both World Wars, and began writing in 1915. He was a correspondent for various newspapers and magazines and made a trip on horseback over Central America. After 1932 he wrote mainly Southwestern history and fiction, such as *Triggernometry*, *Riders of the Night*, etc.

Subject matter: Cunningham and his relations with other writers of Western lore, such as Eugene Manlove Rhodes and his wife; General Thomas Cruse, who was with the Army in Arizona during the Indian campaigns and wrote *Apache Days and After*.

Significant persons: Eugene Manlove RHODES (21), May Louise (Davison) Purple RHODES (104), and Thomas CRUSE (12).

Physical description: letters, manuscripts (including 12 bound volumes), 5 scrapbooks, and 250 photographs (many reproduced from the collection of Noah H. Rose of San Antonio, Texas).

Source: purchased from Mrs. Eugene Cunningham, June, 1959.

CURTIS, SAMUEL RYAN (1807–66)
79 pieces, 1828–66

Samuel Ryan Curtis, Union officer and engineer, graduated from West Point in 1831. Leaving the regular army in 1832, he became a civil engineer and lawyer but organized the Ohio Militia for the Mexican War and served therein in various capacities, including a period as governor of Saltillo, Mexico. From 1848 to 1855 Curtis resumed his engineering career, primarily in Iowa. He represented that state in Congress from 1857 to 1861 and promoted the transcontinental railroad project. During the Civil War he was commander of the Army of the Southwest and of the Departments of Kansas, Missouri, and the Northwest. Curtis ended a career of public service as a U.S. Indian commissioner.

Subject matter: the presidential election of 1828; the Mexican War (particularly battles, troop movements, and the nature and life of the Mexican soldier); the Civil War (including the Battle of Pea Ridge, Arkansas, at which Curtis defeated Confederate forces); Missouri politics; the transcontinental railroad; western Indian affairs; some personal and family life; strongest for the periods 1846–47 and 1862–66.

Physical description: letters and 1 document.

Source: gift of Mrs. Charles D. Seeberger, 1937.

D

DALLAS, GEORGE MIFFLIN (1792–1864)
45 pieces, 1847–59

George Mifflin Dallas, Philadelphia lawyer, politician, diplomat, and vice-president under Polk, was appointed ambassa-
dor to Great Britain by President Pierce in 1856. With George
Villiers, 4th Earl of Clarendon and British secretary of state for
foreign affairs, Dallas negotiated the Dallas-Clarendon Treaty
of 1856 to settle grievances between the two nations concerning a British protectorate over the Mosquito Indians of Nicaragua, British interference in a Nicaragua–Costa Rica boundary dispute, and title to the Bay Islands off the coast of
Honduras. The U.S. Senate ratified the treaty pending certain
changes, but as Great Britain rejected these changes, the treaty
was never implemented.

Subject matter: U.S. diplomacy, Nicaragua, and the Dallas-
Clarendon Treaty.

Significant persons: Lewis CASS (8), William Learned
MARCY (23), and George William Frederick VILLIERS, 4th
Earl of Clarendon (7).

Physical description: primarily letters, with a few documents.

Source: unknown.

DALTON, HENRY (1804–84)
2430 pieces, 1819–1942

Henry Dalton, California land owner and businessman, was born in London and engaged in the coastal trade in Peru and Mexico before acquiring property in California in 1843. After his purchase of Rancho Azusa in 1844, Dalton eventually became the owner of five adjacent ranches. In 1847 he married María Guadalupe Zamorano, daughter of Agustín Vicente Zamorano. During the conflict between Mexico and the United States, Dalton supported the Mexican side and suffered damages and losses of livestock on his properties as a result of the war. After American occupation he lost much of his land to squatters and in litigation with the government. He spent the rest of his life trying to settle his claims against Mexico and the United States.

Subject matter: life in early California, including the daily occurrences at Rancho Azusa; business papers from Dalton's Peruvian trade years (1827–42); litigation about his Mexican War claims and his land in Mexico; land papers and maps of Ranchos Azusa, Santa Anita, San Francisquito, San José and Addition.

Physical description: letters (including 2 letterbooks), manuscripts (including 8 diaries), documents (including 10 memorandum books, 35 account books, and 14 banking and receipt books).

Source: purchased from Mrs. Roger Dalton, January, 1958.

DAMON, JOHN FOX (1827–1904)
63 pieces, 1849–1902

John F. Damon, newspaperman and pioneer of the gold rush days, sailed around Cape Horn in 1849 to California from Massachusetts, where he had been a printer. After working in the gold mines for several months, Damon took jobs with various California newspapers, and in 1858 started on a trip up the Fraser River in British Columbia as a correspondent for the Victoria, British Columbia, *Gazette*. In 1864 he went to Portland, Oregon, where he served as editor of the *Oregonian* for a short time, then entered the ministry, becoming pastor of the Portland Congregational Church. Damon settled in Seattle, Washington, in 1868 and spent the rest of his years in the ministry.

Subject matter: California during the gold rush period (1849–56); the gold rush period in British Columbia (with five letters from Victoria and a diary of a trip up the Fraser River to the Cariboo district in 1859); Oregon (1856–66); Washington (1876–83), with many letters regarding the activities of the Scottish Rite Masons.

Physical description: letters, manuscripts (including 1 diary), documents.

Source: purchased from E. C. Damon, June, 1930.

DANE FAMILY COLLECTION
1030 pieces, 1849–1934

Ezra Dane (1828–1921) crossed the plains to California in 1852 and engaged in mining in the Tuolomne region. He married in 1859, established a home in Sonora, California, and in 1884 acquired a fruit ranch, "Sunny Ridge," near Pasadena, California. George Ezra Dane (1904–41), grandson of Ezra Dane, was a lawyer and a writer of folklore, western history, and humor.

Subject matter: personal correspondence to and from the Dane family, mainly concerning family matters, the largest group being from Ada (Nutting) Baker, written from Decatur, Michigan; letters (1863–64) of James W. Nutting dealing with the Civil War. Includes notes and source material used by George Ezra Dane in editing "Sketches of Old Block," "Sojourn with Royalty," etc.

Physical description: letters, documents, manuscripts, and some newspaper clippings.

Source: gift of George E. Dane, 1934–39.

DANIELL, CHARLES PENNIMAN (1828–61)
47 pieces, 1844–53

Charles P. Daniell, San Francisco merchant, sailed around the Horn from Boston in 1849–50. In San Francisco he opened a hardware store, which he operated until 1853. The next year Daniell returned to Boston, was married in 1860, and came back to California but lived for only one year.

Subject matter: life in San Francisco (1850–53) and Daniell's life and experiences, as seen in his letters from the Boston area, where he helped with his father's dry goods business; from the ship "Marcia Cleaves" as he sailed around the Horn to California; and chiefly from the city of San Francisco.

Physical description: letters, photographs.

Source: gift of Mrs. Austin Jenison, November, 1967.

DANIELL, JOHN, SR. (1839–98)
790 pieces, 1868–1945

John Daniell, Sr., came to the United States from Cornwall, England, in 1863. He supervised a gold mine in California for a short time in 1872 but spent the following twenty-two years

(1872–94) as superintendent of a group of copper mines in Michigan's Lake Superior region, which were owned by the Boston investment firm of A. S. Bigelow and Joseph Clark. In addition to developing the Michigan mines (some of which later became part of the Calumet & Hecla Copper Company), Daniell also made consulting trips to Montana and Arizona for his firm. His advice led to their investment in mines which were later amalgamated to form the Anaconda Copper Company of Montana.

Subject matter: operation and development of the Michigan mines and related railroads, labor conditions, the activities of rival companies, mining finance, stock market speculations, and national and international mining syndicates. There is also some information on mining in Arizona and Montana. Three letterbooks and correspondence belonging to John Daniell, Jr. (1875–1945), son of the above, are chiefly concerned with mining in Finland, Arizona, and Montana, where the younger Daniell worked as a mining engineer from 1899 to 1923.

Significant persons: Albert S. BIGELOW (255).

Physical description: letters (including 26 volumes of letterbooks), documents, and 36 photographs (mainly of the Finnish-American Mining Company).

Source: purchased from Mr. and Mrs. Earl Wiitanen, January, 1973.

DAVIES, GODFREY (1892–1957)
approximately 4500 pieces, 1913–60

Godfrey Davies, historian, was born in England. Educated in history at Pembroke College, Oxford, he became the assistant of Sir Charles Harding Firth. He emigrated to the United States in 1925 and became a citizen in 1939. Davies taught at

Oxford (1919–24), the University of Chicago (1925–30), the University of California at Los Angeles (1938–45), and the California Institute of Technology. In 1931 he joined the research staff of the Huntington Library, serving as editor of its quarterly (1937–48) and chairman of the research staff (1948–51). He had a major role in shaping the research, publication, and acquisition policies of the Library. An authority on seventeenth-century English history, Davies was best known for his *Bibliography of British History, Stuart Period* (1928) and *The Early Stuarts* (1937)

Subject matter: seventeenth-century English history; the Huntington Library; professional matters, such as positions for scholars, academic freedom in the 1950s, the justification of historical studies, and academic publications; a little on contemporary issues and events like World War II and English and Irish life; British foreign policy; a negligible amount of personal material.

Significant persons: Lily Bess CAMPBELL (13), Sir George Norman CLARK (51), Merle CURTI (7), Godfrey DAVIES (ca.2325), Edward Meade EARLE (7), Sir James EDMONDS (7), Max FARRAND (21), Sir Charles Harding FIRTH (47), William HALLER (34), Wilbur K. JORDAN (21), Alfred A. KNOPF (9), Robert Andrews MILLIKAN (10), John Robert MOORE (46), Charles Frederic MULLET (12), William Bennett MUNRO (22), Wallace NOTESTEIN (15), Frederick Maurice POWICKE (27), Conyers READ (14), Caroline ROBBINS (15), Bernadette Everly SCHMITT (18), George SHERBURNE (66), John Ewart Wallace STERLING (19), David Harris WILLSON (11), Frank Percy WILSON (30), Austin WRIGHT (6), Louis Booker WRIGHT (39).

Physical description: letters; documents, such as lecture and research notes, and transcripts of primary sources; manuscripts of scholarly articles and books; a few photographs.

Source: gift of Margaret Gay Davies, 1973.

DAVIS, JEFFERSON (1808–89)
[Autobiographical Sketch to 1846] (1847<)

Autograph MS. 4 pp.

DAVIS, WILLIAM HEATH, JR. (1822–1909)
634 pieces, 1843–1906

William H. Davis, Jr., San Francisco merchant and author, was born in Hawaii, the son of a Boston shipmaster and early trader. He visited California as a boy and returned to stay in 1838, employed as a clerk in his uncle's store in Monterey. Davis established his own store in San Francisco in 1845 and became a prominent citizen of that city. He married María de Jesús Estudillo in 1847 and was associated with many prominent California families. Davis was instrumental in the founding of San Diego and Oakland and in 1889 published his memoirs of early days in California, *Sixty Years in California.*

Subject matter: shipping and commerce before and during the gold rush; land titles (particularly for Rancho San Leandro); manuscripts and source material for Davis' book, *Sixty Years in California* and its later enlarged version, entitled *Seventy-Five Years in California.*

Physical description: manuscripts, letters, documents, and newspaper clippings.

Source: purchased from A. S. McDonald, 1916, and John Howell, August, 1928.

Bibliography: Davis' books were published as: *Sixty Years in California* (San Francisco: A. J. Leary, 1889) and *Seventy-Five Years in California* (San Francisco: John Howell, 1929).

DENSMORE, PARK (fl. 1890)
41 pieces, 1890

Park Densmore, accompanied by other members of the Erie (Pennsylvania?) Cycling Club, toured Great Britain and Europe in the summer of 1890 and wrote numerous, lengthy descriptive letters to his family at home.

Subject matter: travel in Great Britain and on the Continent.

Physical description: letters.

Source: gift of Robert E. Densmore, grandson of Park Densmore, 1973.

DESTOUCHES, CHARLES RENÉ DOMINIQUE SOCHET, CHEVALIER (1727–93)
117 pieces, 1754–1804

Charles René Dominique Sochet, Chevalier Destouches, French admiral, sailed from France in 1780 with the fleet of the Chevalier de Ternay, bringing General Rochambeau and 6000 men to the aid of the American revolutionary forces. On the death of de Ternay in December, 1780, Destouches assumed command of the French squadron at Newport, Rhode Island, and in that capacity engaged the British fleet under Admiral Marriott Arbuthnot, indecisively, off Cape Henry in March, 1781. After taking part in the seige of Yorktown and the attack on the island of St. Christopher, Destouches returned to France, where he died in 1793.

Subject matter: French participation in the American revolution, particularly naval affairs and administration; French and English fleet movements; the Cape Henry engagement. Strongest for the years 1780–81.

Significant persons: Jean Charles d'ARSAC, Comte de HECTOR (5), Anne-CÉSAR, Chevalier de LA LUZERNE (14), Jean François de GALAUP, Comte de LA PÉROUSE (17), PENEVERT (the French agent at New London) (9), Antoine Raimond Jean Gaulbert Gabriel de SARTINE (8), and George WASHINGTON (5).

Physical description: primarily letters, with manuscripts (including 7 maps, 1 journal, and 1 volume of drawings of military and other flags and emblems), and documents. Most of the collection is in French, and a few of the letters are contemporary copies.

Source: purchased from the American Art Association, 1926.

DOCKWEILER, JOHN HENRY (1864–1930<)
69 pieces, 1882–1931

John H. Dockweiler, California civil engineer, was employed in the office of Los Angeles City Surveyor and on railroad surveys from 1880 to 1887. He served as Los Angeles City Engineer for three terms (1891–99) and in this position was instrumental in the development of the Los Angeles water-supply system. From 1899 to 1904 Dockweiler was a consultant in engineering, water projects, and the investigation of Western mining properties. From 1904 to 1916 he was a consulting engineer for the cities of San Francisco and Oakland but by 1925 had returned to Southern California and continued consulting on irrigation and other engineering projects.

Subject matter: surveys of Los Angeles and environs (1882–92) and of water supplies for the San Francisco and Oakland area (1906–16).

Physical description: documents (field books).

Source: purchased from Dawson's Book Shop, July, 1966.

DODGE, FRED JAMES (1854–1938)
2313 pieces, 1890–1938

Fred J. Dodge, special investigator for Wells, Fargo & Co. for forty years, was the first white child born in Butte County, California. He worked with his father's pack train, which took supplies to gold camps, and later served as a stage driver in California and Nevada. He was known for his relentless search for justice during his many years as chief special agent for Wells, Fargo & Co.

Subject matter: material on nine investigations (in Texas, Oklahoma, Arkansas, and Louisiana), from 1893 to 1912. Important chiefly for photographs of outlaws, lists of criminals, and the letters to and from John P. Clum (twenty-three letters, 1930–32).

Significant persons: John Philip CLUM (5).

Physical description: letters, documents, and 116 photographs.

Source: purchased from William Wreden, August, 1963.

DORNIN, THOMAS ALOYSIUS (1800–74)
Journal and Remarks on Board the United States Steam Frigate "San Jacinto" (1860–61)
Autograph MS. volume 119 pp. illus.

The "San Jacinto" patrolled the African coast in search of slave traders. The journal also contains entries Dornin made while on board the "Constellation" sailing from Portsmouth, N.H., to New York City.

Letterbook (1860–1861)
Autograph MS. volume 101 pp.

Kept while on board the "San Jacinto."

DOTY, JAMES DUANE (1799–1865)
[Commonplace Book] (1826–56)
Autograph MS.S. volume 107 pp.

Indian words, summaries of Indian speeches, topographical details of Wisconsin, lyrics, and anecdotes.

[Letterbooks] (1829–39)
Autograph MS. 319 pp. in two volumes.

Northwestern Expedition under Gen. Cass in 1820 (1820)
Autograph MS. volume 151 pp.

Contains a report from Doty to Michigan territorial governor Lewis Cass, Nov. 5, 1820. The report was published as "Northern Wisconsin in 1820" in the Wisconsin State Historical Society *Collections*, 7(1873–76), 195–200. Extracts of the report, with an introduction contained herein, were published as "Notes on the North-Western Part of the Territory of Michigan, 1820–1822" in an 1822 issue of the Detroit *Gazette*. Also contains a narrative headed "On the Manners and Customs of the Northern Indians" and a letter to the editor of the *Gazette*.

[Notes on the History of Wisconsin] (ca.1842)
Autograph MS. volume 243 pp.

Mostly extracts from Alexander Henry, *Travels and Adventures in Canada and the Indian Territories . . . 1760–1776* (New York: I. Riley, 1809). Also extracts from the Pierre F. X. de Charlevoix, *Journal of a Voyage to North-America* (London, 1761).

Words and Sentences Used in a Canoe Voyage and Journey by Land (ca.1820)
Autograph MS. volume 243 pp.

Contains vocabulary and grammar of the Sauk, Fox, Winnebago, and other northern tribes and extracts from various writings on European rights to Indian land.

DOWELL, BENJAMIN FRANKLIN (1826–97)
277 pieces, 1855–69; 1895

Benjamin F. Dowell, Oregon attorney and newspaperman, was born in Virginia and graduated in law from the University of Virginia in 1847. He emigrated to California from Missouri in 1850, then to Oregon where he participated in the Indian wars as a member of the 1st Regiment, Oregon Volunteers. He settled in Jacksonville, Oregon, became proprietor of the Oregon *Sentinel,* and was influential in local politics.

Subject matter: Oregon politics and government, transportation (including some material on pack trains, mail routes, and railroads), and Indian Wars.

Physical description: letters (including a letterbook), documents, and manuscripts.

Source: purchased from Fred Lockley, March, 1924.

DUARTE-MONROVIA FRUIT EXCHANGE
approximately 21,000 pieces, 1892–1937

The Duarte-Monrovia Fruit Exchange in Los Angeles County (originally named the Duarte Fruit Exchange, then the Duarte-Monrovia Citrus Association), was one of the original seven members of the California Fruit Growers Exchange when the latter was formed in 1893.

Subject matter: business records of this cooperative association formed to process and market citrus fruit in Southern California.

Physical description: letters (including 11 letterbooks) and documents (including 164 volumes of ledgers, account books, etc.).

Source: gift of Duarte-Monrovia Fruit Exchange, 1937–38.

DUDLEY, THOMAS HAINES (1819–93)
4684 pieces, 1841–1900

Thomas Haines Dudley, American diplomat and politician, became active in New Jersey Republican circles in the early 1840s, was chairman of the Republican state committee and delegate to the Republican convention of 1860, and in 1861 was appointed U.S. consul to Liverpool. During the Civil War he was active in attempts to prevent Confederate shipbuilding in England and from 1865 until his return to the United States in 1872 was much occupied with settling property claims arising out of the war. His political career continued until 1891, and he died two years later.

Subject matter: Confederate shipbuilding and blockade running, British claims against the United States after the war, efforts to confiscate Confederate property in England, and routine consular matters. Includes Dudley's personal and political correspondence throughout his entire public career, which contains information on various political campaigns, the Republican convention of 1860, contemporary political issues such as slavery, temperance, and protection, and Dudley's own personal and social life.

Significant persons: Charles Francis ADAMS (25), Adam BADEAU (31), John BIGELOW (10), Joseph P. BRADLEY (11), Frederick Carroll BREWSTER (11), John BRIGHT (32), Henry Charles CAREY (110), Charles Dexter CLEVELAND (42), George Hammell COOK (21), Caleb CUSHING (28), John Chandler Bancroft DAVIS (25), William Lewis

DAYTON (24), William Maxwell EVARTS (23), Hamilton FISH (26), Frederick FRALEY (10), Montgomery GIBBS (15), Horace GREELEY (9), Charles HALE (15), William HUNTER (8), Sir Robert LUSH (11), Hugh McCULLOCH (7), Benjamin MORAN (ca.250), Andrew MURRAY (14), Thomas NELSON (13), John Thompson NIXON (8), James Osborne PUTNAM (25), Isaac Fletcher REDFIELD (48), Robert Cumming SCHENK (9), Frederick William SEWARD (12), William Henry SEWARD (39), William Tecumseh SHERMAN (7), Charles Perrin SMITH (6), Erasmus Peshine SMITH (9), Warner Lewis UNDERWOOD (46), Morrison Remick WAITE (6), David Ames WELLS (15), John WELSH (6), and John Ancrum WINSLOW (29).

Physical description: letters (including 22 volumes of diplomatic correspondence and 1 volume of copies of Confederate correspondence), documents (including 8 account books and 2 volumes of memoranda concerning shipping), 6 scrapbooks of newspaper clippings, and miscellaneous pamphlets, photographs, and other printed material.

Source: purchased from E. Lawrence Dudley (grandson of Thomas Haines Dudley) through the agency of Stanley V. Henkels, 1923.

DULING, JOHN F. (fl. 1920s)
approximately 300 pieces, 1925–27

John F. Duling was a Los Angeles mining engineer and real estate developer.

Subject matter: reports and maps of various mines in Arizona, California, Montana, Nevada, New Mexico, and Canada (Cariboo Mining District, British Columbia); tract maps and some reports of land subdivisions in Southern California, chiefly in the Topanga-Malibu, Norwalk-Whittier, Lake Elsinore, Glendale, Lancaster, and Fillmore areas.

Physical description: documents (bound reports), maps (mostly blueprint), and copies of photographs.

Source: purchased from Spencer Moore, July, 1961.

DUMOURIEZ, CHARLES FRANÇOIS (1739–1823?)
Histoire de la Guerre d'Amerique (ca. 1782)
Autograph MS.S. volume 112 pp.

Text in French. Dumouriez's translation of an anonymous narrative written in English.

DUTCH WEST INDIA COMPANY
[Van Rappard Manuscripts] (1624–26)
MS. volume 115 pp.

Five pieces consisting of letters from and instructions to officials at New Netherland. Published in Arnold F. J. Van Laer, ed., *Documents Relating to the History of New Netherland . . . in the Huntington Library* (San Marino: Huntington Library, 1924).

E

EAGLE, JOHN H. (fl. 1850s)
49 pieces, 1852–55

John H. Eagle came to California to mine gold and worked near Auburn, California, from 1852 to 1855.

Subject matter: the daily life of a miner in the California Gold Rush country, 1852–55, including details of prices of commodities, living conditions, and a description of the community; also a few letters describing Eagle's voyage via the Isthmus of Panama.

Physical description: letters.

Source: purchased from Helen L. Dobson, September, 1934.

EATON, WILLIAM (1764–1811)
555 pieces, 1792–1829

William Eaton, army officer and diplomat, graduated from Dartmouth College and served for a time in the army. In 1798 he was appointed consul to Tunis. Successful at renegotiating a treaty, Eaton was unsuccessful in his attempt to restore peace between Tripoli and the United States.

Subject matter: U.S. relations with the Barbary states; the Tripolitan War, 1801–05; James Leander Cathcart; naval operations of the U.S. and the European powers; Eaton's professional and personal affairs, including his army career, business transactions, claims against the U.S., and relations with family and friends.

Significant persons: AHMED II, Bey of Tripoli (13), Samuel BARRON (6), James Leander CATHCART (114), Rufus KING (7), James MADISON (6), Francisco MENDRICE (6), Nicolai Christian NISSEN (37), Richard O'BRIEN (78), and Timothy PICKERING (8).

Physical description: primarily letters and documents (including 9 volumes of contemporary copies), with manuscripts (including 2 commonplace books and 3 sketches). Some of the pieces in French, Itauay Arabic, and code.

Source: purchased from Charles Harbeck through the agency of George D. Smith, 1917.

Bibliography: part of the collection has been published in *Naval Documents Related to the United States Wars with the Barbary Powers . . . ,* 6 vols. (Washington: Government Printing Office, 1939–44).

EATON, WILLIAM P. (fl. 1836–56)
47 pieces, 1836–64

William P. Eaton, of Connecticut, attended both Yale Law School and Harvard Law School before taking up a teaching career in Alabama and Texas. In later life he moved to New York.

Subject matter: education in New England, Alabama, and Texas; family affairs and personal religious beliefs.

Physical description: letters.

Source: gift of Miriam C. Post, 1969.

EDGERTON, R. CURTIS (fl. 1861–62)
46 pieces, 1861–62

R. Curtis Edgerton, Union soldier, of Walnut Grove, Illinois, joined the 26th Illinois Volunteer Regiment in the fall of 1861. Although Edgerton entered the army as a member of the band, he gradually concentrated on hospital work and was eventually acting assistant surgeon. He was stationed in Hannibal, Pleasant, and Commerce, Missouri, and saw some service in Tennessee and Mississippi.

Subject matter: soldier's life and medical and sanitary affairs during the Civil War, chiefly as seen in Edgerton's letters to his wife Lydia.

Physical description: letters.

Source: gift of Mr. and Mrs. Charles L. Carter, August, 1975.

EDWARDS, PIERPONT (1750–1826)
44 pieces, 1753–1876
Pierpont Edwards, lawyer and politician, was the son of Jonathan Edwards. He represented Connecticut in the Continental Congress and in the Constitutional Convention. His son Ogden (1781–1862), also a lawyer, became a judge of the New York Supreme Court and a member of the state legislature.

Subject matter: personal affairs of Pierpont and Ogden; local, national, and international politics. There is no topical coherence to the collection.

Physical description: letters and documents.

Source: gift of Louis N. Boyle, 1953.

EL DORADO COUNTY ARCHIVES
approximately 1600 pieces, 1850–1906

El Dorado County, California, in the Sierra Nevada east of Sacramento in the heart of the gold mining country, was established in 1850 with Placerville as the county seat.

Subject matter: El Dorado County government and administration, as seen in court records (justice court records, 1862–86, and county court records, 1852–69); land records (1871–92); school records (1867–80); treasury records, including tax rolls (1852–69), assessment rolls (1852–69), etc.; merchandising accounts, principally for mining camps (1855–1900); mining papers and records (time books, claim books), many from the El Dorado Water and Deep Gravel Mining Co. (1855–83).

Physical description: documents, (including 227 volumes).

Source: purchased from James H. Sweency, September, 1945.

ELDRIDGE, JAMES WILLIAM (1841–1909)
approximately 15,000 pieces, 1797–1902

James William Eldridge was born in Hartford, Connecticut, and joined the U.S. Volunteers as a first lieutenant during the Civil War. After the war he began an extensive collection of letters, manuscripts, books, photographs, and other papers relating to the major military and civilian figures of the war years.

Subject matter: military history of the Civil War, from both the Union and Confederate sides, concentrating on generals and admirals, military and naval operations and administration, the armed forces of South Carolina and Virginia, and the everyday life of the common soldiers (including prisons and medical care). Includes civilian administration and politics during the war years, concentrating on governors, mayors, and congressmen. Mostly concentrated in the years 1861–65, but there is some material on the both pre- and post-war politics and military affairs, such as the raid on Harpers Ferry and the post-war navy.

Significant persons: John BROWN (17), Jefferson DAVIS (15), Ulysses Simpson GRANT (12), Henry Wager HALLECK (27), Robert Edward LEE (69), George Brinton McCLELLAN (77), John Bankhead MAGRUDER (55), Ely Samuel PARKER (19), Thomas Caute REYNOLDS (103), William Henry SEWARD (5), William Tecumseh SHERMAN (12), Edwin McMasters STANTON (8), and Henry Alexander WISE (83).

Physical description: letters, manuscripts, documents, printed military forms, autographs, and ephemera, also approximately 4000 portraits and contemporary photographs.

Source: purchased from William H. Murray, 1916.

ELLESMERE COLLECTION—AMERICANA
285 pieces, 1594–1700

Sir Thomas Egerton, Baron Ellesmere and 1st Viscount Brackley (1540?–1617), began the large English collection known variously as the Ellesmere, Bridgewater, and Egerton papers. The ELLESMERE AMERICANA is a small portion of that collection and was assembled by John Egerton, 3rd Earl of Bridgewater (1646–1700), a member of the Privy Council and president of the Board of Trade (1696).

Subject matter: colonial politics, piracy and illicit trade in Maryland and Pennsylvania, and Quaker affairs, as described by Sir Francis Nicholson; Bermuda and the British West Indies; Newfoundland fisheries. Includes a letter by Capt. Peter Wyn describing Jamestown, Virginia, in 1608.

Significant persons: Richard COOTE, 1st Earl of Bellomont (10), John EGERTON, 3rd Earl of Bridgewater (160), Francis NICHOLSON (14), Edward WALROND (7).

Physical description: letters; documents, notably memos and notes by the 3rd Earl of Bridgewater. The 285 pieces are bound into 4 volumes.

Source: purchased from the Earl of Ellesmere through the negotiation of George D. Smith and Sotheby's of London, 1917.

Note: for a description of the entire Ellesmere Collection, see the *Guide to British Historical Manuscripts in the Huntington Library.*

ELLIOTT, THOMAS BALCH (1824–81)
approximately 140 pieces, 1873–74

Dr. Thomas B. Elliott, one of the founders of the city of Pasadena, California, formed the California Colony of Indiana in May, 1873, at his home in Indiana, for the purpose of seeking a place to settle in California. He sent Daniel M. Berry in the summer of 1873 to select the site of the new city, and after traveling about Southern California, Berry chose the area which is now Pasadena. He incorporated the San Gabriel Orange Grove Association, which replaced the California Colony of Indiana, and began negotiations with Dr. John S. Griffin (see JOHNSTON-GRIFFIN COLLECTION) and Benjamin Davis Wilson (q. v.) for the purchase of the land on which the new town was established.

Subject matter: description of Southern California, events leading to the founding of Pasadena; also a manuscript by Thomas B. Elliott, "History of the San Gabriel Orange Grove Association."

Physical description: letters, (chiefly from Daniel M. Berry) documents, 1 manuscript, and photographs.

Source: purchased from Whittier Elliott, April, 1925.

Bibliography: described by John H. Parish, *Huntington Library Bulletin*, no. 7 (April, 1935): 54–55.

EMMET (THOMAS ADDIS) COLLECTION
97 pieces, 1729–1905

Thomas A. Emmet (1828–1919), a famous physician, was also an antiquarian specializing in American prints and autographs, and during his life he extra-illustrated 150 books, including four sets of signers of the Declaration of Independence.

Subject matter: the politics, diplomacy, and ideology of the American Revolution; the War for Independence; colonial and state politics; personal business. An autograph collection, it has no topical coherence.

Significant persons: mostly signers of the Declaration, with a few others.

Physical description: letters, with some documents, bound into an eight-volume edition of John Sanderson's *Biography of the Signers of the Declaration of Independence* (New York, privately printed, 1906). This set was Emmet's fourth.

Source: purchased from Anderson Galleries, 1922.

ENGLISH, EDMUND (fl. 1860s)
43 pieces, 1861–66

Edmund English, Union soldier, served as a second lieutenant in the 2nd Regiment of New Jersey Volunteers with the Army of the Potomac during the Peninsular Campaign. He took part in or was a witness to the battles of Bull Run (1st), Seven Days' Battle, South Mountain, Antietam, Fredericksburg, Gettysburg, and The Wilderness.

Subject matter: Civil War campaigns and battles; soldiers' life.

Physical description: letters, documents, and 1 manuscript journal (in 9 parts).

Source: purchased from the Philadelphia Autograph Shop, 1944.

EVANS, GRIFFITH (1760–1845)
[Journal of a Trip from Philadelphia to Ft. Stanwix (N.Y.) and Return to Ft. McIntosh (Pa.)] (1784–85)
Autograph MS. volume 79 leaves.

Concerns treaty negotiations with the Six Nations and other Indians.

F

FALL, ALBERT BACON (1861–1944)
approximately 55,000 pieces, 1887–1941

Albert B. Fall, senator from New Mexico (1912–21) and secretary of the interior (1921–23) under President Harding, came to the West from his native Kentucky, entered the field of law, purchased a large cattle ranch in New Mexico, and entered New Mexico politics. He was one of the state's first senators and became chairman of the Senate Subcommittee Investigating Mexican Affairs, an important position during the Mexican Revolution because of its effect on American investment in petroleum, mining, and land. As secretary of the interior, Fall concentrated his efforts on problems relating to the development of the nation's resources. Important issues were the controversy with the conservationists over the development of Alaskan resources, the transfer of the Forestry Bureau from the Agriculture Department to the Interior, the building of Boulder Dam, and the leasing of the Elk Hills (California) and Teapot Dome (Wyoming) Naval Oil Reserves to Edward L. Doheny and Harry F. Sinclair. These oil leases were to end his career. Fall, deemed guilty of having accepted a bribe, was sentenced to prison and died a broken man in 1944.

Subject matter: Fall's terms of office as senator and secretary of the interior (1912–23), family affairs (1907–41), and personal business (1912–23); politics and government (both in New Mexico and on a national level); New Mexico (especially land, water, forest, and mineral questions); Mexico (including the testimony before the U.S. Senate Subcommittee Investigating Mexican Affairs); reclamation projects (especially the Colorado River Project and Elephant Butte Dam); Indian Affairs (particularly with the Apache, Navajo, and Pueblo tribes); Alaska.

Significant persons: Holm Olaf BURSUM (31), Thomas Benton CATRON (5), George CURRY (20), Harry Micajah DAUGHERTY (15), Henry Ossian FLIPPER (25), Warren Gamaliel HARDING (25), Herbert Clark HOOVER (10), Charles Evans HUGHES (23), Franklin Knight LANE (24), Robert LANSING (21), Henry Cabot LODGE (13), Stephen Tyng MATHER (10), Theodore ROOSEVELT (10), Woodrow WILSON (15).

Physical description: letters and documents (including 82 volumes of testimony for the Senate Subcommittee Investigating Mexican Affairs) over the period 1887 to 1923.

Source: gift of Mahlon T. Everhart, Jr., 1952–63.

FARNSWORTH, CHARLES STEWART (1862–1955)
approximately 9000 pieces, 1883–1955

Charles S. Farnsworth, U.S. general, was born in Pennsylvania and graduated from West Point in 1887. He served in the Dakota Territory, Montana, and North Dakota until 1893, in Alaska from 1899 to 1901, and in the Philippines, Alaska, and at other posts in the period 1904 to 1911. Farnsworth was with Pershing's punitive expedition into Mexico in 1916 and during World War I he commanded the 37th Division of the American Expeditionary Forces. General Farnsworth later retired to Altadena, California, where he became involved in civic affairs.

Subject matter: military affairs and administration (as seen in orders, bulletins, communications, etc., chiefly during World War I); information about Montana, Alaska, and Farnsworth's other posts (from his correspondence and from diaries kept intermittently between 1890 and 1955); the city of Altadena, California (1927–51); the Farnsworth family.

Physical description: letters, documents, and manuscript diaries; a few maps, photographs, and some printed ephemera.

Source: gift of Robert F. Farnsworth, August, 1958, and May, 1961.

FARRAGUT, DAVID GLASGOW (1801–70)
285 pieces, 1826–1913

David G. Farragut, naval officer, joined the U.S. Navy in 1810 as a midshipman and gained experience in a broad range of service. He was with Commodore David Porter during the War of 1812, served in the Mediterranean from 1815 to 1820, the West Indies from 1822 to 1824, the Atlantic from 1825 to 1838, and in Mexican and South American waters through the forties. After working in Washington, D.C., and Norfolk, Va., from 1850 to 1854, and in California from 1855 to 1859, he took command of the Union blockade of the South in the Gulf of Mexico in 1862. In 1864 he made his famous, victorious attack on Mobile Bay, an achievement that earned him a special commission as admiral.

Subject matter: Farragut's activities during the Union blockade of the South; family affairs, including his children; personal business; naval politics; Farragut's efforts for promotion, and his conflict with Oliver Hazard Perry; Mexican War; visit to Haiti.

Significant persons: Nathaniel Prentiss BANKS (6), David Glasgow FARRAGUT (214), Gustavus Vasa FOX (7), Gideon WELLES (20).

Physical description: letters, with some documents and manuscripts.

Source: purchased from Charles Baker, 1918, and Abraham Lincoln Book Shop, 1962.

FARRAND, HIRAM (fl. 1861–64)
75 pieces, 1861–64

Hiram Farrand, Union soldier, was a captain in Company E of the 1st New York Volunteer Engineers, Second Division, Northern District, Department of the South. He participated in the Hilton Head (South Carolina) naval battle of November 1861, the battle of Secessionville of June 1862, and the siege of Forts Sumter and Wagner in the summer of 1863.

Subject matter: Civil War naval and military operations; soldiers' life. Also included is the journal of a delegate of the U.S. Christian Commission at Gettysburg following the battle.

Physical description: primarily letters; documents; 1 bound volume; some newspaper clippings and other ephemera.

Source: acquired from the official Huntington Library archives of Max Farrand, 1953.

FARRAND, MAX (1869–1945)
approximately 233 pieces, 1755–1930

Max Farrand, born in 1869, taught American history at Wesleyan, Stanford, and Yale Universities before accepting, in 1927, the post of director of research at the Huntington Library. Four years later he was named director of the Huntington Library and Art Gallery, in which position he remained until his retirement in 1941. Throughout his career, Farrand continued to research and publish in the history of the American revolutionary and early federal periods.

Subject matter: primary source material for research in American history, particularly in the politics of the revolutionary and early federal periods (especially concerning Benjamin Franklin and the drafting of the U.S. Constitution, on both of which topics Farrand wrote extensively); travel and description of Pennsylvania, Massachusetts, Connecticut, New York, and Maryland at the beginning of the nineteenth century; Mary Cadwallader Jones (Farrand's mother-in-law and the author of "Lantern Slides").

Physical description: letters, manuscripts, documents, and 1 scrapbook. (Many of the pieces are typewritten and photostatic copies.)

Source: gift of Max Farrand, 1936.

FERNALD, CHARLES (1830–92)
8160 pieces, 1852–1904

Charles Fernald, pioneer Santa Barbara (California) jurist, came to California in 1848, tried mining in the Mother Lode, then went in 1850 to San Francisco, where he became a self-taught lawyer and a member of the California Bar at the age of twenty-two. Fernald settled in Santa Barbara and was elected, successively, sheriff, district attorney, and judge of Santa Barbara County, and became recognized as a leading authority on Mexican land grants.

Subject matter: personal, legal, and land papers of Charles Fernald, mainly for the Santa Barbara area. Included are some 600 letters (1870–92) from Thomas R. Bard (q. v.), developer of oil lands in Southern California, addressed to Judge Fernald, his legal counselor.

Physical description: letters (including 14 letterbooks), documents (including 1 account book), and manuscripts (including 3 maps).

Source: purchased from Florence Fernald, January, 1950.

Bibliography: a selection of these letters has been published in Cameron Rogers, *A County Judge in Arcady* (Glendale, Calif.: Arthur H. Clark Co., 1954).

FERNÁNDEZ DE OVIEDO Y VALDÉS, GONZALO (1478–1557)
Natural y General Hystoria d[e] las Indias (1539–48). [Portions of books IV, VI, VII, IX, XI, XXXII, XXXVII only]
Autograph MS. 2 volumes 178 leaves illus.

Text in Spanish. Contains 24 pen-and-ink drawings. These books are included in the published version, *Historia general y natural de las Indias,* ed. José Amador de los Ríos (Madrid: La Real Academia de la Historia, 1851–55).

FILLMORE, MILLARD (1800–1874)
A Statement of Some Facts and Dates Made by Me, Millard Fillmore, in Reference to My Genealogy and Life, at Buffalo This 2d November 1864 [and] Sketch of the Early Life of Millard Fillmore by Himself, Commenced February 8, 1871 (1864 and 1871)
Autograph MS. volume 72 pp.

Published in *Papers of Millard Fillmore,* ed. Frank H. Severance, in Buffalo Historical Society *Publications* 10 (1907), 3–26.

FISKE, JOHN (1842–1901)
1661 pieces, 1850–1901

John Fiske, philosopher, historian, and lecturer, was born Edmund Fisk Green in Hartford, Connecticut, in 1842. While a student at Harvard (from which he received a B.A. in 1863), Fiske became a convert to the advanced views on evolution propounded by Herbert Spencer and worked to popularize these views until the end of his life. After a brief career as a lawyer, and then as assistant librarian at Harvard (until 1870), Fiske turned increasingly to the study of American history, on which topic he published voluminously and delivered numerous popular lectures both at home and in Great Britain. He died in Gloucester, Massachusetts, in 1901.

Subject matter: American history, historiography, education, Fiske's everyday life, financial difficulties. Includes manuscripts of many of Fiske's lectures, articles, and books on American colonial and revolutionary history and on philosophy (for example, the author's autograph manuscripts of *The American Revolution, The Beginnings of New England, The Dutch and Quaker Colonies in America, Genesis of Language,* and a lecture series on "Scenes and Characters in American History").

Significant persons: Charles Robert DARWIN (10), Thomas Henry HUXLEY (9), and Herbert SPENCER (41).

Physical description: letters, manuscripts (including 15 volumes), a few documents, and 3 musical scores (by Fiske).

Source: acquired at various times during the 1920s through Goodspeed and in 1955 from Mrs. Otis D. Fisk.

FONTRANES, ? (fl. 1795)
[Sketchbook of the State of New York] (1795)
MS. volume 47 pp.

Contains ink and color drawings of buildings in New York City, including Jacob Quesnel's house, maps of the French Company land and Castorland (Chassanis Tract), and a plan of Esperanza Town.

FORBES, JAMES MONRO (fl. 1860s)
56 pieces, 1862–67

James Monro Forbes, a Union soldier, served during the Civil War in the 92nd Regiment of Illinois Mounted Infantry, and took part in battles and operations in Kentucky and during the Atlanta Campaign with the Army of the Cumberland.

Subject matter: Civil War military operations, military life, and soldiers' attitudes.

Physical description: letters.

Source: purchased from Miss Mabel Forbes, 1944.

FORD, JOHN ANSON (1883–   )
approximately 35,000 pieces, 1832–1971

John Anson Ford was a member of the Los Angeles County Board of Supervisors from 1934 to 1958 and served as chairman from 1952 to 1954 and in 1957. He attended Beloit College in Wisconsin, taught history and economics, then became a news writer for the Chicago *Tribune* and for the Department of Labor and Agriculture in Washington, D.C. Ford came to Los Angeles in 1920 and entered the public relations business. In 1937, after his election as Los Angeles County supervisor, he was chosen by the Recall Committee as candidate for mayor of Los Angeles but worked instead for the election of Fletcher Bowron (q.v.). Ford retired from the Board of Supervisors in 1958, but continued to write newspaper columns and to serve the community.

Subject matter: primarily Los Angeles County government in the fields of agriculture, education, finance, labor, law enforcement, minority groups, music and art, politics, recreation and welfare. Strongest for the years 1928–71. Includes a series of family diaries beginning in 1832.

Physical description: letters, documents, manuscripts (including 23 bound volumes), photographs, and some printed material.

Source: gift of John Anson Ford, 1961 and 1975.

FORT DALLES
approximately 3070 pieces, 1850–85

Fort Dalles was established in 1850 as a supply depot for the U.S. Army on the Columbia River in Oregon and continued as a military post during the Indian uprisings. After the discovery of gold in 1855 at Fort Colville, Washington Territory, Americans began to arrive in greater numbers, and friction with the Indians increased. Governor Stevens of Washington Territory persuaded several bands of Indians in the Dalles area to agree to a reservation and opened the land to settlers, bringing further troubles. During the Civil War the regular army was removed, and volunteer troops from California, Oregon, and Washington took over the task of protecting the frontier settlements. Although Fort Dalles was abandoned in 1866, Forts Simcoe, Vancouver, Yamhill, and other military camps (whose records also appear in this collection) were important centers of military activity in the Pacific Northwest during the latter half of the nineteenth century.

Subject matter: operation of Fort Dalles and other Northwest military posts such as Fort Simcoe and Fort Vancouver (Washington Territory), and Fort Yamhill (Oregon); Indian wars and campaigns, such as the Yakima expeditions (1855 and 1858), the Snake (Shoshone) Campaigns (1855–64), the Modoc War (including messages and dispatches about the death of Gen. Edward R. S. Canby in 1873), the Nez Percé War (with a draft of Oliver Otis Howard's official report covering the period from August 27, 1877, to the surrender of Chief Joseph in 1877), and the Bannock War (1878).

Significant persons: John T. APPERSON (11), George B. CURREY (37), Oliver Otis HOWARD (4), Winfield SCOTT (31), and George WRIGHT (116).

Physical description: documents (including orders, post returns, quartermaster reports), letters (including 2 letterbooks), and 2 maps.

Source: purchased from A. H. Blaker, March, 1952.

FORT NISQUALLY
approximately 2600 pieces, 1833–1901

Fort Nisqually (Washington Territory), on Puget Sound near the mouth of the Nisqually River, was founded as a Hudson's Bay Company post in 1833. Originally a fur-trading station, it became mainly a supply station for the other company forts in the region. The development of stock raising and farming on the surrounding lands led to the organization in 1838 of the Puget Sound Agricultural Company as a subsidiary of the Hudson's Bay Company, with William Fraser Tolmie as manager. After 1845, when friction developed between the company and the increasing number of American settlers, the U.S. Government bought out the Fort Nisqually holdings of both the Hudson's Bay and the Puget Sound Agricultural companies, and the business was closed in 1870.

Subject matter: activities of the Hudson's Bay Company in the Pacific Northwest, including fur trade; activities of the Puget Sound Agricultural Company at Fort Nisqually and Cowlitz Farm; Indian wars in Washington; the early history of Fort Steilacoom; the papers of Edward Huggins, who succeeded William Tolmie as manager of the fort in 1859 and later wrote historical sketches about it.

Significant persons: Edward HUGGINS (50), John McLOUGHLIN (6), Peter Skene OGDEN (4), and William Fraser TOLMIE (100).

Physical description: letters, documents, and manuscripts, including 111 volumes of journals of daily occurrences, letterbooks, accounts, etc.

Source: purchased from George W. Soliday, May, 1924.

FORT SUTTER
161 pieces, 1845–62

Fort Sutter, a settlement on the Sacramento River in northern California, was founded in 1839 by Swiss emigrant John A. Sutter, who fortified the outpost with arms purchased from the Russians when they abandoned Fort Ross. Sutter's fort became a center of trading activity in California. During the Bear Flag Revolt in 1846 Edward Meyer Kern (1822–63), a young artist and draftsman from Philadelphia who was a member of John C. Frémont's 3rd Exploring Expedition (1845–46), was appointed first lieutenant in the California Battalion and placed in charge of Fort Sutter. The fort served as a focal point for military operations during the revolt. After the annexation of California to the United States, Kern returned home, then later joined Frémont's 4th Exploring Expedition with his brothers Benjamin G. and Richard H. Kern. From 1849 to 1853 Edward and Richard Kern were members of the Simpson and Sitgreaves Expeditions in the southwest. Edward Kern then went to China and Japan as artist and photographer for two U.S. Navy surveys, the North Pacific Exploring Expeditions of 1853–56 and 1858–60.

Subject matter: Edward M. Kern and his activities at Fort Sutter, chiefly during the period of American military activities in California (1846–47); the Bear Flag Revolt and subsequent military action, Indian insurrections, the establishment of the first California mail service, and the relief of the Donner Party. Also includes material concerning Kern's attachment to the 3rd Frémont Exploring Expedition (1845–46) which came to

California ostensibly for exploration purposes but became involved in the California-Mexico conflict, and the 4th Frémont Exploring Expedition (1848–49) which had a disastrous climax in the mountains of Colorado. There is also a printed volume of engravings of drawings by Edward and Richard Kern made during the Simpson and Sitgreaves Expeditions in the region of the Zuni, Little Colorado, Colorado, and Gila Rivers in 1849–53.

Significant persons: John Charles FRÉMONT (2), Edward Meyer KERN (39), Richard Hovenden KERN (6), John Stoney MISSROON (4), John Berrien MONTGOMERY (16), Joseph Warren REVERE (7), Antoine ROBIDOUX (2), James Hervey SIMPSON (3).

Physical description: letters, documents, and 3 maps, in English and Spanish, mounted in 38 bound volumes; 1 volume of engravings and printed maps, and 1 printed introductory volume describing the collection.

Source: purchased from Anderson Galleries, November, 1921.

Bibliography: the collection is described in the *Huntington Library Bulletin,* no. 7 (April, 1935): 42–44.

FOSTER, THOMAS (fl. 1779–83)
Thomas Foster His Book (1779–83)
Autograph MS. volume 101 pp.

A military journal, account book, and commonplace book, kept by a soldier of the 7th and 14th Massachusetts militia regiments between July 7, 1779 and June 3, 1783.

FOY, MARY EMILY (1862–1958)
approximately 500 pieces, 1879–1957

Mary E. Foy, Los Angeles community and education leader, and city librarian from 1880 to 1884, was a pioneer Los

Angeles resident and the daughter of Samuel Calvert Foy (q.v.), early businessman of Los Angeles. She was a member of Los Angeles cultural and historical organizations such as Ina Coolbrith Circle (composed of friends and admirers of Ina Coolbrith, poet laureate of California), First Century Families (descendants of California pioneers), the Women's Democratic League, and the Ladies' Adams Street Women's Investment Company.

Subject matter: Los Angeles history, Samuel Calvert Foy, Democratic politics, women's organizations, and some correspondence and manuscripts of Ina Donna Coolbrith.

Significant persons: Ina Donna COOLBRITH (13).

Physical description: letters, manuscripts, photographs, and clippings.

Source: gift of Foy estate, ca.1959.

FOY BROTHERS
59 pieces, 1854–1925

Foy Brothers, a Los Angeles harness and saddlery firm, was founded in 1854 by Samuel Calvert Foy (1830–1901) and his brother John Moran Foy (>1830–92). Samuel C. Foy arrived in California via Panama in 1852 and worked two years in the mines. He had been trained in saddlery and harness work in Cincinnati and Natchez before coming west. After a visit to Los Angeles in 1854, he rented a shop, bought a full line of goods, and established his business with his brother as partner. The partnership continued until 1865 when John moved to San Bernardino to open his own firm. Samuel continued to direct this early Los Angeles concern for almost fifty years, up to the time of his death in 1901.

Subject matter: the Foy Brothers harness and saddlery firm in Los Angeles from 1854 to 1925.

Physical description: 59 volumes of documents (accounts).

Source: gift of Miss Mary E. Foy, November, 1938.

FRANKLIN, BENJAMIN (1706–90)
Memoirs (1771–90)
Autograph MS. volume 75 pp.

Franklin's life to the year 1757. Published in various editions from 1791 to the present as *The Autobiography of Benjamin Franklin.*

FRENCH CLANDESTINE SLAVE TRADE COLLECTION
106 pieces, 1822–28

Letters and documents concerning a secret slave-trading expedition undertaken by Captain Jean-Baptiste Menard and his ship "Le Jeune Louis," with the backing of François Fernandez of Bordeaux and others. The ship embarked from Nantes, purchased slaves in Nigeria, continued to Havana, and returned to Antwerp, where Jean Donnet was the shipping agent. Menard died during the voyage, and was followed in command by the ship's surgeon Bejaud and, after his death two weeks later, by François Demouy.

Subject matter: slaves and the slave trade, including the purchase and treatment of slaves; the equipment, crew, activities, and finances of a slave ship; precautions taken to disguise the true nature of the voyage.

Physical description: letters (including one volume of the captain's letterbook) and documents (in French).

Source: purchased from John Howell, September, 1958.

G

GALLOWAY, JOSEPH (1731–1803)
64 pieces, 1717–1874

Joseph Galloway, lawyer, statesman, Loyalist, and member of a prominent colonial merchant family with extensive lands in Maryland and Pennsylvania, was a member of the Pennsylvania assembly from 1756 to 1764 and again (as speaker) from 1766 to 1775. As a delegate to the First Continental Congress, Galloway tried repeatedly to effect an Anglo-American compromise, but after the eventual failure of this policy moved in 1778 to England, where he became a spokesman and pamphleteer for American Loyalists. Galloway was accompanied into exile by his daughter, Elizabeth (Galloway) Roberts, but not by his wife, Grace (Growdon) Galloway, the daughter of Lawrence Growdon, Jr., judge of the Supreme Court of Pennsylvania. In later life Galloway turned to writing religious tracts. He died in England in 1803.

Subject matter: Galloway and Growdon social life, business affairs, and family matters; Pennsylvania real estate transactions; life in exile; Napoleon.

Physical description: letters, documents (including 9 land surveys and a genealogical chart), and ephemera.

Source: purchased from Sotheby's, August, 1972.

GÁLVEZ, JOSÉ DE, MARQUÉS DE SONORA (1720–87)
734 pieces, 1763–94

José de Gálvez, Spanish statesman, began his career as secretary to Cardinal Grimaldi, foreign minister to Charles III, and in 1764 was appointed by the king as a member of the Council of the Indies. In 1765 Charles III sent Gálvez to New Spain (Mexico) as Visitador-General in order to effect administrative and financial reforms. Along with the new viceroy, de Croix, Gálvez undertook improvements, including the reorganization of the tax system, the strengthening of the northern frontier, and the Spanish occupation of Alta California.

Subject matter: papers assembled in 1794 for the Conde de Revilla Gigedo, and consisting mainly of official correspondence (1765–72) between Gálvez and the successive viceroys of Mexico, Marqués de Cruillas, Marqués de Croix, and Antonio María Bucareli. They deal with the organization of the expeditions sent to San Diego and Monterey to occupy California, the efforts to enlarge the frontiers of New Spain and subdue the Indians in Sonora and Sinaloa, and the removal of the Jesuit missionaries from Lower California.

Significant persons: Antonio María BUCARELI y URSÚA (38), Carlos Francisco de CROIX, Marqués de Croix (204), José de GÁLVEZ, Marqués de Sonora (291), Juan Vicente de GÜEMES PACHECO, Conde de Revilla Gigedo (5), Joaquin MONSERRAT, Marqués de Cruillas (126).

Physical description: letters, documents, and 1 map (in Spanish).

Source: purchased from Stanley V. Henkels, April, 1925.

Bibliography: the collection is described in the *Huntington Library Bulletin,* no. 7 (April, 1935): 26–29.

GARCÉS, FRANCISCO (1738–81)
[Diary of a journey through Sonora, Arizona, and California in 1775 and 1776] (October 21, 1775—August 12, 1776)
Contemporary copy MS. 1 volume 30 leaves [incomplete]

Text in Spanish.

GARDNER, WILLIAM BUNKER (1811–56)
76 pieces, 1847–1965

William B. Gardner, New England shipmaster, commanded whaling ships which made voyages to the Pacific Coast from 1839 to 1850. In 1852 he became master of the ship "Sarah Parker" and sailed from New Bedford, Massachusetts, to the Pacific Coast. Gardner's wife, Charlotte (Coffin) Gardner, and their son accompanied him on this journey, and another son was born in San Francisco before their return to Nantucket in 1855.

Subject matter: the 1852–55 voyage of the "Sarah Parker" to San Francisco via Cape Horn, visits to North Pacific ports, and the return trip to Massachusetts; a few accounts for the ships "Courier", "Mary Mitchell", and "Flora"; also includes correspondence 1920 to 1965, mainly between Grace Brown Gardner, granddaughter of Charlotte and William B. Gardner, and Eleanor Jane Graves, relative to the journals and to early Nantucket inhabitants.

Physical description: letters (including 1 letterbook), manuscripts (including 1 journal, 1 drawing, and 1 map), and documents (including 1 logbook).

Source: gift of Mrs. Lloyd Graves, October, 1965.

GAY, EDWIN FRANCIS (1867–1946)
approximately 20,000 pieces, 1838–1972

Edwin Francis Gay, historian, achieved eminence for great learning in economic history and for distinguished administrative ability. He wrote little, but transmitted his knowledge through outstanding students at Harvard (1902–08, 1924–36). Gay first revealed his administrative talents as dean of the Harvard Business School (1908–19). During World War I (1917–19) he served as director of the Division of Planning and Statistics of the U.S. Shipping Board, head of the Imports Bureau of the War Trade Board, and member of the War Industries Board. From 1919 to 1924 he edited the New York *Evening Post* and cofounded the National Bureau of Economic Research and the Council on Foreign Relations. Honored with the presidencies of the American Economic Association and the Economic History Association, Gay concluded his career by serving from 1936 to his death as director of research at the Huntington Library.

Subject matter: Gay's family; Harvard University; activities of the Division of Planning and Statistics of the U.S. Shipping Board, the Imports Bureau of the War Trade Board, and the War Industries Board; European economic recovery after World War I; the New York *Evening Post;* a little on the National Bureau of Economic Research; international economic relations after World War II; U.S. business; the Huntington Library; also a large amount of data on English and European economic history.

Significant persons: James Rowland ANGELL (17), Frank AYDELOTTE (14), Henry Moore BATES (43), Isaiah BOWMAN (11), John Harold CLAPHAM (11), Arthur Harrison COLE (107), Archibald Cary COOLIDGE (39), Homer CROTTY (8), William James CUNNINGHAM (25), Edmund Ezra DAY (10), Henry Sturgis DENNISON (114),

Charles William ELIOT (12), Ralph Cecil EPSTEIN (22), Max FARRAND (29), Herbert FEIS (10), John Palmer GAVIT (7), Edwin Francis GAY (ca. 9400)*, Norman Scott Brien GRAS (27), Hubert HALL (28), Earl Jefferson HAMILTON (17), Charles Homer HASKINS (6), Herbert HEATON (18), Herbert HOOVER (25), Vernon Lyman KELLOGG (9), Charles Foster KENT (11), John Maynard KEYNES (8), Julius KLEIN (24), Abbott Lawrence LOWELL (24), Vance Criswell McCORMICK (8), Robert Andrews MILLIKAN (6), Wesley Clair MITCHELL (46), Arthur Ernest MORGAN (17), Christopher Darlington MORLEY (14), William Bennett MUNRO (10), John Ulric NEF (17), Arthur Darby NOCK (36), Charles Dyer NORTON (12), Ralph Barton PERRY (36), Franklin Delano ROOSEVELT (6), Joseph Halle SCHAFFNER (51), Harlow SHAPLEY (6), Archibald Wilkinson SHAW (109), Harold Phelps STOKES (15), Frank William TAUSSIG (17), Richard Henry TAWNEY (7), Mary VAN KLEECK (10), Eliot WADSWORTH (8), Edgar Huidekoper WELLS (11), Joseph Henry WILLITS (45).

Physical description: letters; documents, including lecture and research notes, photographs, and appointment books; manuscripts of essays and speeches.

Source: gift of Margaret Gay Davies, 1973.

* primarily correspondence, excluding research notes and the like.

GEORGE, JAMES HERBERT (fl. 1862–65)
77 pieces, 1862–65

James Herbert George, musician and Union soldier, served as band director for the 10th Vermont Volunteers during operations in Maryland and Virginia.

Subject matter: Civil War military operations, including the Spotsylvania Campaign and the Siege of Petersburg; attitudes toward the war and toward blacks; military life.

Physical description: letters.

Source: purchased from Genevieve L. George, July 5, 1963.

GERSON, THEODORE PERCEVAL (1872–1960)
483 pieces, 1901; 1929–38

T. Perceval Gerson, founder of the Hollywood Bowl, was a physician, the publisher of the *Los Angeles Municipal Newspaper,* and a patron of many community organizations. He was active in the Hollywood Bowl Association, the Theatre Arts Alliance of Hollywood, the National Committee for Planned Parenthood, and the American Civil Liberties Union.

Subject matter: personal and business correspondence of Dr. T. Perceval Gerson, chiefly for the years 1934–37, including letters from conductors and musicians, lecturers on liberal causes, etc.; also two sets of newspaper clippings covering the San Francisco Graft Trial of 1907 and the William Dudley Haywood trial in Idaho in 1907.

Physical description: letters and manuscripts, with some newspaper clippings.

Source: purchased from N. A. Kovach, February, 1948.

GILL, WILLIAM HARRISON (1849–1909)
approximately 300 pieces, 1876–1968

William H. Gill, interdenominational missionary, was sent to the Southwest in 1876 under a contract with the American Sunday School Union. From 1876 to 1896 he organized Sunday schools in Texas, Oklahoma, and Indian Territory, establishing his headquarters in Sherman, Texas, in 1887. Because of his wife's health, Gill moved to Arizona where he worked with the Indians of the Salt River and Fort McDowell Reservations and stayed briefly at the Walker River Paiute Reservation in Nevada.

Subject matter: missionary work of William H. Gill, in Texas from 1876 to 1896 with the Choctaw and Chickasaw Indians, in Arizona from 1896 to 1902 with the Salt River Pima tribe near Phoenix, and from 1902 to 1906 with the Mohave Apaches at Fort McDowell.

Physical description: letters, manuscripts, documents, and photographs.

Source: purchased from Ruth L. Gill Hammond, January, 1970.

GILLESPIE, GEORGE A. (1830–1928)
123 pieces, 1849–99

George A. Gillespie, pioneer California businessman and politician, crossed the plains to California in 1850. After spending two years in the mines in Nevada and California, he settled in Solano County. He became county assessor in 1860 and engrossing clerk of the state senate in 1861. His newspaper activities, which began in 1866 when he purchased the *Solano Press*, brought him some political prominence in his county.

Subject matter: California politics, mainly from 1859 to 1890, and family affairs.

Significant persons: John BIDWELL (4).

Physical description: letters, manuscripts, and documents.

Source: purchased from Henry Stephens of Vacaville, California, February, 1936.

GLAZIER, JAMES EDWARD (fl. 1861–1918)
174 pieces, 1861–1922
James Edward Glazier, of Salem, Massachusetts, enlisted in
the 23rd Regiment of Massachusetts Volunteers in October,
1861. He served in North Carolina under Ambrose Everett
Burnside until February, 1863, and then in South Carolina
and Virginia, including five months in the summer of 1864 in
the U.S. General Hospital in Hampton, Virginia. After leaving
the service, Glazier entered the ministry of the Methodist
Episcopal Church but soon moved with his family to the Pacific Coast, where he homesteaded a small farm. After the
death of his wife he returned to Massachusetts in 1881 and
thereafter spent six years looking for work (as a plasterer and
bricklayer) in several states before finally settling in Ukiah,
California, where he remained for the rest of his life.

Subject matter: U.S. Civil War, including a soldier's life and
experiences, military operations (including battles of Roanoke
Island and New Bern, North Carolina), and life in a military
hospital; farming on the Pacific Coast; work, family, and social life of Glazier.

Physical description: letters (1861–65) and manuscripts (including 48 bound pocket diaries, 1868–1922).

Source: purchased from Mrs. Norina Fletcher, September 12,
1962.

GOFF-WILLIAMS COLLECTION
64 pieces, 1859–65; 1889

James M. Goff and Robert Henry Williams, Union soldiers,
served in the 10th Wisconsin Infantry and 2nd Massachusetts
Cavalry, respectively. Goff served in Maryland, Kentucky,

and Tennessee before his capture by Confederate forces in the fall of 1863, and was then taken to Libby Prison in Richmond, from which he was exchanged the following year. Williams fought in Tennessee, Kentucky, and Virginia and in later years moved to California.

Subject matter: soldiers' lives and activities (including prison experiences) during the U.S. Civil War.

Physical description: primarily letters with photographs, newspaper clippings, and some ephemera.

Source: purchased from Mrs. Wayne Pogue, March, 1961.

GOLD RUSH JOURNALS
125 pieces, 1840–82

Individual diaries of the Gold Rush period and of overland journeys or sea voyages to the Pacific Coast have been placed together in a cumulative collection. The majority of the diaries pertain to California during the 1848–65 period, but the collection includes all single western diaries—a few from either before or after the Gold Rush years, and some relating to other western journeys to Oregon, Washington, Arizona, etc. (with the exception of Mormon journeys to Utah, which are placed in the Mormon File [q.v.]). The collection is subdivided into "Overland Journeys" and "Sea Voyages," with a small additional grouping of "Journeys to Oregon," "Whaling Logs," and "Other Western Journals."

Subject matter: overland journeys to the Pacific, voyages to the Pacific, mines and mineral resources of California, whaling logs, and life in the West.

Physical description: manuscripts.

Source: acquired from many sources over a period of years.

GRABILL, LEVI (fl. ca. 1847–85)
96 pieces, 1861–92

Levi Grabill, Union soldier, enlisted in the 4th Ohio Volunteer Infantry in 1861 and was later commissioned captain in the 22nd U.S. Colored Infantry. At the end of the war Grabill attempted to resign but was posted instead to Brownsville, Texas, where he remained until discharged in November, 1865. He moved to California in the 1880s and settled in Sunnyvale.

Subject matter: Civil War: soldier's life, military affairs, and army administration.

Physical description: documents, letters, manuscripts (2 Civil War journals, April–December, 1861 and February–August, 1865), 51 card photographs, newspaper clippings, and other ephemera.

Source: gift of Amelia Kneass (step-daughter of Grabill's son), July, 1958.

GRAHAM, JOHN LORIMER (1797–1876)
560 pieces, 1786–1875

John Lorimer Graham, lawyer and New York City civic leader, was born in England in 1797 during one of several extended visits to that country by his parents, John Andrew and Margaret (Lorimer) Graham. The senior Graham was active in the Episcopal Church of Vermont and after 1805 was a prominent New York criminal lawyer. His son, John Lorimer, was admitted to the New York Bar in 1821, appointed postmaster of New York City in 1842 (which post he filled until 1845), and in 1861 obtained a position in the Treasury Department. He was a member of the American Bible Society, St. Andrews'

Society, the New York Historical Society, and the Metropolitan Club and took an active part in civic, state, and national politics.

Subject matter: government and politics of New York and New York City; New York Militia; religious life, banking, construction, and real estate in New York City.

Significant persons: John TYLER (7).

Physical description: letters and documents (including some printed forms).

Source: purchased from Philip S. Graham, June, 1958.

GRANT, ULYSSES SIMPSON (1822–85)
345 pieces, 1864–65

Ulysses Simpson Grant, Civil War general and eighteenth president of the United States, graduated from West Point in 1843. Despite distinguished service in the Mexican War, Grant resigned his commission in 1854 and retired to an unsettled civilian life. At the outbreak of the Civil War he joined the 21st Illinois Volunteers as a colonel, was promoted to major general after the capture of Vicksburg in July, 1863, and given command of the Union forces the following November. At the conclusion of the Wilderness Campaign in June, 1864, Union forces began the long siege of Petersburg, Virginia, which exhausted Confederate strength and led to final victory. Grant then entered politics, served as president from 1868 to 1876, and died in 1885.

Subject matter: the Petersburg Campaign in the U.S. Civil War, primarily during the period from August 1864 to February 1865; includes official dispatches to figures such as Henry Halleck, Edwin Stanton, George Meade, Benjamin Butler, Philip Sheridan, William T. Sherman, and Abraham Lincoln.

Physical description: letters and documents.

Source: acquired from William K. Bixby, 1918.

Bibliography: Grant's dispatches are printed in *The War of the Rebellion: A Compilation of the Official Records of the Union and Confederate Armies,* 70 vols. (Washington: Government Printing Office, 1880–1900).

GRAVES, JACKSON ALPHEUS (1852–1933)
approximately 14,000 pieces, 1878–1930

Jackson A. Graves, pioneer Los Angeles lawyer and business-man, was born in Iowa and came to California in 1857. He graduated from St. Mary's College in San Francisco in 1872 and studied law in the firm of Eastman and Neumann. Graves moved to Los Angeles in 1875. In 1888, after membership in various partnerships, Graves joined Henry O'Melveny, and the firm became Graves, O'Melveny and Shankland until its dissolution in 1904. Graves was vice-president of Farmers and Merchants National Bank in 1903 and president from 1920–33.

Subject matter: banking and finance as seen chiefly in the business correspondence of Jackson A. Graves, mainly with Isaias W. Hellman, Sr., president of the Farmers and Merchants Bank (Los Angeles) from 1875 to 1920 and president of Wells Fargo Nevada National Bank in San Francisco from 1890 to 1920; also land papers of the Los Angeles area and papers of California law firms.

Significant persons: Isaias William HELLMAN, Sr. (262).

Physical description: letters (including 23 letterbooks), 3 photographs, and 2 scrapbooks.

Source: gift of Francis P. Graves, July, 1952.

GRAY, JOHN ALEXANDER (fl. 1963–65)
approximately 75 pieces, 1963–65

John Alexander Gray, Los Angeles newswriter, drafted articles relating to the Bureau of Power and Light (later the Department of Water and Power) of the City of Los Angeles.

Subject matter: personal correspondence of John Alexander Gray (1963–65); and information about William Mulholland, Ezra Scattergood, and other engineers connected with the procurement of water and power from the Owens Valley (California) and from Boulder Dam for the City of Los Angeles.

Physical description: letters, manuscripts, and newspaper clippings.

Source: gift of James A. Linck, February, 1968.

GREAT BRITAIN. ARMY. PROVINCIAL FORCES OF CONNECTICUT
[Orderly Book] (1761)
MS. volume 334 pp.

Kept by John Grant of Archibald McNeil's company in the 2nd Connecticut Regiment, commanded by Nathan Whiting. Pertains to the British occupation of Crown Point, N.Y., between June 20 and Oct. 17, 1761. Also contains miscellaneous accounts, verses, and memoranda to 1801.

GREAT BRITAIN. ARMY. PROVINCIAL FORCES OF NEW YORK
Lt. Joseph Bull His Orderly Book (1759)
Autograph MS. volume 134 pp.

Kept by a soldier of the 1st Battalion of the New York Regiment and concerns the actions of the British army at Schenectady and Forts Herkimer, Stanwix, Oswego, and Ontario, between May 25 and Nov. 1, 1759.

GREAT BRITAIN. ARMY. PROVINCIAL FORCES OF PENNSYLVANIA
Col. Bouquet's Orders (1758)
MS. volume 68 pp.

An orderly book of the 3rd Battalion of the Pennsylvania Regiment, containing the orders of Col. Henry Bouquet in connection with Gen. John Forbes's assault on Fort Duquesne. Also pertains to Forts Raystown and Lyttleton, Pa. Covers June 17 to Sept. 14, 1758. Published in *The Papers of Henry Bouquet*, ed. S. K. Stevens, Donald Kent, and Louis Waddell (Harrisburg: The Pennsylvania Historical Museum Commission, 1951–), 2:656–90.

An Orderly Book of Samuel Grubb's Company (1759)
MS. volume 99 pp.

Covers June 18 to July 24, 1759. Concerns the activities of the British army around Fort Bedford (Raystown) and Carlisle, Pa. The volume also contains commercial accounts by William Worrall, 1771–92.

GREAT BRITAIN. ATTORNEY AND SOLICITOR GENERAL
General Reports (1763–67)
MS. volume 88 leaves

Copies of official papers on various American colonial subjects, including Newfoundland fisheries, admiralty courts, the northern boundary of West Florida, and inventions.

GREAT BRITAIN. LORDS COMMISSIONERS FOR TRADE
AND PLANTATIONS
To the Right Hon[ora]ble Lords Spiritual and Temporal in
Parliament Assembled: [A Representation of the State of the
Trade of This Kingdom] (1707)
MS. volume 199 pp.

Published in Historical Manuscripts Commission, *The Manuscripts of the House of Lords, 1706–1708* (London: His Maj-
esty's Stationery Office, 1921), n.s., 7:232–309.

GREAT BRITAIN. PRIVY COUNCIL
Copies and Extracts of All Such Papers and Letters Trans-
mitted to the Councill Office as Relate to the Riots . . . in
America in Opposition to the Putting in Execution the Stamp
Act . . . Likewise Copies of All Orders &c Issued from the
Councill (1765)
MS. volume 148 pp.

Copies of Papers Transmitted to the Council Office re: the
Assemblys of Massachusetts Bay and New York Previous to
the Passage of the [Stamp Act] (1764–1765)
MS. volume 47 pp.

GREELEY, HORACE (1811–72)
Lecture on Abraham Lincoln (1868)
Autograph MS. volume 50 pp.

GREENE, NATHANAEL (1742–86)
107 pieces, 1775–86

Nathanael Greene, Revolutionary general, held various positions in American military forces from 1774. Prior to the southern campaign (1780–82), his most noteworthy service was as quartermaster general from 1778 to 1780. Following the destruction of the American forces under Gates at Camden, S.C., in 1780, Greene successfully organized another formidable army, using it to capture the British posts in the South.

Subject matter: national politics; the southern campaign and the American army; Henry Lee's resignation of his commission.

Significant persons: Nathanael GREENE (47), Henry LEE (12).

Physical description: mostly letters, documents.

Source: purchased from Anderson Galleries, 1919, and George D. Smith, ca. 1919.

Bibliography: The Papers of Nathanael Greene (Chapel Hill: University of North Carolina Press, 1976–   ), ed. Richard K. Showman.

Note: the Library also holds over 2,600 transcripts of Greene letters made by Greene's grandson George Washington Greene in the nineteenth century. Most of the originals are in the Library of Congress.

GREENE, THOMAS SUMNER (1842–1900<)
41 pieces, 1854–1901

Thomas Sumner Greene was born in Cincinnati, Ohio, in 1842, and served as a private in the 5th Ohio Battery at the beginning of the Civil War. In 1863 he was appointed lieutenant and adjutant in the 47th U.S. Colored Infantry and remained there throughout the war, turning down an offered promotion to the rank of major in the 70th Infantry. In June 1865 he was promoted to captain in the 47th and reenlisted for a further three years the following September.

Subject matter: Greene's military promotions and transfers during the period 1861–1865; some personal affairs; one character sketch.

Physical description: mostly documents (many printed forms, filled in), with a few letters.

Source: acquired from Jack R. Brown, October 2, 1969.

GUNNISON, JOHN WILLIAMS (1812–53)
79 pieces, 1832–96; 1926

John Williams Gunnison, army topographical engineer in charge of surveying a route to the West for the Pacific Railroad, was born in New Hampshire and graduated from West Point in 1835. He served as ordnance officer in the Seminole War in Florida and in making surveys in Georgia, where he met and married Martha A. Delony. After further surveying work in the Wisconsin-Michigan area, he was assigned to Captain Howard Stansbury's party to explore the Great Salt Lake region. Gunnison returned to Washington and was then appointed to lead the government survey for the exploration and survey of a railroad route through the mountains of Colorado and Utah. He perished on October 26, 1853, when his party (which included the artist Richard Kern) was ambushed by Indians on the Sevier River in Utah.

Subject matter: three separate groups of papers. The first concerns Gunnison himself: his journal kept in Florida and Georgia in 1840, information about Wisconsin Territory (1841), the

Stansbury Expedition (1849–50), life among the Mormons, the expedition that Gunnison led from St. Louis to Utah (1853), and the official communications relating to his death. The second group concerns the Civil War period as seen in letters written by his wife's family in the South. The third group concerns his nephew, Charles Andrew Gunnison (1861–97), who traveled in Europe and Japan with San Francisco area businessman Timothy Hopkins, the adopted son of Mrs. Mark Hopkins.

Physical description: letters, manuscripts (including 9 journals and 2 sketch books), and photographs.

Source: purchased from Miss Genevieve D. O'Neill, 1952, and Miss Alma Gunnison, 1954.

Bibliography: many of the important items in the collection have been published in Nolie Mumey, *John Williams Gunnison* (Denver: Artcraft Press, 1955).

H

HACK, WILLIAM (fl. 1681–1710)
[Captain Bartholemew Sharp's *South Sea Waggoner:*] A Description of the Sea Coasts in the South Sea of America from the Port of Acapulco to the Straights of Lemaire. [An English copy of the Spanish Atlas: Derrotero general del Mar del Sur . . . of 1669 (q.v.)] (ca.1684)
MS. 1 volume Atlas of 130 charts

HAGUE, JAMES DUNCAN (1836–1909)
approximately 24,000 pieces, 1824–1936

James D. Hague, mining engineer, was born in Boston, graduated from the Lawrence Scientific School of Harvard in 1855, and did graduate work in Gottingen and Freiberg, Germany. In 1859 he was employed by William Henry Webb of New York to explore the coral islands of the South Seas in search of phosphate deposits. After three years there, Hague returned to the United States to become associated with Edwin J. Hulbert in the discovery and early development of the Calumet and Hecla copper mines in Michigan. Hague married Mary Ward Foote, a cousin of Harriet Beecher Stowe and sister-in-law of Mary (Hallock) Foote. In 1867 he was made first assistant to Clarence King on the United States Geological Exploration of the Fortieth Parallel. Hague visited England in 1871 and formed friendships with Charles Darwin, Charles Lyell, and John Tyndall. He returned to San Francisco, where he became a consulting mining engineer and developed many mining enterprises, including the North Star Mine in Grass Valley, California. Hague retired to his home in Stockbridge, Massachusetts, where he died in 1909.

Subject matter: family and business affairs of James D. Hague, mainly mining (including the South Sea Expedition [1858–61], the Calumet and Hecla copper mines in Michigan [1863–1914], and other mining companies, chiefly in the western United States and Mexico). Also small groups of papers of Horace F. Cutter of San Francisco, a friend of Clarence King, and of Edward Singleton Holden (1846–1914), astronomer and Hague family friend who was director of the Lick Observatory, president of the University of California, and librarian of West Point. Also included are a few drawings and letters of Mary Hallock Foote.

THE CLARENCE KING COLLECTION is a sub-collection of the Hague Collection. Clarence Rivers King (1842–1901), geologist, mining engineer, and writer, was born in Newport, Rhode Island. Following graduation from Yale Scientific School in 1862, King and his friend James T. Gardiner journeyed West, arriving in Virginia City, Nevada in 1863. Upon meeting William H. Brewer in California, they joined the California Geological Survey as volunteers. From 1867 to 1877, King directed the geological and scientific survey of the Fortieth Parallel from eastern Colorado to the California border. The next year he was made head of the newly established United States Geological Survey, a position he held until entering private practice as a mining engineer in 1881. The collection contains mainly Clarence King's scientific papers, (including those concerning a reconnaissance in Arizona in 1865 and 1866, and Mexican mining companies), 43 scientific notebooks (including material on the California Geological Survey [1864–66], and the United States Geological Exploration of the Fortieth Parallel [1867–72]), some correspondence, a few manuscripts, and photographs. Also included is material concerning James D. Hague's publication of the *Clarence King Memoirs.*

143

Significant persons: Henry Brooks ADAMS (7), William Earl DODGE (15), Samuel Franklin EMMONS (16), Stuyvesant FISH (8), Mary Hallock FOOTE (72), James Terry GARDINER (7), James Ben Ali HAGGIN (18), Arnold HAGUE (70), Edward Everett HALE (24), Edward Henry HARRIMAN (11), John HAY (18), Edward Singleton HOLDEN (21), HENRY HOLT (11), Edwin James HULBERT (116), Henry JANIN (56), Louis JANIN (98), Clarence Rivers KING (46), John LA FARGE (21), Raphael PUMPELLY (12), George Haven PUTNAM (7), Rossiter Worthington RAYMOND (10), Edmund Clarence STEDMAN (6), John TYNDALL (9), Stanford WHITE (6), Henry VILLARD (7).

Physical description: letters (including 46 letterbooks), manuscripts (including diaries, notebooks, and fieldbooks), documents, photographs, maps, and drawings.

Source: gift of Misses Eleanor and Marion Hague and Mr. James Hague, 1947 and 1971.

HAIGHT, HENRY HUNTLEY (1825–78)
508 pieces, 1846–85

Henry H. Haight, California governor, was born in New York and graduated from Yale University in 1844. He was admitted to the bar in St. Louis, Missouri, where he practiced law until 1850. He then traveled to California and settled in San Francisco. Haight practiced law there until 1867 when, as candidate of the Democratic party, he was elected governor of California. During his term of office he led the fight against railroad subsidies. The University of California was established (1868) during this period also. After losing his bid for reelection in 1871, Haight returned to private practice until his death.

Subject matter: the political history of California, the development of San Francisco, and the business papers of the legal firm of Wells, Haight and Garry.

Significant persons: Eugene CASSERLY (5), Henry Huntley HAIGHT (23), and Bayard TAYLOR (3).

Physical description: letters, documents, and manuscripts.

Source: purchased from Edwin Grabhorn, April, 1941 and January, 1945.

HALE, CHRISTOPHER J. (fl. 1865)
120 pieces, 1865; 1909

Lieutenant Christopher J. Hale served as a recruiting officer for the United States Army during the spring of 1865 at Goldsboro, North Carolina, when ninety-three Negro volunteers were admitted to the 135th Colored Infantry.

Subject matter: volunteer enlistment forms and lists and returns of men and materiel of the 135th Infantry; one private land deed of 1909.

Physical description: documents (printed forms, filled in).

Source: gift of Mrs. R. E. Johannesen, April 14, 1959.

HALE, GEORGE ELLERY (1868–1938)
152 pieces, 1887–1937

George Ellery Hale, astronomer, was born in Chicago in 1868 and educated at the Massachusetts Institute of Technology, Harvard College Observatory, and the University of Berlin. A specialist in solar and stellar spectroscopy, Hale organized the Kenwood Astrophysical Observatory for the University of Chicago (and served as its director until 1896), where he also invented and developed the spectroheliograph, established the *Astrophysical Journal,* and served as the director of the Yerkes Observatory. In 1904 Hale moved to Pasadena, California, where (as a trustee of the California Institute of Technology and with the backing of the Carnegie Institution of Washington) he organized the Mount Wilson Observatory, served as its director until 1923 (and honorary director until his death), and was instrumental in the construction of the 200-inch reflecting telescope at Mount Palomar. Hale was an active member of the international scientific community, the recipient of numerous awards and honors, and a leading force in the cultural and scientific growth of the Pasadena area. He served on the original board of trustees of the Huntington Library. Hale died in 1938.

Subject matter: Hale and his friendship with Harry Manley Goodwin, physicist and graduate dean of M.I.T.; practical and theoretical aspects of astronomical research; information about other scientists (Norman Lockyar, William Whewell, William Jevons, Robert Millikan, Albert Michelson, and Albert Einstein); the administration and finance of scientific research, scientific organizations and publications; Hale's own experiments and theories; the University of Chicago, California Institute of Technology, astronomical observatories, the foundation of the Huntington Library; and Hale's private and family life.

Physical description: primarily letters, with a few documents.

Source: acquired from Richard Hale Goodwin, 1958.

HALLECK, PEACHY & BILLINGS (firm)
80 pieces, 1837–61

Halleck, Peachy & Billings was one of the most prestigious law firms on the Pacific Coast. It was headquartered in San Francisco and specialized in California land cases. The firm was organized by Frederick Billings and Alexander Carey Peachy in 1849, and they were soon joined by Henry Wager Halleck. Halleck (1815–72) was a West Point graduate sent to California at the beginning of the Mexican War. He served as secretary of state under military governors of California and helped frame the California Constitution. He wrote the report on land titles used to formulate the Land Act of 1851, which provided for the official transfer of property titles from Mexican to American jurisdiction. Halleck became active in the firm of Halleck, Peachy & Billings and resigned from the army in 1854. Archibald Carey Peachy (1820–83) was a native of Virginia who came to California in 1849 and joined Billings in forming the law firm. He was elected to the state assembly in 1852 and to the senate in 1860. Frederick Billings (1823–90) graduated from the University of Vermont in 1844, was admitted to the bar in 1849, and was appointed legal advisor to California territory under Governor Mason. The firm was dissolved in 1861 with the coming of the Civil War, and Halleck returned to the army, where he served as general-in-chief (1862–64) and as a top aide to Abraham Lincoln. Frederick Billings returned to Vermont after the war and later became president of the Northern Pacific Railroad.

Subject matter: California land cases—copies of land titles, drafts of briefs, and opinions used in establishing the legal titles of some 36 different land grants. Includes notes on Spanish land law and a few papers relating to other legal cases in California.

Physical description: documents and letters.

Source: purchased from the Argonaut Book Shop, December, 1946.

HALPINE, CHARLES GRAHAM (1829–68)
684 pieces, 1811–89

Charles Graham Halpine, New York author, journalist, and politician, was born Charles Boyton Halpin in Oldcastle, Ireland, was educated at Trinity College, Dublin, and migrated to America in 1851. As a journalist and poet (principally of light and satiric verse), Halpine co-edited the *Carpet-Bag* with B. P. Shillaber, was an associate editor of the *New York Times,* and finally the principal editor of the *New York Leader.* Halpine was active in New York Democratic circles as an opponent of municipal corruption and until the Civil War was a reform member of Tammany Hall. At the outbreak of the war he enlisted in the 69th Regiment and served on the staff of General David Hunter, while continuing to write for northern newspapers (often under the guise of his invented character Private Miles O'Reilly).

Subject matter: Halpine's poetry, prose, and private correspondence dealing with New York political and literary matters and with the Civil War. Includes an 1864 pocket diary, an incomplete novel, an incomplete autobiography by Horace Greeley, and a biographical sketch of Halpine written by his wife.

Significant persons: Horace GREELEY (15), John Milton HAY (9), David HUNTER (23), Christopher Raymond Perry RODGERS (6), Benjamin Penhallow SHILLABER (28), and Alfred Howe TERRY (5).

Physical description: letters, manuscripts (some poetry), and a large collection of ephemera including newspaper clippings and photographs.

Source: acquired from Mrs. Charles G. Halpine, 1966 and from William Hanchett, 1967.

Bibliography: many of Halpine's poems were published in *The Life and Adventures, Songs, Services, and Speeches of Private Miles O'Reilly* (New York: Carleton, 1864) and *The Poetical Works of Charles G. Halpine (Miles O'Reilly)*, ed. Robert B. Roosevelt (New York: Harper & Brothers, 1869).

HAMER, THOMAS LYON (1800–46)
approximately 574 pieces, 1825–90

Thomas L. Hamer, congressman and soldier, was born in Pennsylvania. Mainly self educated, he was admitted to the Ohio Bar in 1821, and served in the Ohio State Legislature for several years. In 1832 he was elected to the House of Representatives as a Democrat, and was reelected twice, serving from 1833 to 1839. A supporter of Polk's Mexican War policy, Hamer enlisted and raised the 1st Ohio Volunteers. He was commissioned a brigadier general by the president and fought under General Taylor at Monterrey, but was stricken by dysentery and died there in December of 1846.

Subject matter: politics in Ohio and Washington, local business in Georgetown, Ohio, and family life as reflected in the correspondence of Thomas L. Hamer in the years 1830 to 1840; also some papers relating to the Mexican War (July to December, 1846).

Significant persons: Lewis CASS (7), James HALL (5), Robert LUCAS (5), and John McLEAN (9).

Physical description: letters, manuscripts, documents, and 3 maps.

Source: gift from Mrs. Mary E. Smith, August, 1976.

HAMILTON, ALEXANDER (1712–56)
Itinerarium (1744)
MS. volume 278 pp.

A narrative of a journey from Annapolis, Md., into Delaware, Pennsylvania, New York, Massachusetts, and New Hampshire from May to September, 1744. Published in Carl Bridenbaugh, ed., *Gentleman's Progress: The Itinerarium of Dr. Alexander Hamilton, 1744* (Chapel Hill: University of North Carolina Press, 1948).

HAMILTON, GIDEON ANTHONY (1841–1922<)
50 pieces, 1874–88

Gideon Anthony Hamilton was an engineer at the Comstock mines in Virginia City, Nevada. In 1878 he moved to a ranch in Mason Valley, Esmeralda County, Nevada, and later to San Francisco.

Subject matter: life in Virginia City and the mines, the growing development of Mason Valley, and Hamilton's great interest in ornithology as reflected in letters to his friend S. Frank Dexter. Includes some comment on life in the San Francisco area.

Physical description: letters and 1 photograph.

Source: purchased from Maxwell Hunley, 1961.

HAMILTON, LAURENTINE (1827–82)
487 pieces, 1858–82

Rev. Hamilton, pioneer missionary preacher in California, was born in Seneca, New York, in 1827. He graduated from Hamilton College in 1850 and from Auburn Theological Seminary in 1853. In 1855 Hamilton accepted a commission as a home missionary of the New School Assembly and went to the mining town of Columbia, California, where he served as pastor until 1859. He was then called to the First Presbyterian Church of San Jose where he served from 1860 to 1864. In 1861, with William H. Brewer and Josiah D. Whitney, he was the first to climb Mt. Hamilton, subsequently named after him. Hamilton went to the First Presbyterian Church of Oakland in 1865 but in 1869 was charged with heresy for his liberal views and resigned. He then established the Independent Presbyterian Church of Oakland, which he headed until his death in 1882.

Subject matter: sermons of Laurentine Hamilton, written from 1858 to 1882, and a few biographical items.

Physical description: manuscripts and some newspaper clippings.

Source: gift of Clark Edward, April, 1961.

HARBECK, CHARLES THOMAS (1850– ?)
539 pieces, 1732–1915

Charles Thomas Harbeck, naval historian, assembled a collection of letters and documents relating to the history of the U.S. Navy and naval officers for inclusion as extra-illustrated material in Edgar Stanton Maclay's *A History of the United States Navy*, although the papers were never in fact so used.

Subject matter: naval affairs in general: naval operations in the American Revolution, the War of 1812, and the Civil War; letters from numerous naval officers, famous and obscure; information about shipping, provisioning and refitting ships; orders, commissions, and other documents of naval administration; information about particular ships, such as the U.S.S. "Constitution"; a small number of items concerning the British navy. Strongest for the period after 1800.

Significant persons: William BAINBRIDGE (6), Isaac CHAUNCEY (7), David Glasgow FARRAGUT (7), John Paul JONES (4), Matthew Calbraith PERRY (5), David PORTER (6), John ROGERS (5), Benjamin STODDERT (6), Thomas TINGEY (6), and Gideon WELLES (5).

Physical description: correspondence, with a few documents, 2 bound volumes, and 1 manuscript poem.

Source: acquired from Charles Thomas Harbeck through the agency of George D. Smith, 1917.

HARBERT, ELIZABETH MORRISSON (BOYNTON) (1843–1925)
approximately 4400 pieces, 1863–1925

Elizabeth (Morrison) Boynton Harbert, feminist, suffragist, author, and lecturer, was born in Indiana in 1843, educated at the Terre Haute Female College, and was active from an early age in support of the rights of women to vote and to obtain a higher education. She served as vice-president of the Woman's Suffrage Association of Iowa. In 1870 she married William Soesbe Harbert, soldier and lawyer, and moved first to Indiana and then (in 1874) to Evanston, Illinois, where she served for eight years as editor of the "Woman's Kingdom" department of the Chicago *Inter Ocean* newspaper and for twelve years as president of the Illinois Woman Suffrage Association. She corresponded extensively with other prominent feminist leaders, wrote pamphlets and books on the topic, and was active in the National Household Economic Association, the National Woman Suffrage Association, the World's Unity League, and numerous other political, religious, and philanthropic organizations. In 1906 the Harberts moved to Pasadena, California, where both continued activities on behalf of women's rights and in various civic associations.

Subject matter: woman suffrage movement (particularly in Iowa, Indiana, Illinois, and California) and related organizations; religious and philanthropic organizations; editorial and journalistic activities of Elizabeth Harbert; Harbert family matters.

Significant persons: Susan B. ANTHONY (85), Rachel (Foster) AVERY (13), Amelia BLOOMER (6), Clara (Bewick) COLBY (16), Matilda (Joslyn) GAGE (13), Helen M. GOUGAR (23), Julia (Ward) HOWE (16), Mary (Ashton) LIVERMORE (8), Caroline Maria (Seymour) SEVERANCE (12), May (Wright) SEWALL (27), Elizabeth (Cady) STANTON (24), Frances E. WILLARD (20).

Physical description: chiefly correspondence, with additional manuscripts (including diaries, address books of woman suffrage workers, and poetry and music composed by Elizabeth Harbert). Includes printed matter and ephemera: large scrapbooks of newspaper clippings, some photographs, and an extensive collection of pamphlets and broadsides on the topic of woman suffrage.

Source: purchased from Mrs. Elizabeth B. Frederick, December, 1969.

HARPER, IDA (HUSTED) (1851–1931)
235 pieces, 1841–1919

Ida (Husted) Harper, journalist, author, and suffragette, was born in Fairfield, Indiana, in 1851, and after her marriage (which eventually ended in divorce) began a career in journalism in Terre Haute and Indianapolis. She eventually moved to New York, acting for a time as department editor for the *Sunday Sun* and for *Harper's Bazaar,* and contributing articles to several other newspapers in various Eastern cities. A firm supporter of the woman suffrage movement, she was director of publicity for the National American Woman Suffrage Association and was chosen by Susan (Brownell) Anthony as the latter's biographer. Several volumes of *The Life and Work of Susan B. Anthony,* written by Harper, were accordingly published between 1899 and 1908.

Subject matter: woman suffrage movement in the late nineteenth and early twentieth centuries.

Significant persons: William Lloyd GARRISON (5), Wendell PHILLIPS (5), Theodore ROOSEVELT (8), Elizabeth (Cady) STANTON (5), and Frances Elizabeth WILLARD (7).

Physical description: letters, with a few documents.

Source: purchased from Thomas F. Madigan, 1926.

HARRINGTON, GEORGE (1815–92)
64 pieces, 1849–91

George Harrington, treasury official and diplomat, served through several administrations as a clerk in the Treasury Department before being appointed chief clerk under his personal friend Salmon P. Chase. In 1861 Harrington was appointed assistant secretary of the treasury and from 1865 to 1869 served as U.S. minister to Switzerland. He then retired from public service to a private life of literary and business pursuits and died in 1892.

Subject matter: U.S. financial administration during and after the Civil War; New York and Maryland politics; arrangements for Abraham Lincoln's funeral; Andrew Johnson's administration; personal affairs.

Significant persons: Salmon Portland CHASE (7), William PITT (12).

Physical description: letters and documents.

Source: acquired from William K. Bixby, 1918.

HARRIS, OBADIAH (fl. 1758)
A Rigmental Jarnul . . . Timothy Ruggles Rigment in the Expedi[ti]on against Canady (1758)
MS. volume 23 leaves

Information on Forts Edward, George and Ticonderoga between May 22 and Oct. 23, 1758.

HASTINGS COLLECTION—AMERICANA
114 pieces, 1610–1823

The Hastings Americana Papers are a sub-collection of the 50,000 piece Hastings Collection of English historical manuscripts at the Library. Although the Hastings earls of Huntingdon and the related Rawdon family (earls of Moira) played no sustained role in American colonial history, at least three members took important if short-lived parts: Henry Hastings, 5th Earl of Huntingdon (1586–1643) "adventured" £120 in the Virginia Company of London in 1610–11 in return for 1,000 acres of land in the new Virginia Plantation; John Rawdon, 1st Earl of Moira (1720–93), invested in lands in Florida; and Francis Rawdon-Hastings, Lord Rawdon (1754–1826), afterwards 2nd Earl of Moira and 1st Marquis of Hastings, served with distinction in the American Revolution from 1775 until the summer of 1781.

Subject matter: the Virginia Company and the early settlement of Virginia; English speculation in American lands in the mid-18th century; and military operations of the American Revolution (in particular the battles of Bunker Hill, Long Island, White Plains, and Kip's Bay, and the Charleston Expedition of 1776).

Significant persons: Francis RAWDON-HASTINGS, 1st Marquis of Hastings (159).

Physical description: letters, documents, and 2 maps.

Source: purchased from Maggs Brothers, 1926.

Bibliography: the collection is briefly described (and a few individual items of interest are noted) in "Summary Report

on the Hastings Manuscripts," *Huntington Library Bulletin,*
no. 5 (April, 1934): 1–67. Much of the correspondence is
calendared in the Historical Manuscripts Commission, *Report
on the Manuscripts of the late Reginald Rawdon Hastings,*
4 vols. (H.M.S.O., 1928–47).

HAY, JOHN MILTON (1838–1905)
52 pieces, 1880–1904

John Milton Hay, statesman, diplomat, historian, and poet,
was born in Indiana in 1838, studied law in Springfield, Illinois, and during the Civil War served as assistant to Abraham
Lincoln's private secretary, John George Nicolay. After holding minor diplomatic and journalistic posts in the postwar
years, Hay was appointed assistant secretary of state in 1878,
and from 1898 until his death in 1905 served Presidents Mc-
Kinley and Roosevelt as secretary of state. Hay collaborated
with Nicolay on the monumental ten-volume *Abraham Lincoln: A History,* published by the Century Company in 1890.

Subject matter: Hay's letters to Richard Watson Gilder and
Clarence Clough Buel, editors of the *Century* magazine, concerning the progress of his history of Lincoln; editorial
changes, recollections of events during Lincoln's lifetime, and
the problems of publishing.

Physical description: letters.

Source: unknown.

HAZZARD, LEMUEL H. (ca.1842–?)
approximately 483 pieces, 1862–1919

Lemuel H. Hazzard, Union soldier, served during the Civil
War in the 12th Regiment of the Indiana Infantry Volunteers,

where he eventually attained the rank of captain. After the war he worked as a carpenter and from 1883 to 1884 was a railway postal clerk.

Subject matter: military administration and life during the Civil War; U.S. postal service.

Physical description: letters, manuscripts (including a 3-volume diary, 1864–65), documents, 1 tintype, medals, and other ephemera.

Source: purchased from T. L. Hazzard, May, 1952.

HELMUTH, HENRY (fl. 1820–60s)
75 pieces, 1820–93

Henry Helmuth was a lawyer practicing in Philadelphia in the decades before the outbreak of the Civil War and was mildly active in civic politics. One of his sons attended, but apparently did not graduate from, the University of Pennsylvania, and another relative, Henry R. Perceval, was an Episcopal clergyman in Philadelphia during the 1870s and 1880s.

Subject matter: family and social matters; also Henry Perceval and ecclesiastical matters and church administration.

Physical description: letters, a few manuscripts (including 3 bound volumes), and documents; also some newspaper clippings.

Source: purchased from Mrs. Forrest S. Fisher, 1953.

HESLOP FAMILY COLLECTION
40 pieces, 1833–58; 1880–1906

Members of the Heslop (often spelled Heslope) family were pioneer landowners in East Pasadena, California. José Heslop

(1835–99) was born of English and Chilean parents in Valparaiso, Chile, and came to California where he married Francisca White. She was the daughter of Michael White, an English sailor who came early to California and married the daughter of Eulalia Pérez de Guillén, through whom Francisca inherited portions of Rancho San Pascual (now Pasadena) and Rancho Muscupiabe near San Bernardino.

Subject matter: Heslop family genealogy; land dealings near the city of Pasadena and the litigation for title of Rancho Muscupiabe.

Physical description: documents (including account books and notebook) and manuscripts (including a diary and a tracing of a diseño map of Rancho San Pascual).

Source: purchased from Burger and Evans, November, 1971.

HIGGINS, ADAM C. (1837– ?)
66 pieces, 1857–89

Adam C. Higgins, army chaplain, was born in Virginia but moved to Illinois, and in August, 1862, enlisted with the rank of captain in the 83rd Regiment of Illinois Infantry Volunteers. He served there as a chaplain until the end of the war, when he returned to the ministry (and possibly to the study of law).

Subject matter: chaplain's activities in the Civil War.

Physical description: letters, documents, manuscripts (including poems); ephemera.

Source: purchased from Fred Lockley, July, 1952.

HILTON, WILLIAM HAYES (1829–1909)
27 original drawings (some in color) and 8 notebooks of sketches of California, Texas, Arizona, and Mexico (1858–70).

Many are published in William Hayes Hilton, *Sketches in the Southwest and Mexico, 1858–1877*, introduction and notes by Carey S. Bliss (Los Angeles: Dawson's Book Shop, 1963).

HINCKLEY, FRANK (1838–90)
221 pieces, 1863–98

Frank Hinckley, civil engineer and rancher, was born in Rhode Island and graduated from Rensselaer Institute. He came to California by the Isthmus of Panama in 1863 and became a civil engineer for the government in San Francisco. He worked as a surveyor for the Western Pacific Railroad in and around the Bay area until 1872, when he became foreman of the Meek Ranch in Hayward, California, owned by his wife's father, William Meek. Hinckley and his family moved to a ranch near Redlands in 1883, where he lived until his death in 1890.

Subject matter: life in San Francisco (1863–66), working for the Western Pacific Railroad (1863–90), and life on the ranch in Hayward and near Redlands.

Physical description: letters, diaries, (29 volumes) and documents (2 volumes).

Source: gift of Mr. and Mrs. George Hinckley, May, 1935.

Bibliography: excerpts from the letters and diaries have been published in Edith Parker Hinckley, *Frank Hinckley* (Claremont, Calif.: Saunders Press, 1946).

HOADLEY, MILO (1809–87)
65 pieces, 1849–86

Milo Hoadley, civil engineer, came to San Francisco, California, from Connecticut in 1849. He served as assistant and deputy county surveyor and was elected state surveyor general in 1851. Hoadley was involved in negotiations for the water supply of the city of San Francisco, served as president of the San Francisco City Board of Civil Engineers (1862–63), and later practiced privately as a civil engineer.

Subject matter: life in and near San Francisco (1850–52), official and private surveys made in San Francisco city and county (1849–62), and land titles in San Francisco city and county; information on the controversy in supplying water to San Francisco (1852–72), in which Hoadley's San Francisco Water Co., organized in 1867, unsuccessfully tried to displace the monopolist Spring Valley Co.

Physical description: letters, manuscripts, and documents (including 7 fieldbooks, journal, account book, and notebook).

Source: purchased from Edwin Grabhorn, January, 1945.

HODGE, BENJAMIN (1797–1868)
approximately 380 pieces, 1795–1892

Benjamin Hodge, the fifth of that name in direct succession, moved with his family to Buffalo, New York, as a small child. He was captured by the British during the War of 1812, later began a career as horticulturalist and nurseryman, and in 1826 opened the Buffalo Nursery. His son Lyman Davis Hodge (b. 1835) was educated at Yale, moved to St. Paul, Minnesota, where, with his brother-in-law Warren Granger, he entered business as a spice and coffee merchant and in the last years of his life planned a move to the Pacific Northwest. Other branches of the Hodge family lived in Ohio and Michigan.

Subject matter: family, social, and business life of the Hodges and related families in New York, Minnesota, Ohio, and Michigan. Strongest for the 1850s, but a few early items relate to

Benjamin Hodge IV, and to the experiences of Benjamin Hodge V as a prisoner of war in the War of 1812.

Physical description: letters, manuscripts (including 6 volumes of journals), some documents, and a few miscellaneous printed items and ephemera.

Source: acquired from Mrs. Ruth S. Hodge through Lindley Bynum, 1937.

HOFFMAN, ELWYN IRVING (ca.1870–ca.1949)
393 pieces, 1893–1947

Elwyn Irving Hoffman was a California writer who lived in Sacramento and the central valley area. A journalist by trade, his great interest was in poetry and in the literary circles attended by Jack London and Ida (Meacham) Strobridge.

Subject matter: Jack and Charmian London; the voyage of the "Snark;" the Londons' ranch at Glen Ellen; literary figures and affairs in and around San Francisco.

Significant persons: Maynard DIXON (13), Charmian (Kittredge) LONDON (39), Jack LONDON (40), and Charles Fletcher LUMMIS (12).

Physical description: letters, notebooks, and 50 photographs.

Source: purchased from Mrs. Marion Stuart, February, 1951.

HOLLIDAY, CYRUS KURTZ (1826–1900)
165 pieces, 1854–83

Cyrus K. Holliday, promoter and railroad builder, was born in Pennsylvania and graduated from Allegheny College in 1852. After practicing law for a short time, he moved to Kansas, where he founded the city of Topeka and succeeded in having it declared the territorial capital. Holliday secured the charter for the Atchison, Topeka & Santa Fe Railroad, which was organized in 1860. He was elected its first president and was director until the time of his death. Holliday was a leader in Republican politics, served in the state legislature, and was active in many business enterprises.

Subject matter: Atchison, Topeka & Santa Fe Railroad Company business matters, development of the city of Topeka, and politics in Kansas.

Physical description: letters (some xerox copies), documents, photographs, and 1 scrapbook.

Source: purchased from Mrs. George W. Burpee, May, 1960.

HOLT, JOSEPH (1807–94)
403 pieces, ca. 1800–93

Joseph Holt, lawyer and politician, practiced law successfully for many years in Mississippi and Kentucky before being appointed commissioner of patents (1857) and postmaster-general (1859) in Buchanan's administration. As secretary of war under Lincoln in 1861, he was instrumental in preserving Kentucky's loyalty to the Union. The following year he was appointed judge advocate general of the army in an attempt to extend military control and jurisdiction over civilian political prisoners. Although Holt's personal popularity rose during the trial of Lincoln's assassins, increasing opposition to the military tribunal he directed and charges that he had suppressed evidence ultimately forced his resignation from the post (1875). Despite failing health Holt continued attempts to prove his own innocence of all charges and died in 1894.

Subject matter: law and politics in Civil War period; Kentucky at the outbreak of the war; military law and the office of judge advocate general; trial of Lincoln's assassins; personal and family life of Joseph Holt; U.S. Patent Office; U.S. Post Office.

Significant persons: Simon CAMERON (5), William CAMPBELL (14), James Abram GARFIELD (6), Henry Stephens RANDALL (7), Winfield SCOTT (5), Edwin McMasters STANTON (10).

Physical description: chiefly letters, with documents, manuscripts, a few printed items, newspaper clippings, and other ephemera.

Source: gift of Joseph Holt Rose, 1970.

HONEYMAN, ROBERT (1747–1824)
[Journal of a Trip from Virginia to New England and Return]
(1775)
Autograph MS. volume 126 pp.

A narrative of Honeyman's journey and description of the countryside, towns, and current events. Published in *Colonial Panorama, 1775: Dr. Honeyman's Journal from March and April,* ed. Philip Padelford (San Marino: Huntington Library, 1939).

HOOKER, JOSEPH (1814–79)
3850 pieces, 1861–64

Joseph Hooker, Union general, was born in Massachusetts in 1814 and had already retired from a military career at the outbreak of the Civil War. He immediately returned to service and was appointed brigadier general of volunteers in 1861, when he was active in the defense of Washington. In the following year he held commands at the battles of Williamsburg, Seven Pines or Fair Oaks, the Seven Days, Second Malvern

Hill, Second Manassas, Chantilly, South Mountain, and Antietam, and was promoted to major general of volunteers. After a celebrated quarrel with his superior, General Burnside, Hooker replaced him in command of the Army of the Potomac in January, 1863. He was defeated by Lee's numerically inferior forces at Chancellorsville in May and, a week before the battle of Gettysburg, in anger over General Halleck's refusal to send reinforcements, Hooker asked to be relieved of his command. He was thereupon transferred to the Department of the Cumberland, and served under Generals Thomas and Sherman from the battle of Chattanooga to the siege of Atlanta, being brevetted major general of the regular army after Lookout Mountain. Upon Sherman's refusal to appoint Hooker to succeed General McPherson, Hooker asked once more to be relieved of command, and in September 1864 ended his service in the field. He continued to hold more peaceful commands in several northern departments of the army until his retirement in 1868.

Subject matter: voluminous and minute details of Hooker's commands from October, 1861, through September, 1864 (excepting only the four important months from October, 1862, through January, 1863, for which there is no material at all). Includes orders and commands from army headquarters, information on tactics and the preparation of campaigns, the use of cavalry, reports from pickets, engineers, and signal corps, reconnaissance reports (including balloon observers), and reports on battles such as Antietam, Chancellorsville, and Second Malvern Hill. Also includes much information on the daily administration of the army, on such topics as discipline and personnel problems, courts martial, civilian relationships, staff work, freed slaves, and contraband goods.

Significant persons: William Woods AVERELL (10), Daniel BUTTERFIELD (94), George Gordon MEADE (13), John Fulton REYNOLDS (8), John SEDGEWICK (71).

Physical description: documents and letters (including some telegrams), and 24 campaign maps.

in the Huntington Library

Source: acquired from Joseph H. Wood, April, 1964.

Bibliography: many, but by no means all, of the papers have been published in *The War of the Rebellion: a Compilation of the Official Records of the Union and Confederate Armies,* 70 vols. (Washington: Government Printing Office, 1880–1900).

HOUGHTON, SHERMAN OTIS (1828–1914)
195 pieces, 1831–1914

Sherman O. Houghton, California lawyer and politician, was born in New York and came to California with Stevenson's New York Volunteers in 1847. In 1849 he settled in San Jose where he became mayor in 1853. Houghton was admitted to the bar in 1857 and used his knowledge of Spanish to specialize in land claims cases brought about by the transfer from Mexican to American jurisdiction. In 1861 he married Eliza Poor Donner, whose parents, George and Tamsen Donner, had perished during the crossing of the Sierra Nevada in 1846. Houghton served in the U.S. House of Representatives from 1871 to 1875. In 1900 he retired to a ranch in Los Angeles County.

Subject matter: primarily correspondence (1879–1904) regarding the publication of *History of the Donner Party* by Charles Fayette McGlashan.

Significant persons: Tamsen Eustace (Dosier) DONNER (6), Charles Fayette McGLASHAN (93).

Physical description: letters, documents, and manuscripts.

Source: acquired by purchase and gift from Miss Eliza P. Houghton, 1935–37.

HOWELL (EVELYN LIONEL VICTOR) COLLECTION
70 pieces, 1831–1905

This collection consists of various legal papers relating to land in California, collected by Evelyn L.V. Howell, weather station observer at Mission San Juan Capistrano. Included are land patents, indentures, mortgages, deeds, etc., principally from Los Angeles and San Diego Counties and in the vicinity of San Juan Capistrano.

Physical description: documents.

Source: gift of Evelyn L.V. Howell, June, 1940.

HOWELLS-FRÉCHETTE COLLECTION
176 pieces, 1844–1934

William Dean Howells (1838–1920), author, journalist, and editor of the *Atlantic Monthly*, was born in Martin's Ferry, Ohio, in 1838, the son of Ohio newspaperman William Cooper Howells. After the Civil War the elder Howells, an acquaintance and client of President James Garfield, served as U.S. Consul in Quebec. The entire Howells family were active in the literary and journalistic circles of the eastern United States, and one of William Dean's sisters, Annie Thomas Howells, married in 1887 the Canadian journalist and politician, Achille Fréchette. Their daughter, Marie Marguerite Fréchette, studied art in New York and later moved with her mother to San Diego, California.

Subject matter: family and social life and activities of the Howells and Fréchette families, some literary and journalistic matters, and occasionally politics. Includes ballot counts from the deadlocked 1880 Republican Convention and medical bulletins from the time of Garfield's assassination, both sent to the elder Howells in Canada by telegraph.

Significant persons: Lucretia GARFIELD (10), William Dean HOWELLS (10), William Henry SMITH (5).

Physical description: mostly letters, with some documents, a few manuscripts (including 1 bound volume), and miscellaneous ephemera including 6 souvenir picture postcards, 1 photograph, visiting cards, and a few newspaper clippings.

Source: purchased from Marie Marguerite Fréchette, 1963.

HUDSON, JOHN T.
Journal of the Schooner Tamana from Woahoo (Sandwich Islands) to the Coast of America. (November 13, 1805–July 13, 1807)
Autograph MS.S. 1 volume 127 pp.

[Also: log of the "Hazard" from Maui (Hawaii) to San Francisco; miscellaneous nautical calculations. (January 4–26, 1804)]

Logbook of the Schooner Tammana, John T. Hudson, Master, from the Sandwich Islands to the Coast of America. (1806–07)

MS. 1 volume 39 pp.

HUNT, GEORGE LUNDY (ca.1842–76<)
approximately 260 pieces, 1864–79

George Lundy Hunt, California miner and rancher, came from Ontario, Canada, to the Cariboo Mining District of British Columbia in 1865. In 1866 he moved to Campo Seco, Calaveras County, California, where he was active in the mines from

1866 to 1872. After this time he moved to Elk Grove, near Sacramento, California, and became a rancher.

Subject matter: life in Ontario, Canada, in Victoria, British Columbia, and in the Cariboo Mining District of British Columbia; mining in Calaveras County, California.

Physical description: letters, a few documents, and 1 manuscript (diary written by Hunt in 1867).

Source: gift of Miss Aurora Hunt, May, 1938.

HUNTER, ROBERT (1764–1843)
[Journal] (1785–86)
Autograph MS. volumes 341 pp.

Contains the observations of an English traveler to America, including a classic word picture of George Washington. Published in *Quebec to Carolina in 1785–1786*, ed. Louis B. Wright and Marion Tingling (San Marino: Huntington Library, 1943).

HUNTINGTON, EBENEZER (1754–1834)
133 pieces, 1737–1898.

Ebenezer Huntington, Revolutionary soldier, was born in Norwich, Connecticut, in 1754, the son of Jabez and Hannah Williams Huntington. At the outbreak of the Revolution, Huntington left his studies at Yale to serve in the army. When he retired at the end of the war in 1783 he had risen to the rank of lieutenant colonel. Huntington continued to serve as a general in the Connecticut militia, was elected to the state legislature, and twice represented his state in Congress.

Subject matter: battles, skirmishes, and other aspects of the Revolutionary war; convicts sent to America; the Constitution and the Constitutional Convention; politics of the early Federal period; business of the port of New London, Connecticut; the War of 1812; the tariff question of 1818; Jacksonian politics; freemasonry; and family matters. Strongest for the period from 1774 to 1818.

Significant persons: Ebenezer HUNTINGTON (76), Jedediah HUNTINGTON (8), and Samuel HUNTINGTON (21).

Physical description: letters, with a few documents.

Source: purchased from Robert H. Dodd, 1916 and from George D. Smith, 1926.

Bibliography: Ebenezer Huntington's letters written between 1774 and 1783 have been printed in a limited edition as *Letters Written by Ebenezer Huntington during the American Revolution,* ed. Charles Frederick Heartman (New York: 1914).

HUSON, NELSON G. (1842–65)
98 pieces, 1862–64

Nelson G. Huson, Union soldier, was born in Starkey, New York, in 1842, the son of George T. and Maria (Gabriel) Huson. By the outbreak of the Civil War the family had moved to Illinois, and Huson enlisted in the 96th Illinois Infantry, probably in 1862. He took part in several minor skirmishes in Tennessee and Georgia during the Atlanta Campaign and died in Columbia, Tennessee, in January 1865.

Subject matter: everyday life of the private soldier, rations, clothing, guarding supply trains, marches and skirmishes, and Huson's opinions of the war.

Physical description: letters, with 1 manuscript, a few genealogical documents, 2 old photographs, 1 tintype, and 1 newspaper clipping.

Source: gift of Harriet E. Pyle, June, 1953.

HUTCHINSON, CALVIN GIBBS (ca.1836– ?)
331 pieces, ca.1861–67

Calvin Gibbs Hutchinson, born about 1836 to a New England seafaring family, enlisted in the Union navy in 1862 as an acting assistant paymaster and clerk. He served from November 1862 to September 1863 on the ferry gun-boat U.S.S. "Commodore Morris" chiefly in patrol and picket duty. He was then transferred to the U.S. Steamer "Pequot," where he served until the end of the war. After the war Hutchinson returned to Massachusetts and settled in Dorchester.

Subject matter: naval operations in the U.S. Civil War; sailor's life and reminiscences; U.S.S. "Commodore Morris"; U.S.S. "Pequot"; U.S. Navy.

Physical description: correspondence (including approximately 300 letters bound in 1 volume), manuscripts (including 3 volumes of journals and diaries), documents, maps (some printed), and ephemera.

Source: purchased from Maury A. Bromsen, October, 1961.

HUTTON, WILLIAM RICH (1826–1901)
147 pieces, 1840–61

William R. Hutton, surveyor and engineer, was born in Washington, D.C., in 1826 and was educated in private institutions. In 1847 Hutton came to California as a clerk with his uncle, Major William Rich, botanist and paymaster for U.S. volunteer troops. For the next six years Hutton was employed as a surveyor and draftsman, and during this time he made watercolor and pencil drawings of California scenes. Hutton returned to the East in 1853 and worked as an engineer on many government projects, including the Washington Bridge and the Hudson River Tunnel in New York City.

Subject matter: drawings and descriptions of early California, Los Angeles, Monterey, Mexico, the Isthmus of Panama, and Peru.

Physical description: 95 drawings (79 of California, 36 of which were made before 1849), 13 letters, and 39 facsimile copies of letters and manuscripts.

Source: purchase and gift from Miss Mary A. Hutton, 1939–46.

Bibliography: of the 95 drawings, 56 have been published in William Rich Hutton, *California Drawings* (San Marino: Huntington Library, 1956). The facsimile copies of letters and diaries have been published in William Rich Hutton, *Glances at California, 1847–1853* (San Marino: Huntington Library, 1942).

I

INDEX TO AMERICAN DESIGN COLLECTION
approximately 260 pieces, 1935–39

The Index to American Design Collection consists of secondary source material and drawings pertaining to Spanish American culture in California, which were produced by the Works Progress Administration Project in Los Angeles.

Subject matter: early American and Spanish American arts, crafts, and costumes (especially those in California); interviews with Los Angeles area pioneers; community studies [including "Los Angeles Negro Survey," 1935; "Racial Elements," and "Parks and Recreation Centers")]; California place names, Indians, and missions; material relating to the Townsend Plan for an Old Age Revolving Pension.

Physical description: manuscripts, drawings, and photographs.

Source: gift of Works Progress Administration of Los Angeles, January 14, 1949.

J

JACKS, DAVID (1822–1909)
approximately 200,000 pieces, ca.1845–1926

David Jacks, pioneer businessman in Monterey, California, came to New York from Scotland in 1841, and sailed around the Horn to California in 1848. In 1850 he settled in Monterey, where he acquired extensive land holdings and became a farmer and stock raiser. Jacks was involved in much litigation concerning his properties, including a suit by the city of Monterey in 1877 to regain land held by Jacks. He was instrumental in the construction of the Monterey and Salinas Valley Railroad in 1874, in establishing the Pacific Grove Retreat, and in founding the city of Del Monte.

Subject matter: correspondence (1855–1919) and business and legal papers (1835–1926) relating to Monterey, California. Includes information about the Pacific Grove Retreat Association (1875–1911).

Physical description: letters, documents (including 307 bound volumes), and some photographs.

Source: gift of Margaret Anna Jacks, April, 1958.

JAMES, GEORGE WHARTON (1858–1923)
266 pieces, 1871–1921

George Wharton James, lecturer and author of books and articles about the Southwest, came from England to Nevada in

1881, where he preached on the Methodist circuit. A self-made man, he became acquainted with many prominent Western personalities. After a sensationalized divorce suit, James was dismissed from the church and turned to the desert to recover his health. He explored the Grand Canyon, studied the Indians, and was made a member of several tribes. In his later years he traveled extensively, lecturing on the Chautauqua circuit. James wrote many books and articles on the Southwest and edited *The Craftsman* (1904–05) and *Out West,* formerly called *Land of Sunshine* (1912–14).

Subject matter: California, Arizona, New Mexico, and Indians of New Mexico; sermons; letters and poems sent to James, some probably intended for publication in *Land of Sunshine* or *Out West* magazines.

Physical description: letters, manuscripts, 2 scrapbooks, and 24 photographs.

Source: purchased from N. Kovach, 1943–44 and Charles Yale, 1968.

JANES (EDWIN B.) COLLECTION
238 pieces, 1746–1900

Edwin B. Janes, together with Andrew J. Williams of Cleveland, Ohio, accumulated an autograph collection devoted primarily to prominent American political, military, and literary figures of the second half of the nineteenth century. A few items are of an earlier date, and a few are written by English politicians and authors.

Subject matter: there is no unifying subject matter for the collection, although 31 of the letters are addressed to Albert Gallatin Riddle.

Physical description: primarily letters, with a few manuscripts and documents.

Source: gift of Edwin B. Janes in memory of his wife Isabelle Kelley Janes, 1942 and 1943.

JANIN, CHARLES HENRY (1873–1937)
15,582 pieces, 1858–1937

Charles H. Janin, California mining engineer, followed the career of his famous father Louis Janin. After working with his father, he established the firm of Janin, Stebbins, and Smith (later Janin & Smith). In 1911 he began working alone as a mining consultant, and in 1914 joined the staff of the U.S. Bureau of Mines in Washington, D.C. Janin traveled to many countries as a consultant and served on assignment in Russia during World War I and again about 1929. He wrote and published many articles on mining and lived with his family on Rancho Marcelino in Santa Barbara County, California.

Subject matter: minerals, mines, and mining, especially in California, Mexico, Alaska, Canada, and Russia. Includes information about gold, silver, tin, platinum, and gold dredging, as well as material on Russian life and politics and on the history of the Santa Inez Valley in California.

Significant persons: Samuel INSULL (14) and Vannoy Hartrog MANNING (18).

Physical description: letters, manuscripts (including diaries and mining reports), photographs, and maps.

Source: gift of Louis and Henry Janin and Elizabeth Janin Evans, December, 1958.

JANIN FAMILY
23,699 pieces, 1735–1932

Louis Janin (1803–74), lawyer, was born and educated in Vienna and in 1828 emigrated to New Orleans, where he became an American citizen, began the practice of law, and invested in sugar plantations. Of his six sons, three became prominent mining engineers, and one, Albert Covington Janin (ca.1844–1928), became a lawyer, practiced law in New Orleans (and later in New York and Washington), entered politics, operated a canal in Louisiana, and later managed Mammoth Cave Estate in Kentucky. Albert Covington Janin married Violet (Blair) Janin (1850–1932), daughter of James Lawrence Blair (1819–53) and Mary (Jesup) Blair (1825–1914). Blair, a U.S. naval officer, was the son of Francis Preston Blair. In San Francisco in 1849, James Blair acquired property and established the first steamship line on the Sacramento River. He died suddenly in San Francisco after resigning from the navy in 1851. James Blair's wife, Mary (the mother of Violet and Lucy James), was the daughter of Thomas Sidney Jesup (1788–1860), U.S. Army officer. The wife of Jesup, Anne Heron Croghan was a member of a Kentucky family and a niece of George Rogers Clark. Her brother John purchased lands containing the Mammoth Cave, which he willed to the descendents of his sister and brothers. Violet (Blair) Janin, Washington, D.C., society leader, lived her entire life in Lafayette Square near the White House except for brief periods following her marriage in 1874 when she lived in New Orleans. She traveled in Europe and elsewhere, and was active in the National Society of Colonial Dames, the National Society of the American Revolution, the National Society Opposed to Women's Suffrage, etc. She and her friends were prominent in Washington, D.C., social and diplomatic circles. Her sister, Lucy James (Blair) Wheeler (1853–1902), married Major George Montague Wheeler (1842–1905), engineer and West Point graduate, and accompanied him to military posts in the U.S. and Europe.

Subject matter: politics and government in Washington, D.C., and Louisiana, and society and customs in Washington, D.C., and New Orleans; Blair House (Washington, D.C.); land titles in Indiana Territory, Kentucky, Louisiana, and Missouri; the

Ocean Canal and Transportation Company (Louisiana to St. Louis); the history of Mammoth Cave (Kentucky) from the time of purchase by John Croghan in 1839 until 1932, when it became a national park (at which time Violet [Blair] Janin was the primary owner); and mining in Australia.

Physical description: letters (including 1 letterbook), manuscripts (including 50 diaries), documents (including 55 account books, 12 cash books, and 5 miscellaneous volumes), and photographs.

Source: purchased from Thomas M. Spaulding, 1936 and 1937; gift of Louis Janin, 1946 and 1968, Howard H. Peckham, 1965, and Elliot A. P. Evans, 1953 and 1968.

JAY, JOHN (1745–1829)
Letters from the Honorable John Jay Esqr., Minister Plenipotentiary from the United States of America to the Court of Spain (1779–82)
MS. volume 314 pp.

Contains the official correspondence of Jay while in Spain.

JAYHAWKERS OF '49
1105 pieces, 1849–1938

The Jayhawker party of 36 single young men left Galesburg, Illinois, in April of 1849 to cross the plains in search of gold in California. In Salt Lake City they joined several other wagon trains and hired Captain Jefferson Hunt, a Mormon guide, to lead them over the Spanish Trail to Los Angeles. The Jayhawkers and a few of the other wagon owners separated themselves from the guide and the main group to try a shortcut by way of the Walker Pass and became lost in what is now known as Death Valley. Struggling with hunger and thirst, with great hardship and the loss of three lives, the party finally made its way to safety at the San Francisquito Ranch near Los Angeles.

Subject matter: the Jayhawker party and its annual reunions (held from 1872 until 1918). Includes some information about the 1849 journey, as reflected in the assembled papers of John Burt Colton (1831–91), a member of the original party.

Significant persons: John Wells BRIER (22), William Frederick CODY (4), Jessie (Benton) FRÉMONT (4), Charles Fletcher LUMMIS (20), William Lewis MANLEY (40 letters and 1 map), Frederic REMINGTON (4).

Physical description: letters, manuscripts (including 1 journal), 1 map, and 8 scrapbooks.

Source: purchased from Edward T. Colton, April, 1930.

Bibliography: some material from the collection has been published in Margaret Long, *The Shadow of the Arrow* (Caldwell, Idaho: The Caxton Printers, 1950).

JEFFERSON, THOMAS (1743–1826)
1046 pieces, 1764–1826

Thomas Jefferson, statesman and scholar, practiced law from 1767 to 1774. During that period he entered public service, becoming in the course of his career a provincial, state, and national legislator, governor of Virginia, envoy to France, and secretary of state and president of the United States. His service also encompassed urban planning, designing government buildings, and founding the University of Virginia. In private life he closely attended his estates, family, scholarship, and technology.

Subject matter: Jefferson's law practice; surveying jobs; management of his plantations, including architectural and landscape designing; architectural and landscape planning of public buildings and grounds; horticulture and agriculture; personal finance; family matters; Jefferson's views on education; the founding of the University of Virginia. Little material concerning politics, government, and political theory.

Significant persons: John Hartwell COCKE (27), Robley DUNGLISON (6), Thomas JEFFERSON (461), James PLEASANTS (12).

Physical description: letters; documents, including accounts (notably Jefferson's daily accounts and memoranda for 1775 written in a copy of *The Virginia Almanac for 1775* and for 1805–09 in his "Day Book"), his "Fee Book," "Casebook," and notes on the twelfth amendment; and drawings.

Source: George D. Smith and William K. Bixby, 1916.

Bibliography: The Papers of Thomas Jefferson, ed. Julian Boyd (Princeton: Princeton University Press, 1950–   ); *The Writings of Thomas Jefferson,* ed. Paul Leicester Ford (New York: G. P. Putnam's Sons, 1892–99); *Thomas Jefferson Correspondence, Printed from the Originals in the Collection of William K. Bixby,* ed. Worthington C. Ford (Boston: privately printed, 1916); *The Family Letters of Thomas Jefferson,* ed. Edwin M. Betts and James A. Bear (Columbia: University of Missouri Press, 1966); *Thomas Jefferson's Architectural Drawings,* ed. Frederick D. Nichols (Boston: Massachusetts Historical Society, 1961).

JEUNOT, PIERRE JOSEPH (fl. 1776–83)
Livre du Bord (1776–83)
Autograph MS. volume 139 leaves illus.

Text in French. A journal of French naval campaigns in the Chesapeake Bay and the West Indies. Contains watercolor drawings of French and English naval vessels. This journal was formerly attributed to Pierre Joseph Jennet. Also contains entries by Pierre Joseph Sordelet, 1791–1832.

JOHNS, JAMES (1797–1874)
Vermont Autographer and Remarker (1849)
Autograph MS. volume 4 pp.

Newspaper in simulated printing.

———————

Vermont Autographer and Remarker (1869)
Autograph MS. volume 4 pp.

JOHNSON, PARISH BARHYDT (1838–90<)
43 pieces, 1864–86

Parish B. Johnson, Western newspaper publisher, became a member of the general committee which controlled the *Walla Walla* [Washington] *Union* when it was founded in 1868. He assumed full editorship of the paper from 1876 to 1890 and pursued a strong Republican policy.

Subject matter: Johnson's family and newspaper work. Included is a journal kept by Captain Parish B. Johnson, United States Army, of a trip from Drum Barracks, Wilmington, California, to Tucson, Arizona, in 1864.

Physical description: letters, documents, and manuscript.

Source: purchased from Mrs. O. C. Hodges, December, 1946.

JOHNSTON, JOSEPH EGGLESTON (1807–91)
532 pieces, 1841–73

Joseph E. Johnston, Confederate general, was trained at West Point. Upon resigning his commission in the U.S. Army, he was commissioned major general by the Confederacy and assigned to oversee operations at Harpers Ferry in May, 1861. After the First Battle of Bull Run, he was given command of northern Virginia and made a full general, fourth in rank. In November, 1862, he took command of all the forces in Tennessee and Mississippi, and in 1863 he headed the Army of Tennessee, which fought Sherman in the Atlanta and Carolinas campaigns. He surrendered in April, 1865.

Subject matter: Johnston's war activities, beginning with his assignment at Harpers Ferry; negligible non-Civil War material.

Significant persons: Pierre Gustave Toutant BEAUREGARD (8), Judah Philip BENJAMIN (9), Braxton BRAGG (21), Samuel COOPER [1798–1876] (13), Jefferson DAVIS (44), Wade HAMPTON [1818–1902] (16), William Joseph HARDEE (7), John Bell HOOD (8), Thomas Jonathan JACKSON (32), Joseph Eggleston JOHNSTON (36), Richard Edward LEE (49), Leonidas POLK (6), James Alexander SEDDON (17), Carter Littlepage STEVENSON (8), Alexander Peter STEWART (9), Zebulon Baird VANCE (6), Joseph WHEELER (11), Louis Trezevant WIGFALL (18).

Physical description: letters, documents, manuscripts (official reports of battles).

Source: purchased from Stan V. Henkels and Son, 1925.

Bibliography: the Jefferson Davis pieces are being published in *The Papers of Jefferson Davis,* ed. Haskell M. Monroe, Jr.

and James T. McIntosh (Baton Rouge: Louisiana State University Press, 1971–   ).

JOHNSTON-GRIFFIN COLLECTION
53 pieces, 1834–1904

William Preston Johnston (1831–99), lawyer, soldier, and educator, the son of General Albert Sydney Johnston (who served in Texas, in Utah, and as commander of the Department of the Pacific in 1860, and as a Confederate general in the Civil War before his death at Shiloh), graduated from Yale University in 1852, and from the University of Louisville law school. He served as an aide to Jefferson Davis in the Civil War, helped found Tulane University and was its president until his death. John Strother Griffin (1816–98), physician and early Los Angeles businessman, served as an army surgeon in Florida, then came to California in 1846 with General Stephen W. Kearny, participating in battles at San Pascual and Los Angeles. In 1858 he took title to Rancho San Pascual, and later sold part of the property, which became the city of Pasadena. Griffin's sister Eliza, wife of General Albert S. Johnston, developed the Fair Oaks Ranch on part of the Rancho San Pascual property.

Subject matter: family matters, chiefly concerning Dr. Griffin and his brothers regarding the Seminole War in Florida and overseas navy cruises; William Preston Johnston, some regarding recruiting in the Spanish-American War; some material on Southern California and family genealogy.

Significant persons: William Preston JOHNSTON (11).

Physical description: letters, photographs (1 volume), and 1 scrapbook.

Source: gift of Mrs. John H. Johnston, November, 1965.

JONES, ELBERT P. (ca.1823–52)
approximately 100 pieces, 1830; 1848–1914

Dr. Elbert P. Jones, early San Francisco lawyer, was a native of Kentucky who came to California in 1847. He was the first editor of the *California Star* and was elected to the San Francisco town council in 1847. Jones became the proprietor of Portsmouth House in San Francisco and was a prominent investor in real estate in the city.

Subject matter: the claim of Jones' heirs, particularly Mrs. Anna M. R. Jones of Westchester, Pennsylvania, to Yerba Buena Island, California, ca.1901–14; also includes records of transfer and diagrams of lots of land in San Francisco sold by Elbert P. Jones, 1848–51.

Physical description: letters and documents (including 1 volume).

Source: gift of Mrs. Lynne F. Saunders, and purchased from David H. H. Felix, 1963.

JONES, JAMES T. (ca.1819–69)
67 pieces, 1843–72

James T. Jones lived in New York before sailing for South America on the U.S. Frigate "Raritan" from 1844 to 1846, and (on other ships) sailing around South America until after 1850. In 1854–55 he settled in San Francisco, returning again to New York from 1857 to 1869, to engage in various business enterprises. In September of 1869, hoping to regain his health, Jones went to the Owens Valley but died within a few months at Independence, California.

Subject matter: life on board ship off the eastern coast of South America and in the cities of Rio de Janeiro and Montevideo, life in San Francisco from 1854 to 1869.

Physical description: letters.

Source: purchased from the Philadelphia Autograph Shop, May, 1942.

JONES, JOHN PAUL (1747–92)
42 pieces, 1776–89

John Paul Jones, naval officer, was commissioned a lieutenant in the U.S. Navy in 1775 and captain in 1776. In 1778 he began raiding the English coast; a year later he commanded the "Bonhomme Richard" in its victory over the "Serapis." After the Revolution he went to Europe, where he acted as an agent for the U.S. government and as a naval mercenary.

Subject matter: a little on each of a wide range of subjects, including Jones's character and personal life, the disposition of prisoners of war, the role of the "Alliance" in the "Bonhomme" affair, the construction of the "America," and Jones as U.S. agent in Europe.

Significant persons: John Paul JONES (23), Paul François de QUÉLEN, Duc de LA VAUGUYON (10).

Physical description: mostly letters, some in French; a few documents.

Source: purchased from the Anderson Galleries, William K. Bixby, Grenville Kane, and Maggs Brothers, before 1920.

Bibliography: some of the pieces have been published in John Henry Sherburne, *Life and Character of the Chevalier John Paul Jones* (New York: privately printed, 1825) and William K. Bixby, *Letters of John Paul Jones* (New York: The De Vinne Press, 1905).

JUDSON-FAIRBANKS COLLECTION
47 pieces, 1852–87

Everitt Judson left his family in New York in 1852, sailing around Cape Horn to seek his fortune in the California mines. Unsuccessful in this, he left Placerville, California, in 1853 to begin fruit ranching in Oakland, California. In 1860 Judson moved to Visalia, California, to engage in ranching and farming, and in 1862 went to the Kern River mining area where he raised vegetables to sell to the miners. During the Civil War Everitt Judson's son, John B. Judson, and his brother-in-law, Martin L. Fairbanks, were members of the Union Army.

Subject matter: the collection is composed of three groups of papers concerning the Judson and Fairbanks families. The first contains letters from California (1852–87), mainly those of Everitt Judson, dealing with life in Placerville and with horticulture and farming in Oakland, Visalia, and the Kern River plateau. The second group consists of letters written from Civil War battlefields by members of the Judson and Fairbanks families. The third group includes letters, receipts, etc., relating to the accidental death of Martin L. Fairbanks and the settlement of his estate.

Physical description: letters and documents.

Source: purchased from Usher L. Burdick, May, 1947.

K

KANE (GERALD JOHN) COLLECTION—AMERICANA
approximately 2000 pieces, 1666–1953

Gerald (Jerry) John Kane was born in Chicago in 1901, but spent most of his life in Nevada, dying in Reno in 1957. In addition to his interest in Nevada and its history [See KANE (GERALD JOHN) COLLECTION—NEVADA], Kane was also an enthusiastic autograph collector.

Subject matter: primarily letters collected for their autographs, with no unifying subject, although there are relatively large numbers of letters from U.S. government officials, members of Congress, soldiers (especially from the Mexican War and the Civil War), clergymen, and actors. [Literary figures are noted separately in the *Guide to Literary Manuscripts in the Huntington Library.*] Includes early documents and land records from Massachusetts, New York, Pennsylvania, and New Hampshire.

Physical description: chiefly letters, with some documents. Among the ephemera are magazine clippings and photographs.

Source: purchased from William Wreden, 1961.

KANE (GERALD JOHN) COLLECTION—NEVADA
approximately 12,500 pieces, 1839–1952

Gerald John Kane (1901–57), collector of autographs and Western lore, was interested in the history and development of the West and particularly in Nevada. To further his interests, Kane operated a small shop in San Francisco called "The Trading Post." He later moved to Reno, Nevada. [See also KANE (GERALD JOHN) COLLECTION—AMERICANA.]

Subject matter: Nevada; mining companies, business firms, land, railroads, stage lines, and politics, centering about Austin, Nevada, and including Virginia City, Nye County, Ormsby County, etc. Includes miscellaneous papers relating to land and mines in California and Arizona and to taxation in Utah.

Physical description: letters and documents (including 1 bound volume).

Source: purchased from William Wreden, January, 1961.

KELLER, MATTHEW (1810–81)
365 pieces, 1851–1959

Matthew Keller, Los Angeles pioneer businessman and ranch owner, was born in Ireland and graduated from Trinity College. In 1832, he went to New York, migrated to Texas in the mid-1830s and spent the next twelve to fifteen years in Mexico. Keller returned to the United States, first to New Orleans, and then to San Francisco (in 1849) before settling in Los Angeles in 1851. He opened a general merchandise store and purchased property on Alameda and Aliso Streets, where he built his home, planted fruit trees and vineyards, and established the Rising Sun and Los Angeles Vineyards winery. He experimented with horticulture, held several public offices, was a director of the Pioneer Oil Company, and became the owner of many pieces of property in Los Angeles, vineyards in Anaheim, and the 13,000 acre Rancho Malibu. His son, Henry Workman Keller, was a director of the Automobile Club of Southern California and was active in the promotion of the Pan American Highway, for which he was honored by the Mexican government.

Subject matter: early Los Angeles after 1850 as seen in the correspondence and land papers of Matthew Keller, especially concerning the wine industry (Rising Sun and Los Angeles Vineyards winery); also a few papers of Henry W. Keller.

Physical description: letters, manuscripts (including 4 diaries and 3 notebooks), documents (including 1 ledger book), and photographs.

Source: gift of Mrs. S. Bartly Cannell, February, 1976.

KENDALL, WILLIAM DEVEREUX (1835–1909)
170 pieces, 1697–1944

William Devereux Kendall, Confederate soldier and physician, was born in 1835, the son of Devereux Jarrett Kendall and Sarah (Ryle) Kendall of Paris, Henry County, Tennessee. Both William and his brother, John Peter Kendall, attended Bethel College in 1851–52, and William graduated from the University of Pennsylvania's medical school in 1858. At the outbreak of the Civil War William Kendall enlisted in the 5th Tennessee Infantry and served in that regiment for the duration of the war, being promoted to lieutenant and (by 1862) to adjutant, and serving also at times as assistant surgeon. He saw active service in Tennessee and Kentucky, and during the Atlanta Campaign. At the end of the war he returned to Paris, married first (in 1868) Ada (Courts) Crawford and second (in 1886) Kate Lamb, and continued his medical practice. He died there in 1909.

Subject matter: the Kendall family, William and John Peter Kendall at Bethel College, and William's career in the Confederate army; the Atlanta Campaign, relations with civilians in wartime, and the everyday life and activities of a fighting regiment. Includes a muster roll for the 5th Tennessee Regiment from May 1861. Contains genealogical information about the Kendall and Courts families, collected at a later date, including typewritten copies of many late seventeenth- and early eighteenth-century land and business papers of the Courts family of Maryland, as well as correspondence of William Kendall's descendants concerning family history. Strongest for the period 1851–1864.

Physical description: letters and documents (including 1 bound notebook), with 14 old photographs, some newspaper clippings, and other ephemera.

Source: purchased from Eric Pointer, December, 1964.

KERN, BENJAMIN JORDAN (1818–49)
[Diary of his trip with Frémont's fourth expedition] (October 20, 1848—January 6, 1849)
Autograph MS. 1 volume 67 pp.

KERN, EDWARD MEYER (1823–63)
[Diary of first part of Frémont's fourth expedition] (October 8—November 11, 1848)
Autograph MS. 30 pp.

_____

[Diary of first part of Frémont's fourth expedition] (October 19—November 9, 1848)
Autograph MS. 1 volume 13 pp.

_____

[Diary of his trip with John Pope's reconnaissance from Santa Fé] (August 9—September 6, 1851)
Autograph MS.S. 1 volume 50 pp. includes small pencil sketches

KERN, RICHARD HOVENDON (1821–53)
[Diary of his trip with Frémont's fourth expedition] (October 20, 1848—February 16, 1849)

Autograph MS.S. 1 volume 78 pp. includes sketches

Notes of a military Reconnaissance of Pais de Los Navajos. (August 17—September 22, 1849) Autograph MS. 1 volume 63 pp.

[Diary of his trip with Sitgreaves' expedition of 1851] (August 13—November 16, 1851) Autograph MS. 1 volume 187 pp. includes small pencil sketches

KIMBALL, THOMAS LORD (1831–99)
approximately 1175 pieces, 1859–1901

Thomas Lord Kimball, railroad executive, was born in Maine in 1831 and worked variously as a farmer, teacher, and jeweler before moving to Cincinnati, Ohio, in 1859 to take a public relations job with the Pennsylvania Railway Co. He was appointed assistant general passenger agent in 1863 and, moving to the Chicago headquarters, general western passenger agent in 1868. Kimball transferred to the Union Pacific Railroad Co. in 1871 to take charge of the General Passenger and Ticket Agency in Omaha, Nebraska, and remained with that company until his retirement in 1897, having risen to the positions of general manager and third vice-president. He also took an active part in the business and civic life of Omaha. Kimball died in 1899.

Subject matter: the railroad business and related industries; Kimball's wife and family; the expansion of the Union Pacific into northern Utah and Idaho; mining in Idaho and Montana; railroad competition; political intrigue involving railroads on both local and national levels; and the prevalent evils of the free-pass system.

Significant persons: Sidney DILLON (9), Jay GOULD (7), Thomas A. SCOTT (6).

Physical description: chiefly letters, with documents, manuscripts (including 53 volumes of diaries kept by Kimball and his wife, Mary Porter Rogers Kimball), and newspaper clippings and other printed ephemera.

Source: purchased from Jack Kimball, March, 1948.

KING, FRANK MARION (1863–1953)
approximately 3500 pieces, 1909–53

Frank M. King, cowboy, ranchman, editor, and author, was born in Los Angeles in 1863. King, who was part Cherokee Indian, went to Texas with his family in 1873, then to Indian Territory. He returned to Texas in 1876, engaging in cattle driving there, and later moved to New Mexico. King wrote books about western folklore and the cattle industry and served as associate editor of *Western Livestock Journal* for many years.

Subject matter: cattle ranching, Indian welfare concerns (particularly relating to the Navajo tribe), and King's books, *Wranglin' the Past, Longhorn Trail Drivers,* and *Pioneer Western Empire Builders.*

Significant persons: Earl Alonzo BRININSTOOL (10), May Louise (Davison) Purple RHODES (16).

Physical description: letters and manuscripts (including drawings).

Source: gift of Mrs. Frank M. King, 1953.

KING,RUFUS (1755–1827)
599 pieces, 1782–1830

Rufus King, statesman and diplomat, was born in Massachusetts. Admitted to the bar in 1780, he became a delegate to the Massachusetts General Court in 1783 and gained prominence among the nationalists. After representing New York in the Constitutional Convention and the new Federal Congress, in 1796 he became U.S. minister to Britain for eight years. He retired from public life in 1825 after serving the Federalist party.

Subject matter: Anglo-American conflict over naval impressment and other violations of American sovereignty, the claim of Maryland to sequestered bank stock, and the execution of the treaty of 1794; Franco-American conflict over commercial relations, the XYZ affair, and Toussaint L'Ouverture's actions in the West Indies; financial transactions with England and Dutch bankers in connection with expenditures for diplomatic purposes, claims, and salaries; Anglo-French wars; the French Revolution; domestic and foreign politics, and personal matters of various diplomats. Strongest for the period from 1797 to 1801.

Significant persons: John Quincy ADAMS (52), John DAWSON (9), Oliver ELLSWORTH (6), Elbridge GERRY (20), James MADISON (6), James C. MOUNT-FLORENCE (39), William Vans MURRAY (156), Timothy PICKERING (94), Charles Cotesworth PINCKNEY (21), Edmund RANDOLPH (16), William Loughton SMITH (47), Charles Maurice de TALLEYRAND-PERIGORD Prince de BENEVENT (10), Oliver WOLCOTT (7).

Physical description: letters, with some documents.

Source: purchased from George D. Smith Book Co., 1927.

KINKADE, JOHN THOMPSON (1828–1904<)
91 pieces, 1829–85

John T. Kinkade, California lawyer, was born in Virginia and attended Bethany College. He then traveled in the midwest with his uncle and guardian, E. Kinkade. Afterward, John T. Kinkade graduated from Wesleyan University in 1844, then returned to Virginia where he was admitted to the bar in 1848. The following year he crossed the plains to California. He engaged in mining along the American River in Placer County until 1869, returning in 1870 to the practice of law in a small mining town, and then in Auburn. Kinkade was active in Republican politics and served as Placer County superintendent of schools for six years.

Subject matter: chiefly living conditions in the Placer County mining district near Auburn (1849–66).

Physical description: letters.

Source: purchased from Fred Lockley, November, 1950 and March, 1951.

KINO, EUSEBIO FRANCISCO (1645–1711)
33 pieces, 1680–87

Eusebio Kino, Jesuit missionary and explorer in Mexico and the American Southwest, was a native of Italy, educated at the Jesuit college at Hall, near Innsbruck, Austria. He became a priest at the age of twenty-one, and in 1681 went to Mexico. Kino led an unsuccessful attempt to settle Lower California in 1683. He was later known for the establishment of missions in Sonora, exploration along New Spain's northern frontier, and the verification that Lower California was a peninsula and not an island.

Subject matter: Kino's experiences in exploring and establishing missions in Lower California (1683–85) and in Sonora (1686–87).

Significant persons: Eusebio Francisco KINO (27).

Physical description: letters (chiefly to the Duchess d'Aveiro d'Arcos y Maqueda, in Spanish, Latin, and Italian).

Source: purchased from Maggs Brothers, December, 1922.

Bibliography: The letters have been published in *Kino Escribe a la Duquesa,* ed. Ernest J. Burrus (Madrid: Ediciones José Porrua Turanzas, 1964) and in *Kino Writes to the Duchess,* ed. Ernest J. Burrus (Rome and St. Louis: Jesuit Historical Institute, 1965).

KOEHLER, MAUDE (ANTHONY) (1866–1950)
114 pieces, 1940–50

Maude (Anthony) Koehler, a niece of Susan B. Anthony, was a co-owner of the *Leavenworth Times* and a seasoned traveler until 1920, when ill health prompted her retirement to Los Angeles. Although not personally active in the woman suffrage movement, her interest in national politics was keen and she took an active role in perpetuating the memory of her famous aunt.

Subject matter: daily life, family affairs, and opinions of Maude (Anthony) Koehler; some reminiscences about Susan B. Anthony.

Physical description: letters (to Una [Richardson] Winter, q.v.).

Source: gift of Mrs. Una Richardson Winter, January, 1952.

KUNZ, GEORGE FREDERICK (1856–1932)
approximately 600 pieces, 1835–1938

George Frederick Kunz, mineralogist and author, was born in New York in 1856, took a Ph.D. at the University of Marburg in 1903 and a Sc.D. at Knox in 1907, and served for many years as a gem expert at Tiffany and Co., the New York jewelers. Kunz wrote numerous books and articles on gems and coins, traveled widely, maintained an active business correspondence with members of the American and international diplomatic corps, and served as an adviser to various governmental agencies. He was a research curator of precious stones at the American Museum of Natural History and founded the American Museum of Peaceful Arts (later the Museum of Science and Industry).

Subject matter: routine business and professional affairs, international mines and mining and the world gem market; reflections on public health, international expositions, preservation of national parks and scenic sites, New York City's economy, civic affairs, and Republican politics. Virtually no information about Tiffany and Co.

Physical description: chiefly letters, with some documents, a very few manuscript poems or speeches, 4 photographs, and ephemera.

Source: purchased from Dawson's Book Shop, May, 1964.

L

LABRANT, JONATHAN (1828–ca.85)
151 pieces, 1862–85; 1917

Jonathan Labrant, Union soldier, was a carpenter in Pierce-ville, Illinois, until 1862, when he volunteered in the Illinois Infantry, 58th Regiment. During the war he attained the rank of corporal, and served in Tennessee, Mississippi, and Louisi-ana.

Subject matter: daily life, family affairs, and living conditions in the Union army; the Fort De Russy area; wartime remi-niscences.

Physical description: letters (to his wife), with a few manu-scripts (including two diaries) and documents. Includes early photographs of members of the Kilty family.

Source: gift of Richard Kilty Heller, January 3, 1973.

LAFAYETTE, MARIE . . . GILBERT DU MOTIER, MAR-QUIS DE (1757–1834)
75 pieces, 1779–1835

The Marquis de Lafayette, French soldier and statesman, served with distinction in the American army during the Revo-lution from 1777 to 1781. Befriended by George Washington, his main role was that of liaison between the American and

French forces, and he won the admiration of the French and American nations alike. An ardent republican, his involvement in the French Revolution led to his incarceration and the loss of his fortune. Americans worked for his release, and Congress awarded him land. In 1824 he made a triumphant tour of the United States.

Subject matter: the efforts to win Lafayette's release from prison in Austria, Lafayette's land in the U.S., his grand tour of the U.S.

Significant persons: Marquis de LAFAYETTE (24).

Physical description: mostly letters, including one volume of letters to Lafayette; documents.

Source: purchased from George D. Smith and others, ca.1916.

L'AINÉ, CHARLES (fl. 1781–82)
Ce cahier appartient à L'Aîné Cuisinier de M. de Bougainville, Chef d'Escadre, commencé a bord de L'Auguste Vaisseau de ligne de 80 canons, dans la Baye de Chesapeake d'en Virginie, le 28 novembre 1781 (1781–82)
Autograph MS. volume 205 pp. illus.

Concerns operations in the West Indies as well as Yorktown, Va. Contains watercolor drawings of a ship, an armillary sphere, and points of the compass. The journal has sometimes been identified by a title on the first page of the text, "Receuil Contenans les Campagnes. . . ." Covers the period from January 1781 to August 18, 1782.

LAKE, ANN (GETZ) (ca.1800–70)
53 pieces, 1820–72

Ann (Getz) Lake, early California resident, first lived in Pennsylvania, Maryland, and (after her marriage in 1835), in

Cincinnati, Ohio. She came to California in 1861 to live with her daughter, whose husband, Dr. Jacob Newton Brown, practiced medicine in San Jose. He was later Professor of Anatomy at Toland Medical College in San Francisco (1864–66).

Subject matter: family life in Pennsylvania and Ohio, some Civil War information.

Physical description: letters and documents.

Source: purchased from Edwin Grabhorn, January, 1945.

LAKE, DELOS W. (1840– ?)
93 pieces, 1862–65

Delos W. Lake, Union soldier, joined the 19th regiment of the Michigan Volunteer Infantry in August, 1862, and served until the end of the war, by which time he had attained the rank of corporal. He took part in campaigns in Tennessee and Kentucky, and with the Army of the Cumberland in the Atlanta campaign.

Subject matter: everyday life and activities of the private soldier in wartime. Includes two officers' farewell addresses.

Physical description: letters and manuscripts.

Source: acquired from Leonard Lake (nephew of Delos W. Lake), September, 1942.

LAKE, STUART NATHANIEL (1890–1964)
approximately 5000 pieces, 1918–61

Stuart Lake, author and motion picture writer, was a native of New York, best known for his writing about the West. He attended Cornell University, then worked as a reporter for the *New York Herald* newspaper (1910–12), where his acquaintanceship with Bat Masterson led to his interest in western lore. After service in World War I, Lake moved to San Diego. He wrote for magazines, was the author of *Wyatt Earp, Frontier Marshal,* and of many motion picture scripts.

Subject matter: western personalities; motion picture companies; publishing firms; political figures, chiefly western subjects, including Wyatt Earp, Eugene Manlove Rhodes; Tombstone, Arizona; and Dodge City, Kansas.

Significant persons: John Philip CLUM (22); Josephine Sarah (Marcus) EARP (43), Wyatt EARP (14), May Louise (Davison) Purple RHODES (16).

Physical description: letters, manuscripts, photographs, and secondary source materials.

Source: purchased from Carolyn Lake, September, 1965.

LAMON, WARD HILL (1828–93)
2490 pieces, 1848–94

Ward Hill Lamon, law partner and close friend of Abraham Lincoln, was born in Virginia in 1828. He moved to Danville, Illinois, in 1847, where he studied law and, five years later, became Lincoln's local partner. In the late 1850s Lamon moved to Bloomington and worked for Lincoln's political career in the newly formed Republican party. In 1861 he followed Lincoln to Washington, D.C., and was appointed Marshal of the District of Columbia. Aside from brief military service (as colonel of a brigade of loyal Virginians, which he personally raised and equipped), Lamon spent the war years in Washington as one of Lincoln's closest personal friends. After Lincoln's assassination Lamon returned to private legal practice, tried unsuccessfully to obtain another official appointment, and began collecting material for a projected biography of the late president. For this reason he purchased copies of extensive source materials gathered for a similar purpose by William Henry Herndon. The first volume, *The Life of Abraham Lincoln from his Birth to his Inauguration as President,* appeared in 1872; the second volume was never published. Lamon moved to Denver, Colorado, in 1876, but returned to Washington ten years later and died there in 1893. Three years later Lamon's daughter, Dorothy Lamon Teillard, published a greatly expanded and revised version of her father's work under the title *Recollections of Abraham Lincoln, 1847–1865.*

Subject matter: documentary materials from which Lamon wrote his biography, including three volumes of copies of Herndon's source materials; numerous letters from contemporaries of Lamon and Lincoln; and the unpublished typescript of Lamon's history of the Lincoln administration. Also includes many of Lamon's own letters and personal papers dealing with such subjects as: requests for patronage from Lincoln addressed to Lamon as intermediary; "Lamon's Brigade" of Virginians; the office of U.S. Marshal of the District of Columbia (1861–65); a political attack on Lamon in 1862 by abolitionist senators; Lamon's family and finances (including wartime speculation and dealings in Colorado mining properties); news of Illinois politics; Lamon's correspondence with Herndon over the purchase of his records; and the controversy over his *Life of Abraham Lincoln* in 1872. Strongest for the period from 1861 to 1879.

Significant persons: David DAVIS (25), William Henry HERNDON (38), Charles Edward HOVEY (12), Abraham LINCOLN (13), Charles H. RUSSELL (10), and John Palmer USHER (11).

Physical description: letters, manuscripts, documents (including 4 bound volumes), newspaper clippings, and other ephemera.

Source: purchased from George D. Smith, 1914.

LAMOUREAUX, THEODORE J. (fl. 1888–1924)
approximately 4370 pieces, 1843–1924

Theodore J. Lamoureaux was a mining engineer and promoter who lived in Oakland, California.

Subject matter: family correspondence and business papers, including mining maps and reports (ca.1888–1923), mostly for California and Nevada, including Elko County, Goldfield, and Tonopah.

Physical description: letters (including 9 letter books), documents (including 21 account books, etc.), and maps.

Source: purchased from Grahame H. Hardy, February, 1950.

LARUE, EUGENE CLYDE (1879–1947)
2543 pieces, 1909–49

Eugene C. LaRue, Los Angeles hydraulic engineer, was born in Riverside, California, and graduated from the University of California in 1904. He was employed by the U.S. Geological Survey making field examinations for power sites and reporting on irrigation projects, first as district engineer for the Great Basin District headquartered in Salt Lake City (1907–11), and then in the Water Resources Branch (1911–27). After this time LaRue entered a private civil engineering partnership in Los Angeles.

Subject matter: irrigation projects in the western states; correspondence, reports, maps, etc., regarding Colorado River projects (including the Colorado River-Los Angeles Gravity Flow Aqueduct); the Klamath Lake Project in Oregon; the Merced Irrigation District in California; the San Juan River, Little Colorado, and Verde projects in Arizona; and many others. Also included are diaries of LaRue's Colorado River trips of 1921, 1922, and 1924, and maps of western areas.

Physical description: letters and documents (including 8 vols.), and 876 maps. (Photograph albums are now filed in Rare Book Department.)

Source: gift of Mrs. E. C. LaRue, 1950–55.

LEE, JOHN DOYLE (1812–77)
99 pieces, 1841–77

John D. Lee, Mormon pioneer, born in Kaskaskia, Illinois, joined the Mormon Church in 1838 and was the leader of one of the Mormon wagon trains migrating to Salt Lake City in 1848. He helped colonize southern Utah, was a probate judge of Iron County, and a member of the territorial legislature. Lee is best known for his part in the Mountain Meadows Massacre—an attack by Indians and Mormons dressed as Indians against a wagon train of settlers from Arkansas passing through southern Utah territory in 1857, at a time of resentment against non-Mormons because of the fear of the invasion of Utah by U.S. troops under General Albert Sidney Johnston. As sentiment within the Mormon community grew against the action taken against the outsiders, blame was centered on Lee. He was excommunicated from the church in 1870 and sent by Brigham Young to a remote spot on the Colorado River, now known as Lee's Ferry. When he returned home for a visit in 1875, he was taken for trial, found guilty, and executed in 1877, maintaining to the end that he was convicted in order to protect others more guilty than he.

Subject matter: early Mormon life in Utah, as reflected in 6 volumes of the diaries of John D. Lee (1846–76), the diary of Rachel Andora (Woolsey) Lee (1856–60), and other letters and papers of John D. Lee.

Physical description: letters, documents, and manuscripts (including 7 volumes of diaries). Many of the items are contemporary copies or facsimiles.

Source: purchased from Miss Esther Nelson, May, 1929, and acquired from various other sources, 1929–68.

Bibliography: the original diaries of John D. Lee, and some of the other items, have been published in *A Mormon Chronicle: The Diaries of John D. Lee, 1848–1876*, ed. Robert G. Cleland and Juanita Brooks, 2 vols. (San Marino: Huntington Library, 1955), and in *Journals of John D. Lee*, ed. Charles Kelly (Salt Lake City: Western Printing Co., 1938).

LEIDESDORFF, WILLIAM ALEXANDER (1810–48)
502 pieces, 1840–67

William A. Leidesdorff, early California trader and official, was born in the Danish West Indies of a Danish father and mulatto mother. In 1841 he came to California as master of the ship "Julia Ann." He engaged in trade between Hawaii and San Francisco, and afterwards began a general exporting business in San Francisco. Leidesdorff became a Mexican citizen in 1844 and received a grant for Rancho Río de los Americanos, east of Fort Sutter. The next year he was appointed vice-consul of the United States, and remained prominent in the affairs of San Francisco until his death in 1848.

Subject matter: letters, mostly received by Leidesdorff in the 1840s, concerning coastal trade and life in the mercantile business in San Francisco. The collection includes considerable correspondence with Thomas O. Larkin, John A. Sutter, and other prominent Californians, as well as with the Russian American Fur Company.

Significant persons: Santiago ARGÜELLO (23), Henry DALTON (19), Thomas Oliver LARKIN (54), William Alexander

LEIDESDORFF (26), William Tecumseh SHERMAN (7), John Augustus SUTTER (39).

Physical description: letters, documents, and 1 map (in English, Spanish, German, and French).

Source: purchased from Holmes Book Co., San Francisco, 1922.

Bibliography: the collection is described in the *Huntington Library Bulletin,* no. 7 (April, 1935): 35, 38–42. Many of the letters have been published in John A. Hawgood, ed., *First and Last Consul, Thomas Oliver Larkin and the Americanization of California* (San Marino: Huntington Library, 1962).

LEVIEN, SONYA (1888?–1960)
approximately 1280 pieces, 1908–62

Sonya Levien, motion picture scenario writer, was a native of Russia who left that country as a young child with her family to escape persecution. They settled in New York City, where Sonya grew up. After receiving her law degree from New York University, Miss Levien was admitted to the bar in 1909, but turned to writing as a career. In 1913 she was sent to England to write an article on the women's rights movement for the *Woman's Journal,* and from 1917 to 1925 she wrote for *Metropolitan Magazine.* She is best known as the author of numerous award-winning screenplays for major Hollywood studios. She was married to Carl Hovey, a writer and executive with the Cecil B. DeMille studio.

Subject matter: correspondence of Carl and Sonya (Levien) Hovey (1931–58) with motion picture and literary personalities; diaries of Sonya Levien (1916–24); and motion picture manuscripts, scenarios, and awards. Also includes papers relating to woman suffrage (1911–13) in the United States and England.

Significant persons: Clarence Shepard DAY (70), Francis Scott Key FITZGERALD (7), Mabel Dodge LUHAN (104), Newton Booth TARKINGTON (16).

Physical description: letters, manuscripts (including diaries and scripts), and photographs.

Source: gift of Mr. and Mrs. Lee Gold, May, 1960.

LEVIN, LEWIS CHARLES (1808–60)
89 pieces, 1849–50

Lewis Charles Levin, lawyer, editor, and politician, was born in Charleston, South Carolina, in 1808 and settled in Philadelphia in 1838 to practice law. He represented that state in Congress for three terms (1845–51), and was one of the co-founders of the Native American Party, a forerunner of the Know-Nothing Party. After 1851 Levin returned to private practice but maintained his political interests, and died in 1860.

Subject matter: the attempt of Levin and his party to secure for William David Lewis an appointment from President Zachary Taylor in 1849 as collector of the Port of Philadelphia; political patronage in Washington, contemporary politics, Senate lobbying (in opposition to the appointment, led by James Cooper); the influence of Henry Clay in the outcome of the struggle.

Physical description: letters.

Source: purchased from the Anderson Galleries, February, 1923.

LIEBER, FRANCIS (1800–72)
approximately 6000 pieces, 1815–88

Francis Lieber, political scientist and educator, was born in Berlin, Germany, in 1800, fought under Blücher at Waterloo, received a Ph.D. at the University of Jena in 1820, and from 1823 to 1824 served as tutor to the son of the German diplomat and historian Barthold Georg Niebuhr. As a liberal, Lieber found the Prussian government uncongenial, and moved first to England (1826) and then (1827) to Boston, Massachusetts, where he founded and edited the *Encyclopedia Americana* and began to establish a wide and lifelong network of friends and correspondents among the most prominent literary and public figures of his day. In 1834 he moved to Philadelphia, and in the following year accepted an appointment to a chair in history and political economy at South Carolina College (now the University of South Carolina), where he remained for the next twenty-one years. During this time Lieber established his reputation as a leader in the field of political science and published numerous books and essays in related fields, including the *Manual of Political Ethics* and *On Civil Liberty and Self-Government.* In 1857 he moved to New York to accept a position at Columbia College (now Columbia University), and remained there for the rest of his life. Lieber became increasingly interested in the field of international law, especially during wartime, and acted as a consultant to the Union government during the Civil War. His *Code for the Government of Armies,* written in 1863, was revised and issued by the War Department as *Instructions for the Government of Armies in the Field, General Orders No. 100.* Prominent as a political philosopher, active in public service, and still corresponding with a wide circle of colleagues at home and abroad, Lieber died in New York in 1872.

Subject matter: Lieber's wide-ranging and continuous correspondence with literary, political, academic, and other leading figures of his day in the United States and in Europe, providing extensive information about his own, and his correspondents' reactions to and thoughts about contemporary events, including: politics and political science (Boston area politics, slavery, the Civil War and Reconstruction, constitutional law, international relations, the "Alabama" Claims case, and penal law and prison reform); contemporary literature (particularly Boston literary circles, Charles Sumner, and Henry Wadsworth Longfellow); and scholarly and academic affairs (higher education, college administration, and the studies of history and culture). Also includes autograph manuscripts of some of Lieber's published works (including *A Code for the Government of Armies*), a substantial number of essays, lectures, and notes on virtually the whole range of Lieber's extensive interests, a fragmentary journal and commonplace books, numerous notes and comments on clippings, and some poetry and plays written by Lieber in Germany in his early years.

Significant persons: Samuel Austin ALLIBONE (9), Alexander Dallas BACHE (15), Edward BATES (25), Horace BINNEY (24), Rufus CHOATE (19), Henry CLAY (8), Henry DRISLER (7), Edward EVERETT (19), Hamilton FISH (31), Simon GREENLEAF (20), Henry Wager HALLECK (104), George Stillman HILLARD (159), Joseph HOLT (12), Samuel Gridley HOWE (34), James KENT (8), Edouard-René Lefebvre de LABOULAYE (22), Henry Wadsworth LONGFELLOW (14), Benson John LOSSING (13), David James McCORD (15), Karl Joseph Anton MITTERMAIER (48), John PICKERING (9), William Hickling PRESCOTT (14), William Campbell PRESTON (21), Gustave ROLIN-JAEQUEMYNS (12), Samuel Bulkeley RUGGLES (13), James SPEED (11), Joseph STORY (42), Charles SUMNER (25), George TICKNOR (8), Alexis CLEREL, Comte de TOCQUEVILLE (13), Samuel TYLER (12), Samuel WARD (9), Emory WASHBURN (9), and Levi WOODBURY (11).

Physical description: letters and manuscripts (some in German or French).

Source: purchased from Miss Mary Lieber (granddaughter), 1927.

Bibliography: many of Lieber's letters were edited, with Mrs. Lieber's assistance, by Thomas Sergeant Perry and published as *Life and Letters of Francis Lieber* (Boston, 1882). The collection is more fully described in Charles B. Robson, "Papers of Francis Lieber," *The Huntington Library Bulletin*, no. 3 (February 1933): 135–55.

LINCOLN FILE
approximately 1275 pieces, 1811–1922

The Lincoln File is an artificially assembled collection consisting of letters and papers written by, to, and about Abraham Lincoln (1809–65), sixteenth president of the United States. It has been augmented by several separate collections of "Lincolniana," notably those of William Harrison Lambert, Mark P. Robinson, and Judd Stewart.

Subject matter: Lincoln's business affairs and legal practice to 1860; his political career from 1832 to 1865, but particularly during his presidency; Mary (Todd) Lincoln; historical studies about Lincoln, including especially those by John Milton Hay and William Henry Herndon; the 1917–18 controversy over the statue of Lincoln by George Grey Grubb Barnard; the collection of "Lincolniana," especially by William Harrison Lambert and Judd Stewart.

Significant persons: Jefferson DAVIS (7), Daniel FISH (77), John Milton HAY (52), William Henry HERNDON (ca.150), William Harrison LAMBERT (ca.155), Abraham LINCOLN (187), Mary (Todd) LINCOLN (75), Robert Todd LINCOLN (107), Fred Wellington RUCKSTUHL (12), Judd STEWART (84).

Physical description: letters, manuscripts, documents, and ephemera (including photographs).

Source: acquired from various sources over a period of years.

Bibliography: some of the manuscripts in the Lincoln File have been published in *The Collected Works of Abraham*

Lincoln, ed. Roy P. Basler (Abraham Lincoln Association, Springfield, Illinois. New Brunswick, N.J.: Rutgers University Press, 1953). Letters of Mary (Todd) Lincoln have been published in Justin George Turner and Linda Levitt Turner, *Mary Todd Lincoln: Her Life and Times* (New York: Knopf, 1972).

LINDBORG, PAUL JAMES (b. ca.1810?)
approximately 100 pieces, 1868–93

Paul James Lindborg, born in Wormland, Sweden, moved early in life to the United States, and fought in the Black Hawk and Civil Wars. By 1870 he was a resident of the National Asylum for Disabled Volunteer Soldiers at Milwaukee, Wisconsin, where he remained until his death. Lindborg was well versed in both classical and modern literature, wrote poetry, and claimed (perhaps as a result of some mental imbalance) to have been secretary to Lord Byron in Greece in the 1820s.

Subject matter: Lindborg's correspondence (chiefly with a younger friend, Charles Lane, at Mount Union College in Ohio); his poetry and other manuscripts. Strongest for the 1870s.

Physical description: letters, manuscripts (including 45 small notebooks, journals, and commonplace books), and a few documents. Some of the letters are in Swedish.

Source: gift of Mrs. Eva F. Hershey, February, 1945.

LLANO DEL RIO COLONY
144 pieces, 1915–ca. 60

The Llano del Rio Co-operative Colony was incorporated in 1914 by Los Angeles attorney Job Harriman, socialist nominee for mayor of Los Angeles in 1911. The settlement was located in the Antelope Valley of California near Pearblossom, where an agricultural community was developed. Because of problems with water rights, transportation for produce, and internal dissention, the colony was discontinued in 1918. One group of the colonists went to Louisiana and reestablished a community under the name Newllano.

Subject matter: the history and administration of the colony; material concerning Job Harriman, Gentry Purviance McCorkle, and members of the Young People's Socialist League of Los Angeles.

Physical description: letters, documents (including minutes of the colony's board of commissioners [1915] and copies of its constitution), manuscripts, and photographs.

Source: gift of Mrs. Nellie (Miller) Calvert, April, 1969 and May, 1972.

Bibliography: material from the collection has been published in Robert V. Hine, *California's Utopian Colonies* (San Marino: Huntington Library, 1953), and in Paul Kagan, "Portrait of a California Utopia," *California Historical Quarterly,* 51 (1972): 131–54.

LOCKLEY, FREDERIC E. (1871–1958)
1520 pieces, 1849–1949

Frederic E. Lockley, Jr. (1871–1958), Oregon historian, editor, and rare book dealer, was born in Kansas and spent his boyhood working on various Western newspapers edited by his father. Lockley, who first gained prominence as editor and manager of the *Pacific Monthly* (1907–11), then as feature writer for the *Oregon Journal* in Portland, also wrote books pertaining to Oregon history, and collected rare Western books and manuscripts. His father, Frederic E. Lockley, Sr. (1824–1905), was born in England, came to the United States in 1848, and worked for Frank Leslie's *Illustrated News* and Horace Greeley's *Tribune* before joining the Union forces during the Civil War. After the war the senior Lockley joined the staff of the *Cleveland Leader*, then (1869–72) worked on the *Evening Bulletin* of Leavenworth, Kansas (where he became interested in the Indian Council and Indian affairs). He was editor of the Salt Lake City *Tribune* (1873–75), and of the Salem (Oregon) *Capital Journal* (1888–99). He spent the remainder of his life in Missoula, Montana, where he wrote his memoirs.

Subject matter: the papers of Frederic E. Lockley, Sr., contain: his memoirs; his Civil War diary; letters to his wife written from the field during the Civil War, from Kansas concerning Indian affairs (1871–72), and from Salt Lake City about Mormons and Mormonism (1873) which include his observations of the trial of John D. Lee (1875); and other correspondence, mainly with Eastern editors. The papers of Frederic E. Lockley, Jr., contain items relating to the *Pacific Monthly* magazine, including letters concerning literary figures, such as Jack London, Edwin Markham, and others and a record book of payments made to contributors from 1907 to 1911. The collection also contains Lockley's interviews with Oregon pioneers and items he collected regarding Oregon history.

Significant persons: Frederick Ritchie BECHDOLT (6), Maynard DIXON (8), Charmian (Kittredge) LONDON (6), and Charles Warren STODDARD (5).

Physical description: letters, manuscripts (including 2 diaries), documents, and photographs.

Source: purchased from Frederic E. Lockley, Jr., and his estate, 1944–60.

LONG, OSCAR FITZALAN (1852–1925)
approximately 800 pieces, 1874–1941

General Oscar F. Long, U.S. Army officer, was born in New York and graduated from West Point in 1876. He saw active service during the Indian Campaigns of 1876–79 and was aide-de-camp to Colonel Nelson A. Miles, then in charge of the Yellowstone Command. Long was appointed general in 1901 and served as general superintendent of the Army Transport Service during the Spanish American War and the Philippine Insurrection. He was married to Amy Requa, daughter of California financier Isaac L. Lequa (q.v.).

Subject matter: Long's life and career, as seen in his correspondence (mainly from 1898–1902), and other papers. Included are a journal of an expedition from Ft. Keogh under Colonel Miles in 1879, a manuscript of Long's "History of the Quartermaster Department, U.S. Army," and scrapbooks of life at West Point. There are also letters and diaries of his wife, Amy (Requa) Long.

Physical description: letters (including 6 letterbooks), manuscripts (including 32 volumes), and photographs.

Source: purchased from Argonaut Book Shop, December, 1960.

LONGINOS MARTÍNEZ, JOSÉ (d. 1803)
Extracto de las Noticias y observaciones que ha echo en las Expediciones que acaba de ejerzer en la Antigua y Nueva California, Costa del sur y viaje de Mexico a San Blas, el Naturalista de la Expedicion Botanica Don José Longinos Martínez. (July 17<, 1792)
MS. 1 volume 168 leaves

Text in Spanish. Translation published by Lesley Byrd Simpson, *California in 1792: The Expedition of José Longinos Martínez* (San Marino: Huntington Library, 1938).

LÓPEZ DE HARO, GONZALO (d. 1823)
Diario de Navegacion que con el Aucilio Divino y proteccion de Nuestra Señora del Carmen, Espera haser el Primer Piloto

de la Real Armada, y Capitan del Paquebot de S[u] M[ajestad] nombrado S[a]n Carlos (Alias el Filipino) bajo las ordenes de la Fragata de S[u] M[ajestad] nombrada la Princesa su Comandante el Alferez de Navio y Primer Piloto de la Armada D[o]n Estevan Jose Martinez con destino ambos Buques de Explorar la Costa Septentrional de la California hasta los 61 grados de Lati[tu]d N[orte] y otros asuntos del Real Servicio; —El Capitan del Referido Paquebot; D[o]n Gonzalo Lopez de Haro. (March 8–October 22, 1788)
Autograph MS.S. 1 volume 217 pp.

Text in Spanish.

LOS ANGELES FLOWER FESTIVAL SOCIETY
approximately 70 pieces, 1885–91

The Los Angeles Flower Festival Society was originally organized in 1885 to raise funds for the support of the Woman's Exchange, a boarding home for women in Los Angeles, and later also benefited other charitable organizations. Mary Widney, the wife of Judge Robert Maclay Widney, was founder and president of the group. The flower shows, immensely popular during the eight years of their presentation, were held in Hazard's Pavilion in Los Angeles.

Subject matter: mainly the correspondence and papers of the Los Angeles Flower Festival Society, including printed programs and memorabilia, and also some material dealing with related activities.

Physical description: letters, manuscripts (including 1 notebook), photographs, and ephemera.

Source: purchased from Dawson's Book Shop, April, 1958.

LOS ANGELES RAILWAY CORPORATION
176 pieces, 1888–1938

The Los Angeles Railway Corporation, formed in 1910, was the final result of various mergers and consolidations of the numerous local and interurban railways which developed in Los Angeles and adjacent communities. One of the early merged companies was the Los Angeles Railway Company, incorporated by the bondholders of the Los Angeles Consolidated Railway Company. In 1898 a group of San Francisco investors including Collis P. and Henry E. Huntington and banker Isaias W. Hellman purchased the system, and in 1901 they incorporated the Pacific Electric Railway Company, with plans to absorb some of the existing lines, and to extend other lines throughout Southern California. In 1910, the commingled interests of the companies were consolidated, and Henry E. Huntington yielded his interests in the Pacific Electric Company to the Southern Pacific Railroad Company, which took control of the interurban lines. At the same time, Huntington's Los Angeles Railway Company and his other interests were incorporated as the Los Angeles Railway Corporation, which subsequently consolidated and operated the Los Angeles city lines.

Subject matter: source material, mainly statistics, reports, etc., collected by Edwin L. Lewis, who had begun working for the Los Angeles Cable Railway Company in 1888, and became vice-president and manager of the Los Angeles Land Company and manager of the Los Angeles Railway Building in 1921. Includes Lewis' two-volume typescript, "Street Railway Development in Los Angeles and Environs, 1895–1938."

Physical description: letters, manuscripts (including 2 typewritten volumes and 4 notebooks), and documents.

Source: gift of Edwin L. Lewis, 1935–39.

LOSSING, BENSON JOHN (1813–91)
2350 pieces, 1740–1928

Benson John Lossing, wood-engraver, author, and editor, was born in New York, where his only formal education was in country schools. At the age of 13 he was apprenticed to a watchmaker, but continued to read and study, especially history. When Lossing was 22, he became joint editor and proprietor of a newspaper and later joint editor of a literary fortnightly, from whose illustrator he learned wood-engraving. In 1838 he moved to New York City, where he edited periodicals and wrote and illustrated books. *The Pictorial Field Book of the Revolution,* published 1850–52, a narrative sketchbook describing scenes and objects relating to the American Revolution, was Lossing's most well-known work. In the following years, until his death in 1891 at his home "The Ridge" in Dover Plains, New York, he wrote many historical and biographical works on popular American subjects, including the War of 1812 and the Civil War.

Subject matter: mainly Lossing's search for information for his pictorial histories, collected at historical sites during his travels around the United States; strongest in the years 1848 to 1885.

Physical description: letters, manuscripts (including 5 diaries, 1 journal, and 23 notebooks), documents, and 1117 drawings.

Source: purchased from Anderson Galleries, 1917, Paul F. Hoag, 1960–64, and Seven Gables Bookshop, 1973.

LOUDOUN COLLECTION—AMERICANA
approximately 8000 pieces, 1682–1780

The papers of the Campbell family, Earls of Loudoun, comprise some 16,000 pieces, roughly half of which relate to Scottish affairs and will be described in the *Guide to British Historical Manuscripts in the Huntington Library*. The remainder of the collection (including a supplementary group of maps and plans and the subcollection of VAUDREUIL-CAVAGNAL PAPERS is the subject of the following entry.

John Campbell, 4th Earl of Loudoun (1705–82), commander-in-chief of British forces in America from 1756 to 1758, was born in 1705 and entered the army in 1727, five years before succeeding to his father's earldom. He rose rapidly in rank: captain in the Queen's Own regiment of dragoons by 1734, governor of Stirling Castle by 1741, and lieutenant colonel and aide-de-camp to George II with the allied army in Germany by 1743. In the Jacobite rebellion of 1745 Loudoun raised and commanded his own regiment of Loyal Highlanders, and in 1747 returned to the Continent to serve under the Duke of Cumberland in Holland. He was commissioned major general in 1755, appointed the following year to replace General Braddock as commander-in-chief of British forces in America during the French and Indian War, and named titular governor of Virginia. The inept earl lost Forts Oswego and William Henry in New York to Montcalm, and led an abortive attack on Fort Louisbourg before being recalled to England in 1758. He served in Portugal in 1762, was promoted to general in 1770, and died at Loudoun Castle (the family seat in Ayrshire) in 1782.

Subject matter: chiefly the personal and official papers of Lord Loudoun during his command of British forces in America from 1756 to 1758, focusing on the state of the war at his arrival, campaigns along New York's northern frontier, and the expedition against Louisbourg. Includes information about: the establishment and administration of the British army in America (including command, recruitment, provisioning, and financing); engineers; activities of General Braddock and Governor Shirley (including expeditions against Fort

Duquesne, Crown Point, and Niagara); Loudoun's selection as commander-in-chief and his arrival in July 1756; Indian affairs (including alliances and treaties, relations with the Six Nations, and the roles of Sir William Johnson and Edmond Atkin); frontier defenses; the fall of Forts Oswego and William Henry and general military retrenchment during 1756 and 1757; preparations for an offensive expedition against Louisbourg (including general strategy, the assemblage of troops and supplies in New York, and Loudoun's shipping embargo); and Loudoun's recall and replacement by Major General James Abercromby (see also JAMES ABERCROMBY). Letters and papers dating after Loudoun's recall provide some additional information about the commands of Abercromby and his successor Jeffrey Amherst and about the American Revolution (including lists, returns, and accounts of the British army establishment, an inquiry into the failure of Burgoyne's expedition from Canada, and the general progress of the war).

Significant persons: James ABERCROMBY (major general and commander-in-chief in 1758) (96), James ABERCROMBY (agent for Virginia in England) (32), William ALEXANDER, later styled Lord Stirling (12), John APPY (18), Edmond ATKIN (20), William Wildman BARRINGTON, 2d Viscount Barrington (83), George BARTMAN (19), Jonathan BELCHER (29), Henry BOUQUET (35), Edward BRADDOCK (12), John BRADSTREET (36), Ralph BURTON (22), John CALCRAFT (80), John CAMPBELL, 4th Earl of Loudoun (1218), William COTTERELL (15), Charles CRAVEN (26), WILLIAM AUGUSTUS, Duke of CUMBERLAND (10), Robert D'ARCY, 4th Earl of Holderness (15), James DE LANCEY (29), Oliver DE LANCEY (16), William DENNY (29), Robert DINWIDDIE (55), Arthur DOBBS (12), George Montagu DUNK, 2d Earl of Halifax (14), Henry ELLIS (8), William EYRE (12), Francis FAUQUIER (6), Thomas FITCH (28), John FORBES (52),

Henry FOX, 1st Baron Holland (40), Simon FRASER (10), Thomas GAGE (18), GEORGE II, King of Great Britain (36), Sir Charles GOULD (afterward MORGAN) (12), Thomas HANCOCK (22), Sir Charles HARDY (51), Francis HOLBURNE (25), Stephen HOPKINS (12), Peregrine Thomas HOPSON (40), Richard HUCK-SAUNDERS (29), Thomas HUTCHINSON (18), Sir William JOHNSON (82), Christopher KILBY (16), Charles LAWRENCE (41), William Henry LYTTELTON, 1st Baron Lyttelton of Frankley (25), James F. MERCER (14), Nathaniel MESERVE (14), Robert MONCKTON (24), George MONRO (15), James Gabriel MONTRESOR (31), Robert Hunter MORRIS (9), Abraham MORTIER (17), Alexander MURRAY (13), Sir William PEPPERRELL (14), Spencer PHIPS (17), James PITCHER (12), William PITT, 1st Earl of Chatham (18), Thomas POWNALL (93), James PREVOST (60), John REYNOLDS (9), James ROBERTSON (39), Thomas ROBINSON, 1st Baron Grantham (39), Robert ROGERS (31), Sir John ST. CLAIR (25), Horatio SHARPE (31), William SHIRLEY (105), John STANWIX (52), George WASHINGTON (10), Daniel WEBB (53), Benning WENTWORTH (27), William WILLIAMS (21), George WILLIAMSON (28), John WINSLOW (44), John YOUNG (31).

Physical description: letters, documents, and manuscripts (including 12 volumes of Loudoun's notebooks and military journals, 1753–60). [Note also LOUDOUN MAPS AND PLANS —SUPPLEMENT, below.]

Source: purchased from the Campbell family through the agency of Sotheby's and Sir Joseph Duveen, 1923.

Bibliography: the collection is more fully described in Stanley M. Pargellis, "Loudoun Papers. (a) Colonial, 1756–1758," *The Huntington Library Bulletin,* no. 3 (February 1933): 97–103; and in *American Manuscript Collections in the Huntington Library,* compiled by Norma B. Cuthbert, Huntington Library Lists, no. 5 (1941).

LOUDOUN MAPS AND PLANS—SUPPLEMENT TO LOUDOUN
AMERICANA

Supplementing the Loudoun Americana papers (and acquired
separately, in 1924, from the Museum Bookstore in London)
is a collection of 62 original and contemporary copies of military maps, plans, and charts used by Lord Loudoun during
his American command. The maps range in date from 1690 to
1761, and concentrate on towns, forts, and waterways in New
York and Nova Scotia, including (among others) maps of the
towns of Albany, Saratoga, Halifax, Louisbourg, and Quebec,
and of Forts George, William Henry, and Cumberland (formerly Beauséjour).

VAUDREUIL-CAVAGNAL PAPERS
383 pieces, 1740–53

Pierre Rigaud, Marquis de Vaudreuil-Cavagnal (1698–
1764), was born in Canada, trained to military service, and
appointed governor of Trois Rivieres in 1733. Nine years later
he was sent to Louisiana to succeed Jean Baptiste Le Moyne,
Sieur de Bienville, as governor of the colony, and was instrumental in implementing the French policy of territorial expansion through the establishment of frontier trading posts. Vaudreuil left Louisiana in 1753, spent two years in France, and
returned to his native Canada in 1755 as governor and lieutenant general of New France. His administration there was
brought to a close by the English conquest of 1760, and Vaudreuil retired to France, where he died four years later.

Subject matter: the Vaudreuil papers (which fell into Loudoun's hands through the French double agent Thomas Pichon,
Vaudreuil's secretary in Louisiana) consist chiefly of Vaudreuil's personal correspondence, his correspondence and dispatches to the court of France as governor of Louisiana, and
papers relating to Indian and colonial affairs. They deal with
the French control of the Mississippi Valley, and include information about civil administration, communications with

Canada, defenses (including troop distribution and the establishment of frontier forts), Indian relations, English encroachments, and the economy of the area (including fur trading, mines, and coastal trade).

Significant persons: Jacques Pierre TAFFANEL, Marquis de la JONQUIÈRE (5), Antoine Louis ROUILLÉ, Comte de JOUY (19), MACARTY-MACTIGUE (15), Jean Frédéric PHÉLYPEAUX, Comte de MAUREPAS (82), Honore Michel de VILLEBOIS (8).

Physical description: letters (including 3 volumes of letterbooks), documents, and manuscripts (in French).

Source: purchased with the Loudoun Collection from the Campbell family through the agency of Sotheby's and Sir Joseph Duveen, 1923.

Bibliography: the collection is described in further detail in Norma B. Cuthbert, "Loudoun Papers. (b) French Colonial, 1742–1753," *The Huntington Library Bulletin*, no. 3 (February 1933): 104–07; and in *American Manuscript Collections in the Huntington Library*, compiled by Norma B. Cuthbert, Huntington Library Lists, no. 5 (1941). See also Bill Barron, *The Vaudreuil Papers: A Calendar and Index of the Personal and Private Records of Pierre de Rigaud de Vaudreuil, Royal Governor of the French Province of Louisiana, 1743–1753* (New Orleans: Polyanthos, Inc., 1975).

LOVELL, MANSFIELD (1822–84)
1205 pieces, 1835–86

Mansfield Lovell, Confederate general and civil engineer, was born in Washington, D.C., in 1822, the son of the surgeon general of the army, Dr. Joseph Lovell. Lovell graduated from West Point in 1842, served in the Mexican War, and in 1854 resigned from the army to work at a Trenton, New Jersey, iron works and later as deputy street commissioner for New York City. In September, 1861, he was appointed a major general in the Confederate army, and given the command of Department No. 1 at New Orleans. There his efforts to provide an adequate garrison and supplies for the defense of the city were unsuccessful, and in April, 1862, he evacuated the garrison before David Farragut's Union fleet. Although subsequently exonerated by a military court of inquiry of all responsibility for the loss of New Orleans, Lovell never again received high command, and by 1864 was serving as a volunteer staff officer for Gen. Johnston. After the war, and a brief venture in Georgia rice farming, Lovell returned to a career in civil engineering and surveying. He died in 1884.

Subject matter: operation of Department No. 1, relations between the army and the state of Louisiana, the strengthening of Forts Jackson and St. Philip, outfitting the gunboat "Arkansas," and ordnance and supplies. Also includes family letters, notably from Mrs. Emily (Plympton) Lovell describing everyday life in wartime, and from Lovell's brother describing his life at boarding school and at Williams College (1837–43). Strongest for the period 1860–65.

Significant persons: Pierre G. T. BEAUREGARD (9), Judah P. BENJAMIN (25), Braxton BRAGG (8), James CHESNUT (16), Samuel COOPER (6), Johnson K. DUNCAN (20), Joseph Eggleston JOHNSTON (23), Roswell S. RIPLEY (7), Earl VAN DORN (14), Leroy Pope WALKER (13).

Physical description: documents (including 10 volumes of Confederate letter-, telegraph-, and order-books), letters, and a few manuscripts (including 5 volumes of diaries and journals and 7 military diagrams and plans).

Source: acquired from Paul Haydon, 1934.

Bibliography: much of the Civil War period material has appeared in *The War of the Rebellion: A Compilation of the Official Records of the Union and Confederate Armies*, 70 vols. (Washington: Government Printing Office, 1880–1900).

LOWDEN, WILLIAM SPENCER AND HENRY L.
approximately 12,500 pieces, 1856–1929

William S. Lowden came to Sacramento from Massachusetts by wagon train in 1849. After working as a carpenter for Samuel Brannan for several months, Lowden went to Weaverville, California, in 1850, where he engaged in mining. Following work as a trader, contractor, surveyor, and express rider, he settled in Grass Valley, California. In 1857 he founded the Weaverville and Shasta Wagon Road Company. Lowden's son, Henry L. (1857– ?), worked with his father in a surveying company for many years and served at one time as U.S. deputy county surveyor.

Subject matter: family and business correspondence and records of the Weaverville and Minersville Wagon Road Company, the Weaverville and Shasta Wagon Road Company, and the Lewiston Turnpike Company; miscellaneous land and legal papers; mining and surveyors' reports.

Physical description: letters and documents (including 57 volumes of account books).

Source: purchased from Leo J. McGlynn, November, 1951.

LOWE, GEORGE W. (? –1862)
86 pieces, 1861–65

George W. Lowe, Union soldier, joined the 5th Regiment of Iowa Volunteers at the outbreak of the Civil War and served principally in Missouri and Mississippi. He was present at the battles of New Madrid and Corinth, and was killed at Iuka, Mississippi, in September 1862.

Subject matter: chiefly letters from Lowe to his wife, Lizzie (Palm) Lowe, dealing with family affairs and with the everyday life of a soldier; accounts of the battles of New Madrid and Corinth; letters written to Lizzie Lowe by other members of her family, including other soldiers, on similar topics.

Physical description: letters, with 2 manuscript poems and a pencil map of the battle of New Madrid.

Source: gift of Mrs. Merlyn Lowe, September 1974.

LUKENS, THEODORE PARKER (1848–1918)
approximately 3600 pieces, 1869–1942

Theodore P. Lukens was a conservationist and pioneer community leader in Pasadena, California. He was born in Ohio and came to California with his wife in 1880. He became active in business and municipal affairs, serving as president of the Board of Trustees of the city of Pasadena in 1890–92 and 1894–95. Lukens was a friend of John Muir (q.v.) and promoted many conservation causes, including the first experiments with reforestation. He served as supervisor of the Angeles National Forest in the San Gabriel Mountains (1905–07), and throughout his career held many important positions in private and government forestry organizations. From 1909 to 1911 he operated the Los Berros Forest Co., a commercial tree farm near San Luis Obispo, California. Lukens remained prominent in civic affairs in Pasadena until his death in 1918.

Subject matter: personal and business affairs; conservation, the botanical study of local forests, and commercial tree farming; material concerning the establishment of the Mt. Wilson Observatory.

Significant persons: Thomas Robert BARD (7), George Ellery HALE (6), Abbot KINNEY (12), Theodore Parker LUKENS (80), John MUIR (80), Harrison Gray OTIS (8), Gifford PINCHOT (101).

Physical description: letters (including 7 letterbooks), manuscripts (including 20 diaries), and 10 photograph albums.

Source: purchased from Mrs. Helen Lukens Gaut, January, 1954.

LUMMIS, CHARLES FLETCHER (1859–1928)
140 pieces, 1900–25

Charles F. Lummis, journalist, author, ethnologist, and founder of the Southwest Museum, attended Harvard University, and edited a newspaper in Ohio. He came west in 1884, crossing the country on foot. Upon arrival in Los Angeles in 1885, he became city editor for the *Los Angeles Times,* but returned to New Mexico in 1887 to recover his health following a stroke. In New Mexico, Lummis studied and wrote about Southwestern history and Indian ethnology. When he returned to Los Angeles, he became editor, in 1894, of the magazine *The Land of Sunshine* (later *Out West*); founded the Southwest Museum in 1903 to preserve material on Indian culture; and served as librarian of the Los Angeles Public Library from 1905 to 1910, laying the foundation for their large collection of California and Western history.

Subject matter: mainly Lummis' work in the Los Angeles Public Library and his efforts to collect the autographs of well-known writers and artists of his own time, for deposit in that institution.

Physical description: letters.

Source: purchased from Argonaut Book Shop, December, 1960.

LUNGREN, FERNAND HARVEY (1857–1932)
75 pieces, 1897–1928

Fernand H. Lungren, a Western artist who originally came from Maryland, studied mining engineering until encouraged by a friend to enter the field of art. He enrolled in the Pennsylvania Academy in Philadelphia in 1876, and his first illustrations were published in *Scribner's Magazine* in 1879. Following a trip to Europe, Lungren visited the western United States for the first time in 1891, returning to live permanently in Los Angeles in 1903. Many of his illustrations appeared in *Century, St. Nicholas, Harper's,* and other magazines. The author Stewart Edward White, for whom Lungren had illustrated stories, persuaded Lungren and his wife to make their home in Santa Barbara in 1906, and in 1920 Lungren became president of the Santa Barbara School of the Arts.

Subject matter: art and artists, as seen in the correspondence of Fernand H. Lungren, mainly with authors and magazine editors.

Significant persons: Stewart Edward WHITE (14).

Physical description: letters, manuscripts, and documents.

Source: purchased from Dawson's Book Shop, November, 1959.

M

McCALL, GEORGE ARCHIBALD (1802–68)
49 pieces, 1831–53

George A. McCall, career soldier, rose from lieutenant to lieutenant colonel in the regular U.S. Army, was aide-de-camp to General Edmund Pendleton Gaines (1831–36), fought in the Seminole War of 1835–42, and served as inspector general of Philadelphia until 1853. He was a brigadier general in the U.S. Volunteers from 1861 to 1863.

Subject matter: the Seminole War of 1835–42, brevet honors for McCall, and miscellaneous military matters of the antebellum Western Department.

Physical description: letters and documents.

Source: acquired from G. S. Macmanus, 1935.

McCLINTOCK, JAMES M. (1839–1921)
84 pieces, 1861–1909

James McClintock, a Union officer from Coshocton, Ohio, joined the 51st Ohio Volunteers in 1861, and was assigned the following year to the U.S. Signal Corps, with which he remained for the duration of the war. McClintock served at several headquarters, most notably with Grant during the Vicksburg campaign and with Sherman during the March to the Sea.

Subject matter: primarily general and special orders pertaining to the operation of the Signal Corps in Kentucky, Mississippi, and Georgia. Also includes a journal by McClintock kept from 1861 to 1869 giving weather, locale, and troop movements, a code sheet, and a report on McClintock's military career.

Physical description: documents, with a few letters and manuscripts, and 14 photographs.

Source: acquired from Maxwell Hunley, 1959.

Bibliography: some of the pieces in the collection have been published in *The War of the Rebellion: A Compilation of the Official Records of the Union and Confederate Armies,* 70 vols. (Washington: Government Printing Office, 1880–1900).

McCULLOH, HENRY (fl. 1730–78)
General Thoughts, Endeavoring to Demonstrate that the Legislature here . . . Have a Right to Tax the British Colonies (1765)
MS. volume 14 pp.

Concerns the Stamp Act.

McCULLOUGH, SAMUEL (1826–ca.90)
72 pieces, 1854–86

Samuel McCullough, California businessman and state assemblyman, came in 1855 from New Jersey to Sacramento, California, where he practiced his trade as a carpenter. In 1858 he joined the gold rush to the Fraser River in Canada, but in 1860 returned to San Francisco where he worked as a building contractor and hotel proprietor. McCullough served in the California state assembly from 1871 to 1873, and was superintendent of U.S. Government buildings in San Francisco from 1873 to 1878.

Subject matter: personal and business papers, mostly relating to the construction of federal buildings in San Francisco from 1873–78; the Sutter New Helvetia title and a trip to the Fraser River mines.

Physical description: letters, documents, and 2 volumes.

Source: purchased from Edwin Grabhorn, January, 1945.

McHENRY, JAMES (1753–1816)
116 pieces, 1776–1815

James McHenry, statesman, soldier, and physician, emigrated from Ireland in 1771 to Philadelphia, where he studied medicine under Benjamin Rush. During the Revolution he served as secretary to Washington and as aide-de-camp to Lafayette. A delegate to the Continental Congress (1783–86) and the Constitutional Convention, he also replaced Timothy Pickering as secretary of war in 1796 and held the office to May 1800. McHenry withdrew from public life in 1802.

Subject matter: American Revolution, especially British treatment of American prisoners of war, military plans, and Washington's military "family"; domestic and foreign affairs after the Revolution, particularly candidates to elective and appointive offices, federal and state elections, the break with France, and the postwar army; strongest for 1796–99.

Significant persons: James McHENRY (7), William Vans MURRAY (14), Timothy PICKERING (9), Benjamin TALLMADGE (6), Uriah TRACY (7), George WASHINGTON (16), Oliver WOLCOTT (7).

Physical description: mostly letters, some documents and manuscripts, including a journal by McHenry while with Washington's army July 10–15, 1778, and a list of prisoners at Yorktown.

Source: purchased from George D. Smith in 1919, after the papers were used by Bernard C. Steiner for his *Life and Cor-*

respondence of James McHenry (Cleveland: The Burrows Brothers Co., 1907).

Bibliography: over twenty-five pieces have been published, primarily in Steiner's book, but also in the *Writings of George Washington,* ed. John C. Fitzpatrick, 39 vols. (Washington: Government Printing Office, 1931–44) and the *Writings of George Washington,* ed. Worthington C. Ford, 14 vols. (New York and London: G. P. Putnam's Sons, 1889–93).

McKEIGAN, ALEXANDER (1874–1958)
approximately 500 pieces, ca. 1912–48

Alexander McKeigan, Los Angeles real estate appraiser, was a native of Sydney, Nova Scotia, who came to Los Angeles in 1906. He was employed by the city and county as an appraiser after 1910.

Subject matter: chiefly notes and appraisal reports, tract maps, and correspondence relating to property in and around Los Angeles.

Physical description: letters, documents, and maps (including 1 volume of a subdivision mapbook).

Source: gift of Mrs. Margaret C. MacKay, May, 1958.

MACLAY, CHARLES (1821–90)
approximately 850 pieces, 1841–1922

Charles Maclay, California legislator, landowner, and pioneer businessman, came to California from Pennsylvania as a Methodist missionary in 1851. He settled in the Santa Clara Valley, where he engaged in farming and various other businesses. As state assemblyman (1861–62) and state senator (1868–73),

Maclay introduced bills encouraging construction of the Southern Pacific Railroad and the establishment of the University of California. In 1874 he purchased, along with George and Benjamin Porter, the northeast portion of Rancho Ex-Mission de San Fernando, where Maclay was instrumental in the founding and development of the town of San Fernando and the surrounding farm lands of the Valley. He endowed the Maclay School of Theology in 1885, which became part of the University of Southern California.

Subject matter: California politics in the 1860–70 period, Methodism in Pennsylvania and California, the Southern and Central Pacific Railroads, the University of Southern California, and the development of the San Fernando Valley in California.

Significant persons: Charles CROCKER (8), Leland STANFORD (6).

Physical description: letters, manuscripts, and documents, including 30 bound volumes.

Source: gift of Mrs. Catherine Dace, March, 1938, and November, 1939.

MADISON, JAMES (1750/51–1836)
and DALLAS, ALEXANDER JAMES (1759–1817)
104 pieces, 1815–16

James Madison, fourth president of the United States, was nearing the end of his second term when these pieces were written. Alexander James Dallas, secretary of the treasury, was looking forward to retirement from his duties, which he assumed in 1814. (Dallas was also secretary of war in the spring and summer of 1815.) In 1815 and 1816 Madison and

Dallas were mainly concerned with organizing a peacetime military establishment and in solving a national financial crisis.

Subject matter: organization of a peacetime military establishment; economic and financial affairs, including the Second Bank of the United States; American relations with England, France, Russia, and Algeria; Indian affairs; Jacob Jennings Brown, Andrew Jackson, Winfield Scott, Thomas Sidney Jessup, Joseph Bonaparte, William Jones; an astronomical observatory.

Significant persons: Alexander James DALLAS (47), James MADISON (57).

Physical description: letters.

Source: unknown.

Bibliography: the entire collection is published in George Mifflin Dallas, *Life and Writings of Alexander James Dallas* (Philadelphia: J. P. Lippincott, 1871).

MANAHAN, CHARLES F. (1871–1955)
approximately 320 pieces, 1898–1946

Charles F. Manahan, first sergeant with the U.S. Volunteers during the Philippine Insurrection of 1899–1901, collected military records, correspondence, and papers dealing particularly with the 34th Infantry Regiment during that action.

Subject matter: military records and papers of the 34th Infantry Regiment, U.S. Volunteers, active during the Philippine Insurrection (1899–1901); and correspondence, including that of General Julius Augustus Penn, commander of the regiment; a small group of letters dealing with World War II.

Physical description: letters, manuscripts, and documents.

Source: gift of Donald F. Manahan, 1956.

MANDEVILLE, JAMES WYLIE (1824–76)
approximately 725 pieces, 1848–66

James W. Mandeville, California politician and surveyor, was a schoolteacher in his native New York before coming to San Jose, California, in 1849. A year later, he left teaching there to engage in mining in Tuolomne County. He was elected to serve in the state assembly from 1853 to 1854 and in the state senate from 1855 to 1857. Mandeville became U.S. surveyor from 1857 to 1861, and afterwards held the offices of state commissioner of immigration and state controller in 1875.

Subject matter: state and local politics and mining in California in the 1850s; letters dealing with the Broderick-Gwin rivalry (1855–57).

Significant persons: William McKendree GWIN (11), Milton Slocum LATHAM (5), James Wylie MANDEVILLE (10).

Physical description: letters, manuscripts, and documents.

Source: purchased from Holmes Book Co., February, 1922, and from Edwin Grabhorn, January, 1945.

Bibliography: the collection is described in the *Huntington Library Bulletin,* no. 7 (April, 1935): 49–50.

MARION, FRANCIS (ca. 1732–95)
The following are generally known as the Marion orderly books:

U.S. ARMY (CONTINENTAL). 2ND SOUTH CAROLINA REGIMENT
General Francis Marion's Orderly Book (1775–77)
MS. volume 555 pp. in two parts
Covers from June 1775 to May 6, 1779.

U.S. ARMY (CONTINENTAL). 2ND SOUTH CAROLINA
REGIMENT
[Orderly Book kept by Francis Marion and others] (1778–89)
MS. volume 263 pp.
Covers from August 14, 1778 to December 28, 1779.

SOUTH CAROLINA. MILITIA. BRIGADE COMMANDED
BY FRANCIS MARION
[Orderly Book] (1781–82)
MS. volume 160 pp.
Covers from February 16, 1781 to December 5, 1782.

MARKHAM, HENRY HARRISON (1840–1923)
approximately 2494 pieces, 1867–99

Henry H. Markham, governor of California, was born in New
York and was educated at Wheeler's Academy in Vermont. He
served in the Civil War, and afterward studied law in Wisconsin. Markham practiced law in Wisconsin until 1879, when
he moved to California, settled in Pasadena, and became a
prominent and influential citizen. His business enterprises
were varied, but his chief interests were in gold and silver
mining in Arizona and California. Markham was elected a
representative to Congress in 1884 and governor of California
in 1890, which office he held until 1895.

Subject matter: political trends in California, the California
gubernatorial campaign of 1890, the 1896 election of President McKinley, and mining in California and Arizona, including some deeds of mining claims and reports.

Significant persons: Charles Frederick HOLDER (6), Henry
Harrison MARKHAM (84), Harrison Gray OTIS (20).

Physical description: letters and documents.

Source: gift of Mrs. Hildreth Markham West, February 25,
1936.

233

MARSTON, OTIS REED (1894–   )
approximately 1000 pieces, 1889–1973

Otis R. Marston, U.S. naval officer and leader of many Colorado River expeditions, was born in Berkeley, California, and graduated from the University of California in 1916. He received a mechanical engineering degree from Cornell University in 1917. After special training at the Naval Academy he became an officer in the submarine service during World War I, and passed the examinations as submarine commander. Marston made the first of his many trips down the Colorado River with Norman Nevills by skiff in 1942, piloted the first motor boat through the Grand Canyon in 1949, and led the only party to run boats all the way up the canyon in 1960. Marston is also known as an authority on the Colorado River and the history of its fast-water navigation.

Subject matter: the Colorado River expeditions (1927–60) of Otis Marston and others; secondary source material on the Colorado River and related subjects.

Physical description: letters, manuscripts (including diaries and journals), documents, and photographs.

Source: gift of Otis Marston, 1950–77.

MARTENET, JEFFERSON (1828–92<)
357 pieces, 1837–92

Jefferson Martenet, emigrant to the California mines in 1852, spent about two years in Jacksonville, then went to San Francisco where he opened a book stand in 1855. He became a clerk in 1857 in the Antiquarian Bookstore, owned by his friends Epes Ellery and Augustus Doyle. From 1866 to 1867,

Martenet was associated with Dr. T. W. Brotherton, rector of Trinity Episcopal Church, in the publication of the *Pacific Churchman,* official newspaper of the Episcopal Diocese in California. After 1867, Martenet engaged in a collection agency business.

Subject matter: life and events in San Francisco, chiefly during the years 1854–70, as reflected in the correspondence between Jefferson Martenet and his mother Catherine M. Richardson in Baltimore, Ohio, and with Simon J. Martenet, a Baltimore surveyor and civil engineer; the Civil War.

Physical description: letters.

Source: purchased from the Argonaut Book Shop, June, 1954.

MARTÍNEZ, ESTEBAN JOSÉ (fl. 1789)
Diario de la Navegacion que Yo el Alf[ere]z de Navio de la R[ea]l Arm[a]da D[o]n Estevan Josef Martínez boy a executar al P[un]to de S[a]n Lorenzo de Nuca, mandando la Frag[a]ta Princesa Y Paquebot S[a]n Carlos de Or[de]n del Ex[celentisi]mo S[eñ]or D[o]n Manuel Ant[oni]o Florez Virrey, Govern[ad]or y Capitan G[ene]ral de N[or] E[ste] en el Pres[en]te Año de 1789. (January 12–December 6, 1789).
Contemporary copy 1 volume 292 pp. (Certified by Martínez)

Text in Spanish.

MATHER, COTTON (1662/63–1727/28)
79 pieces, 1645–1807

Cotton Mather, Puritan clergyman, was pastor of the Second Church of Boston his entire professional career. A scholar and an activist, he produced many writings, most notably *Magnalia Christi Americana,* and worked to alleviate poverty and educate slaves. He was also for a while a leading politician.

Subject matter: theology, evangelization of the Indians, current events in Europe, economic conditions in New England.

Significant persons: Cotton MATHER (29), Increase MATHER (10).

Physical description: manuscripts (two groups of about 90 sermons by various Boston clergymen, including Increase and Cotton Mather), letters, documents.

Source: purchased from Robert Dodd, George D. Smith, Anderson Galleries, Wilberforce Eames, J. B. Learmont, George P. Marsh, and William K. Bixby, 1905–27.

Bibliography: Selected Letters of Cotton Mather, ed. Kenneth Silverman (Baton Rouge: Louisiana State University Press, 1971) contains some of the letters from Cotton Mather to William Ashurst.

MAYO, CLARENCE HASTINGS (fl. 1880s)
95 pieces, 1879–82

Clarence H. Mayo, cattle ranch manager, went to Colfax County, New Mexico, in 1880 as overseer of the Kiowa Ranch, which was owned by U.S. Senator William Windom. After Windom sold the ranch to another member of the senate, Stephen Wallace Dorsey, Mayo left for the Dakota, Wyoming, and Montana Territories and later tried mining in Colorado.

Subject matter: discusses cattle ranching in New Mexico and Wyoming Territory; also material concerning William Windom, and Mayo's life in Wyoming Territory and Colorado.

Physical description: letters.

Source: purchased from Dawson's Book Shop, September, 1959.

MEGQUIER, MARY JANE (COLE) (fl. 1848–56)
89 pieces, 1822–56

Mary Jane (Cole) Megquier and her husband, Dr. Thomas Lewis Megquier, were early San Francisco residents. Dr. Megquier had practiced medicine in Winthrop, Maine, until 1848, when the prospects of gold lured them to California. The Megquiers left their children with relatives and traveled via the Isthmus of Panama to San Francisco, and family tradition tells that Mrs. Megquier was the first American woman to cross the Isthmus. Dr. Megquier became one of the first American physicians in San Francisco, and his wife ran a boarding house there. They made return visits to Maine in 1852 and 1854. In 1855 Dr. Megquier died, and Mrs. Megquier returned to San Francisco alone, once more to open a boarding house.

Subject matter: the voyage to California by way of Panama and life in the San Francisco area during the Gold Rush era, as reflected in letters from Mary Jane Megquier to her children.

Physical description: letters and documents.

Source: purchased from Mrs. C. H. Lund, April, 1937.

Bibliography: the letters have been published in Mary Jane Megquier, *Apron Full of Gold,* ed. Robert Glass Cleland (San Marino: Huntington Library, 1949).

MELLEN, WILLIAM S. (fl. 1880s)
52 pieces, 1889

William S. Mellen of Milwaukee, Wisconsin, general manager of the Wisconsin Central Railroad, was traveling with his daughter Gertrude from Chicago to Washington when their train was trapped in the Johnstown (Pennsylvania) Flood on May 31, 1889. The Mellens and many of the other passengers (including the wife and daughter of President Harrison's private secretary) left the train at Conemaugh and took to the hills, where most of them were saved.

Subject matter: the Johnstown Flood; telegrams and letters concerning the fate of the Mellens, and subsequent congratulations from friends on their escape. A large collection of newspaper clippings gives further details of the flood and its aftermath.

Physical description: letters and telegrams with newspaper clippings.

Source: gift of Mrs. Gertrude Mellen Fuller, April 21, 1939.

MELLISH, GEORGE H. (b. ca.1844)
187 pieces, 1862–65

George H. Mellish, of Woodstock, Vermont, served during the Civil War as a corporal in the 6th Vermont Volunteers. His regiment saw action in the Peninsular and Gettysburg campaigns and at the sieges of Richmond and Petersburg.

Subject matter: all aspects of the life of a Union soldier, including skirmishing and picket duty, everyday life, the Gettysburg and Peninsular campaigns, and the battles of Fredericksburg and Spotsylvania; as well as family affairs, opinions of the war, and comments about commanding officers. Also includes letters to Mellish from his mother, Mary.

Physical description: letters and some ephemera (including a card photograph of General Ulysses S. Grant).

Source: acquired from C. E. Tuttle, June, 1965.

MEXICAN INQUISITION COLLECTION
88 volumes, 1525–1822

The Mexican Inquisition was an extension of the institution in Spain which had been originated by the papal bull of Sixtus IV in 1478. The Supreme Council of the Spanish Inquisition originally controlled both the local tribunals in Spain and those in the colonies. In 1571 the Holy Office was established as a separate body in Mexico, where it was never as severe as in Spain. The purpose was to detect and try heretics or persons guilty of any offense against the church (including violations by priests) and to investigate the blood lines and genealogy of individuals aspiring to positions of trust in the Church or government.

Subject matter: the original records of 93 trials from the archives of the Holy Office of the Inquisition in Mexico. The testimony of these trials (for heresy, blasphemy, violation of ecclesiastical vows, witchcraft, Judaism, and other charges) reveals much information about ethnic groups and manners and customs in colonial Mexico.

Physical description: 88 volumes of documents (in Spanish).

Source: gift of W. F. Stuart-Menteth, 1932, and Walter Douglas, 1944.

Bibliography: a partial list of cases has been published in *Hispanic American Historical Review,* 44 (November, 1964): 565–67.

MEXICAN WAR COLLECTION
89 pieces, 1829–48

Relations between the U.S. and Mexico, troubled by diplomatic failures during the 1830s, disintegrated completely after the annexation of Texas by the U.S. in 1845. In November of that year, President James K. Polk's emissary to Mexico, John Slidell, failed to negotiate the differences, and in January 1846 the president sent American troops under General Zachary Taylor into the disputed territory bounded by the Nueces and Rio Grande Rivers in Texas. When the Mexicans attacked and captured an American patrol party, Polk urged Congress to declare war. Following the occupation of Matamoros, Mexico, Taylor proceeded inland with his army, and reached the town of Monterrey, where he engaged in battle with the defending troops of General Pedro de Ampudia. After three days of rugged combat in and around the city, the Mexicans surrendered and negotiated an armistice with General Taylor. The Americans occupied the city of Monterrey until the end of the war.

Subject matter: primarily the Battle of Monterrey and the occupation of that city by U.S. forces during the Mexican War. The papers are unusual in that they shed light on the events from both sides of the conflict. Most of the papers fall within the period 1846–48, and a few concern the settlement, independence, and annexation of Texas (1829–45).

Significant persons: Pedro de AMPUDIA (4), Isaac Hull WRIGHT (9).

Physical description: letters and documents (mostly in Spanish), with 2 photographs.

Source: purchased from Lawrence Lingle, August and November, 1973.

MEYERS, JACOB A. (fl. 1905–17)
106 pieces, 1893–1917

Jacob A. Meyers, of Myers Falls, Washington, was interested for many years in collecting information concerning the history of Washington and Oregon. He became a trustee of the Spokane (Washington) Historical Society in 1916.

Subject matter: correspondence of Jacob A. Meyers with Thompson C. Elliott, Joseph B. Tyrrell, and William S. Lewis, authors of historical works about the Northwest; information about Ranald McDonald and the areas surrounding Fort Colville, Washington.

Physical description: letters (typewritten copies).

Source: purchased from G. F. Hollingsworth, May, 1961.

MITCHELL FAMILY
193 pieces, 1858–87

The Thomas Mitchell family came to Coloma, California, in the 1850s, and they and their six daughters were active participants in the life of El Dorado County. One daughter married George W. Kinney, an accountant and mining agent in San Francisco (who often visited various Nevada mining towns). Another daughter married William J. Forbes, editor and printer, and a widely known journalist whose humor appeared under the pen name of "Semblins." Forbes came to California in 1852 and became the editor of newspapers in the gold rush country, then went to Nevada, where he published several newspapers including the Uniontown *Humboldt Register* (1863–67), the Virginia City *Daily Trespass* (1867–68), and the *White Pine News* in Treasure City (1869–73). After 1875 the Mitchell family lived in San Francisco where the sisters earned their living by keeping a boarding house.

Subject matter: centering in the period 1860–71, life in the California gold region of El Dorado County as well as mining areas in Nevada, such as Austin, Virginia City, Treasure City, Hamilton, etc.; life in San Francisco in 1866 and from 1876 to 1887.

Significant persons: William J. FORBES (11).

Physical description: letters and documents.

Source: purchased from Edwin Grabhorn, January, 1945.

MONTEIRO DE BARROS, FRANCISCO XAVIER
(1778–1855)
approximately 100 pieces, 1813–41

Francisco X. Monteiro de Barros, Portuguese statesman and U.S. businessman, received his degree in both philosophy and mathematics from the University of Coimbra. He was appointed cosmographer of Santarém in 1802, served as secretary to the Lisbon Commissariat, and was elected in 1820 to the Portuguese Congress (where he worked diligently for the organization of the Bank of Lisbon). In opposition to the growing influence of a reactionary absolutist movement, Monteiro de Barros moved first, with his family, to England. In 1824, losing hope for the future of liberal Portuguese institutions, he moved to New York to try his fortune in business and subsequently became a banker in Goochland County, Virginia. With the reimposition of the liberal constitutional charter in Portugal in 1834, however, Monteiro de Barros was offered the position of state counselor. This he refused, on the grounds that he had opposed royal control of the office in 1820, and thereafter elected to remain in the U.S., where his children became naturalized citizens.

Subject matter: letters to Francisco X. Monteiro de Barros concerning political matters in Portugal (1813–22) and manuscripts by Monteiro de Barros on scientific subjects and mathematics. There are also 18 letters (1834–38) from Joaquim Cesar Figaniere e Morao, Portuguese minister to the U.S., commenting on the commercial and diplomatic relations between the U.S. and Portugal and on Portuguese politics.

Significant persons: Joaquim Cesar FIGANIERE E MORAO (18), Caetano José PEIXOTO (20).

Physical description: letters and manuscripts (in Portuguese).

Source: unknown.

MONTEREY COLLECTION
1337 pieces, 1785–1877

The town of Monterey, California, founded by the Spanish as a presidio in 1770, remained under the rule of New Spain until the Mexican government took control in 1822. During the Mexican period, when Monterey was the capital of the province, the city was governed by an Ayuntamiento and an alcalde. Walter Colton became the first American alcalde of Monterey on July 28, 1846, serving during this formative period when the territory was under the rule of U.S. military governors. California officially became a U.S. possession in 1848, and after statehood in 1850 the Ayuntamiento became the Common Council, and a mayor was elected in place of the alcalde.

Subject matter: the government of the municipality of Monterey, primarily during the period 1828–54. Includes minute books, election results, and records of disbursements of funds and of ordinances passed.

Physical description: letters and documents (mainly in Spanish until 1846 and in English thereafter).

Source: purchased from Mr. and Mrs. W. R. Holman, February, 1959.

MOORE, DOROTHEA (RHODES) LUMMIS (1860?–1942)
84 pieces, 1883–84

Dorothea Moore was secretly married to Charles Fletcher Lummis [q.v.] (later a well-known writer and editor in Cali-

243

fornia) in 1880 while she was still a student at the Boston University School of Medicine. After graduation, she began the practice of medicine in Los Angeles in 1885. She later became the president of the Los Angeles County Homeopathic Medical Society, was dramatic critic for the *Los Angeles Times,* and was a lifelong friend of Mary Austin and others in the literary world. Dorothea was divorced from Lummis in 1891, and later married Dr. Ernest Carroll Moore, provost of the University of California at Los Angeles.

Subject matter: the life of a woman in medical college in the 1880s, bringing out a little-known period in the life of Charles F. Lummis.

Physical description: letters.

Source: purchased from Ronald Woodlin, August, 1974.

MOORE, JOHN (1765–ca.1824)
303 pieces, 1760–1848

John Moore was a New York City shipping merchant whose varied financial interests and activities flourished in the last two decades of the eighteenth century.

Subject matter: information on the business and commerce of New York and on American mercantile practices; some family letters from sons and other relatives on purely personal matters. Strongest for the period 1785–95.

Physical description: letters, documents (including 2 account books), and manuscripts, with some printed material and other ephemera.

Source: gift of Carl H. and Norma Peine, September, 1958.

MOORE, WILLIAM (1827–91<)
approximately 100 pieces, 1851–91

Captain William Moore, Los Angeles surveyor, worked for the Los Angeles city surveyor's office with George Hansen in the 1850s, when the early surveys of the area were being made. Moore served as Los Angeles county surveyor in 1857, 1858–59 and 1861, and as Los Angeles city surveyor in 1868 and 1873. Moore was given a contract in 1878 to build a tunnel in central Los Angeles to supply irrigation water—the tunnel was completed but never used. In 1874 he married Mary Elizabeth Hall, a teacher in the first Los Angeles public school, and sister of Charles Victor Hall, early Los Angeles land developer and editor of *Hall's Land Journal* (1878–80).

Subject matter: maps and surveys of Los Angeles; field books (25 volumes, 1851–89), diaries (8 volumes, 1869–91), time books (5 volumes), "Maps and Field Notes and Surveys" (2 volumes, 1858); also family letters and documents.

Physical description: letters, documents (including 38 volumes), and maps.

Source: gift of Florence Moore Kreider, 1935–46.

MORAN, BENJAMIN (1820–86)
54 pieces, 1870–75

Benjamin Moran, American diplomat, was born in Pennsylvania in 1820, studied literature, and took a walking tour of Great Britain in 1851 and 1852 before accepting, in 1854, a position as clerk to James Buchanan, minister at the American legation in London. Moran subsequently served as clerk and secretary of the legation, and acted frequently as chargé

245

d'affaires during his twenty years at that post. In 1874 he was appointed resident minister in Portugal and, when that office was discontinued two years later, he was named chargé d'affaires at Lisbon. He retired from the diplomatic service in 1882, returned to England, and died at Braintree, Essex, four years later.

Subject matter: personal and diplomatic affairs, information about British perceptions of President Grant, the "Alabama" Claims issue, the Irish Question, and British Columbia, as well as personal and diplomatic gossip. Strongest for the years 1869–70, when the historian John Lathrop Motley was minister of the U.S. legation at London.

Physical description: letters.

Source: purchased from the Abraham Lincoln Bookshop, February, 1966.

MORGAN, DALE LOWELL (1914–71)
approximately 2000 pieces, (1809–ca.57)

Dale L. Morgan, Western historian, was born in Salt Lake City and educated at the University of Utah. He was state superintendent for the Utah Writers' Project of the Works Progress Administration (1940–42) and information specialist with the Office of Price Administration during World War II. As a Guggenheim Fellow for 1947–48, Morgan did research on the subject of Mormonism throughout the United States. He went to the Bancroft Library of the University of California in 1954 as editor and author for a projected guide to their manuscript collections. Morgan has written books on many Western subjects, including Mormonism and Jedediah Smith.

Subject matter: Morgan's projected book on the Mormons and the Far West; other related Western subjects, such as the opening, exploration, and settlement of the West; the fur trade; Indians of the middle and southwestern states; the Santa Fe trade, California Gold Rush; etc.

Physical description: typewritten copies of newspaper articles.

Source: purchased from Dale L. Morgan, December, 1949.

MORGAN, WILLIAM R. (ca.1832–1901<)
187 pieces, 1852–86

William R. Morgan came to California from Bennington, Vermont, in 1852 to seek his fortune in the mines, and later became a state legislator. He settled in St. Louis, Sierra County, California, where he engaged in mining activities, eventually becoming secretary of the Sierra Union Water and Mining Company. Morgan served as state assemblyman from Sierra County in 1873 and 1874.

Subject matter: mining, mostly in St. Louis, Sierra County, California, and with the Sierra Union Water and Mining Company.

Physical description: letters and documents.

Source: purchased from Dawson's Book Shop, December, 1958.

MORMON FILE
approximately 1500 pieces, 1807–1962

The Church of Jesus Christ of Latter-Day Saints was founded by Joseph Smith of New York, who experienced a vision in 1823, and published the Book of Mormon in 1830. Persecution caused the members of the church to move continually westward, to Kirtland, Ohio, and Independence, Missouri, in

1831, to Far West, Missouri, in 1833, and to Nauvoo, Illinois, in 1838. After Smith was murdered in Nauvoo in 1844, the Mormons were guided by their new leader, Brigham Young, to Salt Lake City, where they settled in 1847. The Mormon followers were encouraged by the Church to keep diaries and journals, which provide a panorama of the travel experiences and daily life during the Westward Movement. In the 1940s the Huntington Library, with the help of Mrs. Juanita Brooks, began a project of gathering together available journals and life sketches to be photocopied for preservation and research. Since that time additional material relating to this subject is continually being added to the collection.

Subject matter: Mormon diaries, reminiscences, biographical sketches, family histories, correspondence, and miscellaneous papers.

Significant persons: Joseph SMITH (4), Brigham YOUNG (5).

Physical description: 118 reels of microfilm, 156 bound volumes of photostatic copies of diaries, etc., and about 1200 letters and manuscripts (some of which are facsimiles or later copies).

Source: acquired from many sources over a period of years.

MORRIS, ROBERT (1734–1806)
320 pieces, 1774–1837

Robert Morris, merchant and statesman, played the leading role in financing the American Revolution. His commercial and financial position was built as a partner in the firm of Willing, Morris and Co. Morris committed himself to the Revolutionary cause in 1775, taking on various public offices. His major governmental contribution was as superintendent of finance for the Confederation, 1781–84. Afterward he continued to engage in commerce and hold public posts, but his land speculation led to poverty and imprisonment.

Subject matter: commercial transactions between Richard Champion, merchant of Bristol, England, and the Willing, Morris and Co., 1774–76; land speculation; Morris family affairs and local gossip; financing the Revolution; Morris' debts and imprisonment; litigation over the estate of Richard Champion, 1825–37.

Significant persons: George Lloyd CHAMPION (28), Richard CHAMPION (30), Mary (White) MORRIS (21), Robert MORRIS (221).

Physical description: mostly letters; documents.

Source: purchased from Anderson Galleries, Thomas F. Madigan, Charles Sessler, and George D. Smith, 1917–25.

Bibliography: The Papers of Robert Morris, 1781–1784, ed. E. James Ferguson (Pittsburgh: University of Pittsburgh, 1973–); Richard Champion, *The American Correspondence of a Bristol Merchant, 1766–1776* (Berkeley: University of California Press, 1934); pieces pertaining to Morris' debt and imprisonment were published in the *Philadelphia North American,* issues dated Feb. 8, 15, 25, and Mar. 1, 1925.

MOTT, EDWARD (fl. 1775)
[Military Journal: Expedition to Ft. Ticonderoga] (1775)
Autograph MS. volume 13 pp.

Covers period from April 28 to May 10.

MOUNT WILSON TOLL ROAD COMPANY
approximately 100 pieces, 1903–53

The Pasadena and Mt. Wilson Toll Road Co., incorporated in 1889 by Judge Benjamin Eaton and others, was reorganized in 1890 with the purpose of building a ten mile wagon road from Eaton Canyon up the west flank of the San Gabriel Mountains to Mt. Wilson, above Pasadena, California. The road was completed and put into use in 1891, and the company gradually acquired control of the Mt. Wilson area. A syndicate took control in 1904, and the Mt. Wilson Hotel was built. The road was later improved for automobile traffic and continued in use until its closure in 1936. The Mt. Wilson Toll Road Co. then became the Mt. Wilson Hotel Co.

Subject matter: the operation of the Mt. Wilson Toll Road; the Mt. Wilson Toll Road Co. (1913–30); one register book for the Mt. Wilson Hotel (1925–28); a description of a trip via the Mt. Wilson Trail to Mt. Wilson (ca. 1903); miscellaneous business papers (1903–53).

Physical description: letters and documents (including 9 volumes of ledgers and journals and one hotel register book).

Source: gift of Jerome Schwimmer, July, 1968.

MOURELLE, FRANCISCO ANTONIO (1755–1820)
22 pieces, 1774–1846<

Letters and official papers of Francisco Antonio Mourelle, Spanish naval officer and explorer who figured prominently in the Hezeta expedition to the northwest coast of North America in 1775 (in Spanish).

[MOURELLE, FRANCISCO ANTONIO ?] (1755–1820)
Segunda Exploracion de la Costa Septentrion[a]l de Californ[ia]s hecha en 1775 con la Fragata Santiago y Goleta Sonora mandadas por el Teniente de Navio Don Bruno de Ezeta, y el de Fragata Don Juan de la [Bodega y] Quadra desde el Puerto de S[a]n Blas hasta los 58 gr[ado]s de latitud N[orte]. (1775<) MS. 1 volume 162 pp. [Incomplete]

Text in Spanish.

MUIR, JOHN (1838–1914)
86 pieces, 1902–55

John Muir, naturalist, conservationist, and writer, came to the United States from his birthplace in Scotland at the age of eleven. His family settled on a Wisconsin farm where the young Muir became an inventive genius. After studying at the University of Wisconsin, Muir set out to travel in South America, but instead arrived in California in 1868. He fell in love with the mountains, and spent the next four years in the Sierra Nevada working as a shepherd and exploring the mountains in solitude. In 1879 his explorations in Alaska led to the discovery of the Muir Glacier. He married Louie Wanda Strentzel in 1880 and moved to Martinez, California, but spent most of his later years traveling in many parts of the world and in working for the preservation of the mountains of California. Muir wrote extensively about the mountains, his best known works being *The Mountains of California, Our National Parks, The Yosemite,* and *My First Summer in the Sierra.*

Subject matter: family affairs (1902–13) chiefly in letters to his daughter Helen; correspondence with Enos Abijah Mills and with J. Marshall Watkins and the John Muir Association. In addition, the Library has Xerox copies of a small collection of correspondence (155 pieces, 1860–1906) of John Muir and his family, mainly letters to his brother Daniel H. Muir and from his mother. These letters may be used at the Library for reference purposes only.

Significant persons: John MUIR (24).

Physical description: letters and 2 manuscripts.

Source: gift of J. Marshall Watkins, May, 1961.

MUNRO, WILLIAM BENNETT (1875–1957)
170 pieces, 1806; 1877–1959

William Bennett Munro, historian and political scientist, was born in Ontario, Canada, in 1875, educated at Queens University (B.A. 1895, M.A. 1896, LL.B 1896) and Harvard (M.A. 1899, Ph.D. 1900), and studied in Edinburgh and Berlin before accepting a post at Williams College in 1901. From 1904 to 1929 he taught American history and government at Harvard, and wrote editorials for the *Boston Herald*. In 1929 he moved to Pasadena, California, to become a professor of history and government at the California Institute of Technology. Munro published numerous books in history and political science (specializing in municipal administration and government); served as president of the American Political Science Association (1927) and the American Association of University Professors (1929–31); was a trustee of the Huntington Library and Art Gallery, Cal Tech, and Scripps College; and was a member of the board of overseers of Harvard. He retired from teaching in 1945 but continued to be active in civic affairs. He died in Pasadena in 1957.

Subject matter: primarily letters to Munro from his academic colleagues, dealing with reactions to his research and publications, with his professional and social activities, and with the administration of universities and other institutions in which Munro was interested. A few letters after Munro's death are addressed to Prof. Harvey Eagleson concerning a memoir of Munro.

Significant persons: Charles Austin BEARD (8), Max FARRAND (5), Herbert Clark HOOVER (5), Walter LIPPMAN (7), Abbot Lawrence LOWELL (5), Robert Andrews MILLIKAN (6), and Sir George Walter PROTHERO (5).

Physical description: primarily letters, with a few manuscripts and some ephemera.

Source: gifts from Dr. and Mrs. Munro at various times after 1951.

MURRELL, GEORGE McKINLEY (1826–72)
66 pieces, 1849–54

George M. Murrell, California gold seeker, left Bowling Green, Kentucky, in 1849, accompanied by his Negro slave Reuben. They traveled by steamer on the Ohio and Missouri Rivers, and continued from Independence, Missouri, by wagon train with the Green River California Company. Murrell left the company and traveled to the Sacramento Valley by way of Lassen's Route, eventually joining the rest of the party in the mining country. He and Reuben settled in El Dorado County, where they engaged in mining and business.

Subject matter: Murrell's journey in the spring of 1849 as far as Fort Kearny, Nebraska; river travel, life along the wagon trail, wagon train organization, Indians; and in September of 1849, after his arrival in Sacramento, California, mining and business ventures in the California Gold Rush country near Coloma.

Physical description: letters and 2 photographs.

Source: gift of Clifford C. Burton, 1969.

MYRICK, HERBERT (1860–1927)
approximately 300 pieces, 1903–26

Herbert Myrick, editor and publisher, was educated at Massachusetts Agricultural College. After spending several years in Colorado, he returned to Massachusetts in 1877. He became president and editor of Phelps Publishing Company, publisher of *Good Housekeeping Magazine*, and of the Orange Judd

Company, publisher of books and articles on agricultural subjects. Myrick collected western historical material, some of which he incorporated into a novel, *Cache La Poudre*.

Subject matter: western history, mainly the Custer battle at Little Big Horn; also material dealing with T. B. Whitmore, who claimed to have witnessed the battle of the Little Big Horn with the Cheyenne Indians.

Physical description: letters, manuscripts, photographs, 1 cloth map, and a few artifacts.

Source: gift of Miss Christine Myrick, April, 1950.

N

NAST, THOMAS (1840–1902)
69 pieces, 1851–1916

Thomas Nast, cartoonist, was born in Germany in 1840, but moved six years later to New York, where he early developed an interest in drawing. Nast contributed drawings to *Frank Leslie's Illustrated Newspaper*, the *New York Illustrated News* (for which he covered the Heenan-Sayers fight in England in 1860 and Garibaldi's rebellion in Italy in the same year), and *Harper's Weekly* (in which appeared his Civil War cartoons, his attack on the "Tweed Ring," and his later political cartoons). In 1861 Nast married Sarah Edwards of New York; they lived first in New York and later in Morristown, New Jersey. His attempt at establishing his own newspaper, *Nast's Weekly* (1892–93), proved unsuccessful, and he later suffered from financial difficulties. In 1902 Theodore Roosevelt appointed him U.S. consul general at Guayaquil, Ecuador, where he died of yellow fever on December 7 of that year.

Subject matter: Nast's visit to England and Italy, trips to Washington, D.C., during Lincoln's and Grant's administrations; Nast's death at his consular post in Ecuador. Strongest for the years 1859–73 and 1902–03.

Physical description: chiefly letters, with a few documents and 1 manuscript.

Source: purchased from P. P. Appel, 1960 and William F. Kelleher, 1962.

Bibliography: some of Nast's letters have been printed in Albert Bigelow Paine, *Th. Nast. His Period and His Pictures* (New York: The Macmillan Co., 1904).

NELSON, DONALD MARR (1888–1959)
approximately 7000 pieces, 1909–50

Donald Marr Nelson, corporation executive and chairman of the War Production Board during World War II, was born in Hannibal, Missouri, in 1888 and received a B.S. degree in chemical engineering from the University of Missouri in 1911. In 1912 he moved to Chicago, Illinois, to begin a lengthy career at Sears, Roebuck & Co., serving during the 1930s as vice-president in charge of merchandising and from 1939 to 1942 as executive vice-president and chairman of the executive committee. In 1940 and 1941 Nelson helped to coordinate defense purchases for the government, and in January 1942 resigned his work at Sears to become chairman of the War Production Board, in which capacity he served until October 1944. In 1943 and 1944 he also served as President Roosevelt's personal representative to China and Russia and continued thereafter as a presidential adviser on Chinese affairs and on the Pacific Theater. At the close of the war Nelson returned to a private career as a business executive, including work for Spiegel, Inc., and moved to Los Angeles, California, where he died in 1959. He was the author of *Arsenal of Democracy*, published in 1946.

Subject matter: chiefly concerned with the organization, development, objectives, and operation of the War Production Board from 1941 to 1944. Includes departmental reports, directives, memoranda, and correspondence, over 100 lectures and addresses given by Nelson on behalf of wartime production, and material relating to wartime industrial production and to the relation of the Board with other governmental agencies. Also includes prewar and postwar material relating to merchandising and to Sears, Roebuck & Co. and Spiegel, Inc., and a few papers relating to Nelson's two trips to China in 1944.

Physical description: letters, manuscripts, and documents, many of which (particularly War Production Board reports and directives) are mimeographed; 31 scrapbooks of newspaper clippings and photographs relating to the War Production Board; some family photographs, and other ephemera.

Source: acquired from Mrs. Donald M. Nelson, 1961.

NEVADA MINING COMPANIES (Savage, and Hale and Norcross Silver Mining Companies)
approximately 12,000 pieces, 1862–1901

The rush to mine the Comstock Lode in Nevada during the two decades after 1860 brought about a proliferation of mining companies whose shafts and tunnels interlaced the mountainside behind Virginia City. One of the earlier successful mines was the Savage, first supervised by Robert Morrow. The mine commenced producing in 1863, yielding over $3,000,000 worth of ore for the next two years, and almost $8,000,000 at its peak from 1865 to 1869. The Bank of California combine of William Sharon, William C. Ralston, and Darius O. Mills initially controlled the majority of the mining operations in the Comstock, but were challenged from within their own ranks by John P. Jones and Alvinza Hayward, who had acquired ownership of the Crown Point Mine in 1870. Jones and Hayward then gained control of the Savage in 1871, but the boom collapsed when Hayward manipulated the stock of the mine. The Hale and Norcross Mine, also controlled by the Bank of California combine, was producing $2,000,000 worth of ore in 1866–67, but its stock fell rapidly in 1868. James Fair, who had been involved in the management for a short time in 1867, returned in 1868 and persuaded John Mackay and James Flood to challenge Sharon's ownership. The future Bonanza Kings (Fair, Flood, and Mackay) succeeded in buying up the stock and in taking control of the Hale and Norcross in 1869, and the mine prospered until 1872. Many of the Comstock mines continued to operate for several years, but never again produced the wealth that flowed during the boom of 1860–80.

Subject matter: legal and business affairs of the Savage Mining Co. and the Hale and Norcross Mining Co., including such items as receipts and disbursements, payrolls, bank books, time books, stockholders' statements and accounts, reports on ore extracted, and assays, vouchers, etc. Also includes letters to mining superintendents, a few pertaining to the mining town of Bodie, California, and some material concerning operations of the U.S. Mint in Carson City, Nevada (1888–98).

Physical description: letters and documents, including 27 bound volumes.

Source: purchased from William P. Wreden, August, 1961.

NEVADA RAILROADS COLLECTION
approximately 9000 pieces, 1862–1950

The Nevada Railroads Collection contains material relating to railroads built in Nevada and eastern California in connection with the Comstock Lode in Virginia City, Nevada, and other mining booms in Nevada and California, mainly in the period from 1870 to 1890. It includes papers concerning the Virginia and Truckee Railroad, the Carson and Colorado Railroad, the Carson and Tahoe Lumber and Fluming Company, and the Lake Tahoe Railway and Transportation Company. The Virginia and Truckee Railroad, which ran from Virginia City to Reno, Nevada, was incorporated in 1868 by the principals of the Bank of California, Darius O. Mills, William C. Ralston, and William Sharon, manager of the Virginia City branch. The banking combine became the owner of mines and mills by absorbing into their own Union Mill and Mining Company those independent companies which defaulted to the bank. The railroad was built to reduce the costs of hauling ore from the mines to the mills and to bring lumber to Virginia City. The railroad company, managed by H. M. Yerington, ran its first train in 1869, and was in full operation from Virginia City to Reno by 1872. After the decrease of mining activity, the line was abandoned from Virginia City to Carson City in 1938, and finally ceased operation in 1950. The narrow-gauge Carson and Colorado Railroad was built in 1880 as an adjunct to the Virginia and Truckee Railroad. It ran from Mound House, near Carson City, to Hawley (later Keeler), California, connecting mining towns in Nevada and eastern California. The line was sold to the Southern Pacific Railroad in 1900. The Carson and Tahoe Lumber and Fluming Company was formed in 1873 by Mills, Yerington, and Duane L. Bliss to assure a lumber supply for the mines of the Comstock. A narrow-gauge railroad, the Lake Tahoe Railroad, was built as part of the operation in 1875. When it closed in 1898, the equipment was used to build the Lake Tahoe Railway and Transportation Company, incorporated by the Bliss family. The train operated as a tourist line from Truckee to Lake Tahoe, California, until its purchase by the Southern Pacific Railroad in 1925.

Subject matter: the railroad, mining, and lumber industries, chiefly the Virginia and Truckee Railroad, including correspondence, business papers, and operating statistics from 1862 to 1950; also letters and business papers of the Carson and Colorado Railroad (1880–1900); the Carson and Tahoe Lumber and Fluming Company (1870–1910); and the Lake Tahoe Railroad and Transportation Company (1907–10).

Significant persons: James Graham FAIR (5), Darius Ogden MILLS (10), William SHARON (21), Henry Marvin YERINGTON (8).

Physical description: letters, documents, 15 volumes, and 5 maps.

Source: purchased from H. A. Levinson, February, 1963.

NEVINS, ALLAN (1890–1971)
approximately 7800 pieces, ca.1950–72

Allan Nevins, American historian, was born in Illinois in 1890 and received an A.B. and M.A. from the University of Illinois and an M.A. from Oxford. After several years on the editorial staffs of various New York newspapers, Nevins became professor of American history at Cornell in 1927–28, and moved the following year to Columbia University, where he remained for the next thirty years. He was senior research associate at the Huntington Library from 1958 to 1969, during which time he completed his eight-volume series, *Ordeal of the Union.* Nevins was also noted for his biographies of Hamilton Fish, Henry Ford, John D. Rockefeller, and other important American figures, for beginning Columbia's influential oral history program, and for his attempt to bridge the gap between professional and popular historians. He twice received the Pulitzer Prize.

Subject matter: Nevins and the study of American history, with particular reference to the writing and publication of *The Organized War, 1863–1864,* the third volume in the *Ordeal of the Union* series; primarily Nevins' notes and drafts for this volume, with some manuscript lectures and professional correspondence.

Significant persons: John Edwin BAKELESS (8), Fred Delbert SCHWENGEL (6), Arnold TOYNBEE (8), and the publishing firm CHARLES SCRIBNER'S SONS (9).

Physical description: letters and manuscripts.

Source: gift of Mrs. Dorothy Graham, the daughter of Nevins' secretary, Mrs. Lillian K. Bean, October, 1976.

NEW ALMADEN MINE
45 pieces, 1853–86

The New Almaden Mine, the mercury mine in Santa Clara County, California, named for the Almaden Mine in Spain, ranked behind it as third richest in the world in extent and quality. For forty-five years the New Almaden produced an almost constant yield. The mine was visited in 1846 by Andrés Castillero, an engineer and representative of the Mexican government, who formed the New Almaden Company, composed of several part-owners. An official survey of the property was not made until after the Civil War, and title to it had passed through several hands when the New Almaden Company brought its petition before the U.S. Land Commission in 1852. Litigation continued for twelve years, eventually reaching the U.S. Supreme Court. In 1857 the firm of Halleck, Peachy and Billings defended the New Almaden Mine Company against U.S. government charges that Castillero's claims were fraudulent. Government counsel Edmund Randolph's success helped bring about the verdict finally given in favor of the government in 1864, in a case in which even President Abraham Lincoln had at one time intervened. Although the claims of the Quicksilver Mining Company of New York, which had acquired partial title to the mine, were upheld by the ruling in favor of the government, public opinion forced the New York company to purchase the assets of the New Almaden Company. The Quicksilver Mining Company continued to operate the mine successfully until 1890, followed by a period of gradual decline and bankruptcy in 1912.

Subject matter: operation and business affairs of the New Almaden Mine, including legal documents (some concerning the land ownership case), reports on production and business accounts of the New Almaden Mine (1868–86), reports to directors of the Quicksilver Mining Company (1868–86), and correspondence relating to the mine.

Physical description: letters and documents (including 1 volume).

Source: acquired from various sources, 1954–69.

NEW YORK. DUTCHESS COUNTY. COMMITTEE OF SAFETY
[Minute Book of the Committee for the Northeast Precinct of Dutchess County] (1778)
MS. volume 33 leaves

Covers the period from January 20 to April 6.

NEWCOMB-JOHNSON COLLECTION
111 pieces, 1769–1863

Daniel Newcomb, schoolmaster and lawyer, was born in Massachusetts in 1746 and had moved to Keene, New Hampshire, to practice law by 1778. His son, Henry S. Newcomb, was a naval lieutenant during the War of 1812 and died in 1825. Daniel's daughter Patty married first, by 1825, Dr. Marlin Johnson and moved to Middlebury, Ohio, where her husband died in 1827, leaving his widow and a son, Henry N. Johnson. She then married, before 1835, David Garrett of Middlebury, and the family moved to Cleveland by 1844. Henry N. Johnson graduated from Western Reserve College, studied law, taught school in Louisiana, and returned to Cleveland, Ohio, where he was admitted to the bar in 1851 and became active in civic affairs.

Subject matter: the numerous members of the Johnson and Newcomb families and their in-laws, and particularly letters to and from Patty (Newcomb) Johnson Garrett and her son Henry Johnson; chiefly family affairs and local gossip.

Physical description: primarily letters, with a few manuscripts and documents, also newspaper clippings and other ephemera.

Source: acquired from N. A. Kovach, 1953.

NEWMAN, EMMA E. (ca.1835–1921?)
approximately 200 pieces, ca.1845–1921

Emma E. Newman (Mrs. Nicholas Newman-Emerson), minister and "Christian metaphysician," grew up in Massachusetts, where she attended the Abbot Academy in Andover. She was a minister at the Congregational Church in Algonquin, Illinois, in 1876, and as a "mental healer" practiced in the middle-western states before moving, about 1896, to California, where she lived in Garvanza and Sierra Madre.

Subject matter: Emma Newman's life, ministry, and religious beliefs, chiefly as seen in her diaries, commonplace books, lectures, and sermons.

Physical description: chiefly manuscripts (including 29 volumes of diaries, notes, and records of "physical ministrations,"), with a few letters and some ephemera.

Source: acquired from Mrs. Martha Caroline Pritchard, December, 1949.

NICHOLS, JOSEPH (fl. 1758–66)
[Military Journal of the Massachusetts Provincial Forces During the Expedition to Ticonderoga] (1758–66)
Autograph MS.S. volume 130 pp.

Covers the period from March 27, 1758 to May 12, 1766.

NICHOLS, SAMUEL S. (d. 1850)
approximately 53 pieces, 1753–1890

Samuel Nichols, California gold seeker, left Buffalo, New York, with his son George to journey overland to California in 1849. After George's death, near Independence, Missouri, Samuel returned home, then resumed his trip to California by the Panama route in 1850. He died of cholera in Sacramento in the fall of the same year.

Subject matter: the preparation for and beginning of an overland journey in 1849; a sea voyage to San Francisco via Panama in 1850; also a diary (1821–22) and autobiography (1821) written by Benjamin Hodge (q.v.) of Buffalo, New York, a relative of a member of the Nichols family.

Physical description: letters, documents, and manuscripts (including 1 diary).

Source: purchased from Mary E. Nichols, May, 1936.

NICHOLSON, GRACE (1877–1948)
approximately 2560 pieces, 1822–1951

Grace Nicholson, Pasadena, California, dealer in North American Indian and Chinese art, came to California from Philadelphia in 1901. She soon began collecting American Indian baskets and other artifacts, opening a small studio and shop in Pasadena in 1902. During her extensive travels visiting the Indians of the American Far West she kept diaries and notes on Indian lore. She gave many pieces of American Indian work to leading museums in the U.S. After a trip to the Orient in 1929, her long-time interest in Oriental art was renewed, and she turned almost exclusively to collecting Oriental art. She designed a building which was an authentic replica of a Chinese temple, and had it built in Pasadena in 1929 for the display of her Oriental art objects. Miss Nicholson gave the building to the city of Pasadena in 1943. It was leased by the Pasadena Art Institute (later the Pasadena Art Museum) until 1971, when it became the Pacificulture-Asia Museum.

Subject matter: business and personal correspondence, notes on Oriental art, American Indians of various tribes in California, Oregon, Washington, Arizona, and New Mexico, travel in the Orient and American West, construction of the gallery in Pasadena. Strongest for the period 1902–48.

Significant persons: Avery BRUNDAGE (12), George Byron GORDON (10), Grace Carpenter HUDSON (58), Otis Tufton MASON (10).

Physical description: letters, manuscripts (including 11 diaries), documents, and photographs (in Rare Book Department).

Source: gift of Thyra H. Maxwell, October, 1968.

NICHOLSON, JOHN PAGE (1842–1922)
995 pieces, 1861–1921

John Page Nicholson, Civil War veteran and manuscript collector, was born in Philadelphia in 1822. During the Civil War he served as regimental quartermaster with the 28th Pennsylvania Infantry regiment during Sherman's March to the Sea and through the Carolinas, and was breveted lieutenant colonel in 1865. On his return to Philadelphia Nicholson began a huge collection of books and manuscripts relating to the military history of the Civil War, and was the editor and translator of volumes three and four of the Comte de Paris' *History of the Civil War in America.* He also served as recorder in chief of the Military Order of the Loyal Legion of the U.S. from 1885 until his death in 1922.

Subject matter: military history of the Civil War, including contemporary dispatches, reports, diaries, maps, and records of individual actions and campaigns as well as later letters and memoirs containing reminiscences and accounts of activity during the war.

Significant persons: James BEALE (95), Daniel BUTTER-FIELD (6), David McMurtie GREGG (26), Winfield Scott HANCOCK (10), Joseph Eggleston JOHNSTON (10), Abraham LINCOLN (5), James LONGSTREET (6), George Brinton McCLELLAN (5), Louis Philippe Albert D'ORLEANS, Comte de Paris (7), Fitz-John PORTER (10), John McAllister SCHOFIELD (5), William Tecumseh SHERMAN (8), Daniel Edgar SICKLES (8), and Francis Amasa WALKER (7).

Physical description: chiefly letters and documents, with some manuscripts (including 3 journals and diaries and 36 military maps). 70 volumes.

Source: purchased from Mrs. Gertrude M. Nicholson (widow of John Page Nicholson), 1922.

NOREN, C.A. (fl. 1930s)
approximately 300 pieces, 1932–39

C. A. Noren was a collector of, and dealer in, minerals in Fresno, California.

Subject matter: mostly inquiries about and information pertaining to California minerals, many from universities and museums.

Physical description: letters.

Source: acquired from Patterson, September, 1966.

NORRIS, ISAAC (1701–66)
[Journal and Account Book] (1733–49)
Autograph MS. volume 119 pp.

Particularly significant for the Albany Indian conference of 1746.

NORTH, JOHN WESLEY (1815–90)
approximately 1400 pieces, 1849–1947

John Wesley North, lawyer, politician, industrialist, and pioneer colonizer, was born in New York. As a young man, he taught school, became an ardent abolitionist, and attended a seminary before his graduation from Wesleyan University in 1841. He practiced law in New York, and, at various times during his career, in Minnesota, Nevada, and California. He became active in politics, holding many Republican Party offices, and was appointed surveyor general (1861) and associate justice of the Supreme Court (1862) of the Territory of Nevada by President Lincoln. North was instrumental in the settlement of St. Anthony, later Minneapolis (1849), and Northfield (1855), Minnesota, and Washoe City, Nevada (1861), before his interest in business opportunities and social reform in the postwar South led him to take his family to Knoxville, Tennessee. Following political harassment and the failure of his southern enterprises, he organized the Southern California Colony Association, and brought members from Chicago to settle the town of Riverside, California. After North was forced to give up his leadership of the colony, he practiced law in San Francisco for a short time, then promoted the founding of Oleander, near Fresno, California, where he died in 1890.

Subject matter: early history and settlement of Minneapolis and Northfield, Minnesota (1849–61); pioneer life in Nevada (1861–65); southern reconstruction in Tennessee (1865–69); the promotion of the settlement of Riverside, California and in Fresno County, California (1870–90)

Physical description: letters, manuscripts, 1 letter book, and 1 photograph album.

Source: purchased from Mary North Shepard, June, 1945, and gift of Anne North Shepard, August, 1955.

Bibliography: much of the material has been published in Merlin Stonehouse, *John Wesley North and the Reform Frontier* (Minneapolis: University of Minnesota Press, 1965).

NOURSE, GEORGE FRANCIS (1831–66?)
42 pieces, 1848–60

George F. Nourse, early California resident, came to California in 1849, seeking gold. He arrived in San Francisco on the brig "Sterling," and worked for Ritchie, Osgood and Co. and the Mercantile Hotel. In 1853 he, George W. Hedges, and Lathiel L. Chace bought a ranch, the "Oasis Rancho," in Santa Clara County. Nourse returned to the mines at various times, and from 1877 to 1886 was again living in San Francisco.

Subject matter: news, in letters to Nourse, of Boston and Beverly, Massachusetts, the temperance movement in 1849 in Massachusetts, the sale of the cargo of the Brig "Sterling," and some information on the "Oasis Rancho" in Santa Clara County.

Physical description: letters.

Source: purchased from Edwin Grabhorn, January, 1945.

NOWLAND, JAMES (1810?–86?)
69 pieces, 1847–1924

James Nowland, of Liverpool, England, moved to the U.S. before 1848 and became a farmer in Houlton, Maine, where his first wife died in 1848. Financial problems caused him to sell his farm in 1854, and by 1856 he had taken a post as a clerk in the shipping office of a timber firm in Saint John, New Brunswick. At the outbreak of the Civil War Nowland left Canada, joined the 15th Maine Volunteer regiment, and served in the Mobile Bay (Alabama) area until 1863. He then resigned his commission as adjutant and returned to farming in Ashland, Maine, where he died shortly after November, 1885.

Subject matter: Nowland's life in Houlton and Saint John and the difficulties of farming; his wartime service, dealing with a soldier's daily life and giving some information about troop movements; and, after 1879, his old age and family.

Physical description: chiefly letters, with a few documents.

Source: acquired from Helen Nowland (granddaughter), 1960.

NUTT, RUSH (1781–1837)
approximately 1000 pieces, 1805–1933

Dr. Rush Nutt, southern planter, physician, and traveler, left his birthplace in Virginia to study medicine at the University of Pennsylvania under Dr. Benjamin Rush. He received his degree about 1801, and in 1805, after returning home to Virginia, started West on horseback, settling in Jefferson County, Mississippi, where he began the practice of medicine. Dr. Nutt bought a plantation and was successful in the application of scientific principles to agriculture and in the development of a

269

new brand of cotton seed. He also wrote about his extensive travels in the United States and abroad. His son, Dr. Haller Nutt (1816–64), after receiving his medical degree at the University of Louisville, joined his father in the management of the plantation. Haller Nutt was also interested in scientific investigations in agriculture and worked with his father in the improvement of the cotton gin. The son's octagonal plantation house, "Longwood," designed by Philadelphia architect Samuel Sloan, was left unfinished with the outbreak of the Civil War, and Dr. Haller Nutt died at the age of 48, his health broken by the losses suffered in the war.

Subject matter: cotton culture, manufacture, and trade; slaves; plantation life; medicine; early Civil War events; and the construction of Longwood Plantation House, mainly within the years 1817–62. Also religion, and a variety of scientific subjects.

Physical description: letters, manuscripts, and documents.

Source: purchased from James E. Smalldon, 1964 and 1971.

O

ODDIE, TASKER LOWNDES (1870–1950)
5783 pieces, 1864–1914

Tasker L. Oddie, Nevada governor and U.S. senator, was a native of New York, where he studied law and was admitted to the bar in 1895. After coming to Nevada in 1898, he engaged in mining, agricultural, and livestock interests. Oddie was instrumental in the development of the Tonopah and Goldfield silver and gold mining districts. He entered politics in 1901 as a Republican, served as governor of Nevada from 1910 to 1914, supported Theodore Roosevelt's Progressive party, and was elected U.S. senator from 1921 to 1933.

Subject matter: mining, politics, and government in Nevada (including divorce laws), women's rights, the financial panic of 1907, Roosevelt and the Progressive party, and the Panama–Pacific International Exposition of 1915. Strongest for the years 1873 and 1910–14.

Significant persons: James H. HAWLEY (7).

Physical description: letters, documents, and one scrapbook, with ephemera.

Source: purchased from Grahame H. Hardy, January, 1953.

O'FARRELL, JASPER (1817–75)
76 pieces, ca.1845–1924<

Jasper O'Farrell, pioneer California politician and surveyor, was born in Ireland, where he received an education in civil engineering. In 1841 he joined a surveying expedition to South America and spent a year in Chile before his arrival in San Francisco in 1843. O'Farrell was employed as a surveyor by the Mexican authorities from 1844 to 1846, continued in government service under American rule, and made an official survey of San Francisco in 1847. He later engaged in mining on the Yuba River and in farming, ranching, and surveying in Sonoma County. He was active in politics, and was elected state senator from Sonoma and Mendocino Counties. O'Farrell died in San Francisco at the age of fifty-eight.

Subject matter: personal, business, and political matters (1846–75); rough survey notes and a few sketch maps of California ranchos and towns (ca.1845–ca.1850); and land papers pertaining to O'Farrell's property in Sonoma County (1855–70).

Physical description: letters, documents, 7 sketches, maps, and 1 manuscript.

Source: purchased from Edwin Grabhorn, January, 1945.

OJAI FESTIVALS, LTD.
approximately 9110 pieces, 1946–53

The Ojai Festivals, Ltd., was an organization founded in 1946 by John Leopold Jurgens Bauer for the production of annual music, theater, and dance festivals at Ojai, California, and was patterned after the Salzburg and similar festivals in Europe.

Subject matter: the years of the Ojai Festival under the directorship of John Bauer: correspondence with sponsors and patrons, artists and their managers; financial records, publicity material, programs, and records of projects in other cities.

Significant persons: Aaron COPLAND (5), Lotte LEHMANN (9), William Grant STILL (6), William STEINBERG (17), Bruno WALTER (14).

Physical description: letters, documents, manuscripts, 10 scrapbooks, and photographs.

Source: gift of Mr. and Mrs. John J. L. Bauer, June, 1955.

OLIVER, PETER (1713–91)
Origin and Progress of the American Rebellion in the Year 1776, in a Letter to a Friend (ca.1825)
MS. volume 496 pp.

A late variant of a Loyalist narrative published in *Peter Oliver's Origin & Progress of the American Rebellion: A Tory View*, ed. Douglass Adair and John A. Schutz (San Marino: Huntington Library, 1961).

OLIVER-GOWEN COLLECTION
approximately 1100 pieces, 1833–1928

Frederick Oliver (d. 1883) of Quebec, Canada, served as secretary and treasurer of the Megantic Mining Company, and, together with his brother-in-law Hammond Gowen and associates such as Dr. James Douglas, also of Quebec, was involved in various projects for developing the mines and mineral resources of the area. After Oliver's death his widow, Dame Charlotte Maria (Gowen) Oliver, moved to Toronto; her investments and other business affairs were handled by her son-in-law Edward Holloway.

Subject matter: business affairs of Frederick Oliver, James Douglas, Charlotte Maria (Gowen) Oliver, and Edward Holloway; the sale, purchase, or lease of lands involved in mining; mining and assay reports; and private financial and legal affairs of the Gowen and Oliver families.

Physical description: chiefly documents and letters, including 6 volumes of memoranda, diaries, and letterbooks, and a 1833 journal of a trip across New York. Also includes a few mining sketch maps and some ephemera.

Source: acquired from R. R. Oliver, 1957.

O'NEIL, HUGH F. (1901– ?)
55 pieces, 1857–1937

A collection of miscellaneous papers regarding Utah, including typescripts of oral interviews and reminiscences, mainly concerning Utah and Mormon history, assembled by Hugh F. O'Neil, editor of a Works Progress Administration Historical Records Survey.

Physical description: letters, manuscripts, and documents.

Source: gift of Hugh F. O'Neil, June, 1942.

ORANGE COUNTY (CALIFORNIA) LAND PAPERS
approximately 1200 pieces, 1887–1915

Orange County, California, was created in 1889 from part of Los Angeles County, and was named for the orange groves which were a predominant agricultural feature of the area. The county seat is Santa Ana. The earliest settlement in the county was at Mission San Juan Capistrano in 1776, and much of the land in Orange County, acquired by Spanish and Mexican grants, changed hands frequently. The predecessors of the Orange County Title Company, consolidated in 1894, transcribed the complete record of all Los Angeles County documents pertaining to Orange County land titles at the time of the county's creation.

Subject matter: land ownership and transfers in Orange County, California, mainly by the Orange County Title Company of Santa Ana.

Physical description: letters, documents, and maps.

Source: gift of Wayne Gibson, February and August, 1974.

ORCUTT, CHARLES RUSSELL (1864–1929)
642 pieces, 1882–99

Charles R. Orcutt, botanist and editor, came to San Diego in 1879 from his birthplace in Vermont. His father established the Orcutt Seed and Plant Company near the ruins of the San Diego mission. From an early age he collected and studied plants, making many contributions to the Smithsonian Institution during his lifetime. He was also interested in the study of shells. Orcutt edited the *American Botanist* (1898–1900), *American Plants* (1907–10), and *The West American Scientist* (1884–1919). He died in Haiti in 1929.

Subject matter: mostly the flora of California and Mexico, in letters to Orcutt.

Significant persons: Asa GRAY (17), Edward Lee GREENE (8), George Frederick KUNZ (24), Charles Christopher PARRY (48), George VASEY (27), Sereno WATSON (15).

Physical description: letters, documents, and manuscripts.

Source: purchased from W. T. Genns, August, 1959.

OSBORN, LUTHER (fl. 1864–65)
approximately 380 pieces, 1864–65

Captain Luther Osborn served as quartermaster of Company "H" of the 22nd U.S. Colored Infantry, which served in Virginia, Maryland, and Texas during the last two years of the Civil War.

Subject matter: regimental administrative matters: muster rolls, requisitions, and returns of clothing, camp, and garrison equipment.

Physical description: documents, mostly printed forms filled in.

Source: acquired from Katherine Osborn, August, 1939.

OVERLAND MAIL COLLECTION
166 pieces, 1850–98

The Butterfield Overland Mail Company, organized in 1857, carried mail along the southern route between St. Louis and San Francisco until the outbreak of the Civil War, when Confederate disruptions caused it to be moved north to the central overland route. It was known as the Central Overland and Pike's Peak Express Company until, in a reorganization of the company, General Bela M. Hughes was elected president of the Overland Mail Company in 1861. The collection is composed of two sections. The first part (seventy-five pieces, 1850–67) contains the papers of Hiram S. Rumfield, an officer of the Overland Mail Company, who began as a mail agent at Fort Smith, Arkansas, in 1860, and was then transferred to the Salt Lake City office as assistant treasurer of the company from 1861 to 1866. Rumfield was greatly concerned with the problems of the Indians in Utah Territory. The second section (ninety pieces, 1880–98) contains the papers of L. P. Williamson of Independence, Missouri, superintendent of the North Western Overland Mail Company and president of the Western Mail and Stage Company in 1884.

Subject matter: Section I: Rumfield family matters, business affairs of the Overland Mail Company, the condition of Indians in Utah Territory. Section II: reports from stage drivers concerning conditions on the road and business policies of the North Western Overland Mail Company.

Physical description: letters, documents, 1 manuscript, 2 photographs, and a scrapbook of newspaper clippings (1865–66).

Source: purchased from H. C. Revercomb, June, 1946.

OWEN, ALBERT KIMSEY (1840–1916<)
320 pieces, 1885–1909

Albert K. Owen, civil engineer and utopian reformer, was the son of a Quaker physician. In 1873, on a surveying trip to Mexico for the future Mexican Central Railroad, he first saw Topolobampo Bay, Sinaloa. Owen dreamed of a railroad linking the U.S. through Texas to this Mexican port as the shortest distance to the Orient for American products, and planned a cooperative colony to be founded on the rich agricultural land nearby. When the Mexican government granted him permission to form the Texas, Topolobampo & Pacific Railway and Telegraph Company in 1881, and the first colonists began to arrive in 1886, Owen's dream seemed to be realized. Little progress was made on the railroad, however, and it was not until 1961 under President López Mateos that the line linking Chihuahua and northern Mexico to the Pacific Coast finally was completed over the Sierra Madre range. The agricultural colony eventually failed when the members were divided in their views on the ownership of land and water rights. In addition to his activities in Mexico, Owen wrote books and articles on a variety of subjects, including cooperatives, woman suffrage, and currency questions.

Subject matter: rise and fall of the Topolobampo utopian colony in Sinaloa, Mexico (1886–ca.1903), and railroad development in Mexico under the regime of Porfirio Díaz.

Physical description: documents and letters (mainly contemporary copies, some in Spanish).

Source: purchased from Ray Reynolds, 1964 and 1974.

P

PACIFIC MAIL STEAMSHIP COMPANY
approximately 190,550 pieces, 1851–1925

The Pacific Mail Steamship Company was incorporated in 1848 to engage in the steamship business after receiving a contract from the United States government to provide mail service between Panama and the Oregon coast. The organizer and first president of the company was William H. Aspinwall, a wealthy New York merchant and exporter-importer. The company had three ships built to begin the operation. The first, the "California," reached San Francisco in February, 1849, and a fleet of three steamships was in full operation from June of that year. The company prospered as a result of business from the California, Fraser River (British Columbia), and Klondike gold rushes, and added sixty steamers between 1860 and 1875. After 1867, the Pacific Mail Steamship Company entered the trans-Pacific trade and by 1876 there were thirty-three steamers sailing between the United States and the Orient, calling at forty-seven ports in the Pacific. The Occidental and Oriental Steamship Company, formed in 1874 by western railroad interests in order to gain control of trans-Pacific shipping, was eventually merged with the Pacific Mail Steamship Company in 1900.

Subject matter: business operations (1851–1925) of the Pacific Mail Steamship Company; articles of incorporation, by-laws, minutes of directors meetings, etc., of the Occidental and Oriental Steamship Company (1874–1908).

Physical description: letters and documents, including 640 volumes of ledgers, journals, logs, and cash books.

Source: gift of the Pacific Mail Steamship Company, 1937–38.

PARK, ALICE LOCKE (1861–ca.1950)
795 pieces, 1798–1953

Alice Locke Park, feminist, reformer, and pacifist, was born in Boston in 1861 but lived most of her life in California. She was active in both national and international organizations for the improvement of prison conditions, labor laws, humane education, wild life conservation, and the preservation of natural resources. Her primary interest, however, was in women's rights and she was assistant director of the Susan B. Anthony Memorial Committee. She wrote and promoted the California law, adopted in 1913, granting to women equal rights of guardianship over their children.

Subject matter: family matters and Alice Park's reforming interests, centering on the cause of women's rights and including papers relating to the passage of a constitutional amendment granting suffrage to women. Also includes her autobiography and a biographical sketch of Katherine Marie ("Kitty") Marion. Strongest for the period 1902–20.

Significant persons: Frederick BAKER (14), Alice Stone BLACKWELL (7), Henry Brown BLACKWELL (6), Clara (Shortridge) FOLTZ (12), Ida (Husted) HARPER (6), Mary McHenry KEITH (13), Sofia M. LOEBING (14), Katherine Marie ("Kitty") MARION (25), Frances MUNDS (10), Estelle Sylvia PANKHURST (23), Agnes E. RYAN (17), Henry Stephens SALT (31), Ellen Clark SARGEANT (42), Caroline M. S. SEVERANCE (14), and Elizabeth Lowe WATSON (16).

279

Physical description: chiefly correspondence, with some documents and a few manuscripts.

Source: acquired as part of the Susan B. Anthony Memorial Collections, donated between 1945 and 1956.

PARKER, ELY SAMUEL (1828–95)
135 pieces, 1802–94

Ely Samuel Parker, full-blooded Seneca Indian and sachem of the Six Nations, was born in 1828 in Indian Falls, New York, and grew up on a reservation while attending a Baptist mission school. From 1846 to 1886 he represented his race in the prosecution of Indian claims, and actively championed their cause against removal to the West. During the Civil War Parker served as Grant's military secretary, and won the brevet appointment of brigadier general. He was appointed commissioner of Indian affairs in 1869, but was forced by political enemies to resign in 1871. In later years Parker ventured into business, with mixed results, and held positions on the New York Police Department.

Subject matter: deals primarily with the Seneca Indians of western New York, and in general with Indian political and cultural affairs. Includes a census of Seneca Indians 1855–57, a list of Indians of the Six Nations who fought in the war of 1812, and a dictionary of the Seneca language; also the papers of Parker's brother Nicholson Henry Parker (d. 1892), who served for many years as an official interpreter for the U.S. government.

Physical description: chiefly letters, with documents and manuscripts.

Source: acquired from Arthur C. Parker, grandson of Nicholson Henry Parker, through Walter C. Wyman, 1920.

PARKER, LUCIEN B. (fl. 1834–66)
50 pieces, 1834–66

Lucien B. Parker was a resident of Clarendon, Vermont.

Subject matter: family matters; a few letters from the Parkers' soldier-son pertaining to Mexico, the Mexican War, and General Gideon Johnson Pillow.

Physical description: letters.

Source: acquired through C. F. Heartman, 1937.

PARSONS, GEOFFREY (1879–1956)
61 pieces, 1876–1937

Geoffrey Parsons, newspaperman and author, was born in 1879, received a B.A. from Columbia in 1899, and worked with the *New York Evening Sun* and *New York Tribune* before becoming, in 1924, chief editorial writer of the *New York Herald Tribune.* Parsons occupied this last position until his retirement in 1952, and was awarded the Pulitzer Prize for journalism in 1942. He was also the author of *Land of Fair Play* (1919) and *Stream of History* (1928), and in 1929, with the encouragement of the Columbia historian Allan Nevins and the publishing firm of Dodd, Mead & Co., began research for a biography of President William McKinley, never completed.

Subject matter: primarily Parsons' correspondence with Nevins, with Frank C. Dodd, and with potential sources of information for the projected McKinley biography. Includes a few personal papers, one McKinley letter, a report of McKinley's speech to the Hayes Club in 1876, and extracts from a diary of Charles G. Dawes (regarding McKinley's assassination) and

281

from U.S. State Department dispatches (concerning the Spanish-American War.)

Significant persons: Allan NEVINS (7).

Physical description: letters (many of which are typewritten carbon copies), with a few printed pamphlets and newspaper clippings.

Source: acquired from Mrs. John C. Long, February, 1964.

PARTEARROYO, JOSÉ MARÍA GIL DE (1811–68<)
162 pieces, 1826–68

José María Gil de Partearroyo, Mexican brigadier general and minister of war and navy, was born in Mexico City and attended military school before entering military service at an early age. He was commissioned second lieutenant by Guadalupe Victoria in 1827, captain by Anastasio Bustamante in 1832, served in the Mexican–U.S. war of 1845–48 as colonel, and was promoted to the rank of brigadier general in 1853 for his services in that war. Sympathetic to the Liberal cause of Benito Juárez during the War of the Reforma (1857–59) and the three-year war known as the European Intervention of 1860–62 which followed, he was offered the position of minister of war and navy to fill the vacancy left in 1859 by Santos Degollado, and was officially sworn in on January 9, 1860. Unhappy in the position, Gil de Partearroyo submitted his resignation in April of the same year to President Benito Juárez, who accepted very reluctantly, but appointed him brigadier general and director of the artillery corps. Three years later, in May, 1863, Gil de Partearroyo retired from military service to attend to his own affairs, although he was only fifty-one years of age and his country was at war (French Intervention, 1862–67). He had served for thirty-nine years.

Subject matter: chiefly military matters dealing with the Mexican War, 1845–48, the War of the Reforma, 1857–59, the

European Intervention, 1860–62, and with Benito Juárez and Miguel Miramón.

Physical description: letters and documents (in Spanish).

Source: purchased from Mr. and Mrs. W. R. Holman, February, 1959.

PASADENA ORANGE GROWERS' ASSOCIATION
approximately 3,500 pieces, 1893–1938

The Pasadena Fruit Growers' Association was formed in 1893 to provide centralized marketing for the produce of the members of the organization. The name was changed to the Pasadena Orange Growers' Association in 1898. The first packing plant was located on California Street in Pasadena until 1913, when a new building was erected on South Marengo Avenue. The organization prospered, realizing a profit of $200,000 in the years 1916–17.

Subject matter: letters, etc., of Orrin Peck and his sister, Miss sociation, its organization, operation, and accounts.

Physical description: letters and documents.

Source: gift of the Pasadena Orange Growers' Association, 1938.

PASCAL, CHARLES LACROIX (fl. 1860–68)
275 pieces, 1836–90

Charles Lacroix Pascal, of the firm of Sullenden and Pascal, lived in Philadelphia during the Civil War and developed a new design of army hat, which he attempted to have adopted by the Union army in 1861 and 1862. Pascal's two nephews,

Amos and Charles Holahan, both served with the Pennsylvania Cavalry. About 1864 Pascal began to collect autographs of Civil War officers and government officials.

Subject matter: Pascal's army hats and his nephews' careers; mostly autographs of Civil War generals and lesser officers, both Union and Confederate, along with governors of states and other civilian officials. Only a few of the letters have substantive content, most having been written in response to requests for autographs.

Physical description: letters, with a few documents. Many of the letters have been mounted for scrapbooks, and some include photographs or etchings of their authors. Also included is one album containing newspaper clippings, etchings, and copies of letters of prominent Civil War generals. Additional photographs acquired with the collection have been transferred to the portrait collection in the Library's Rare Book Department.

Source: unknown.

PEALE, CHARLES WILLSON (1741–1827)
[Military Journal] (1776–77)
Autograph MS. volume 17 leaves

Kept while on duty with the Philadelphia Militia during Washington's retreat through the Jerseys, December 4, 1776 to January 20, 1777. Published in Horace W. Sellers, "Charles Willson Peale: Artist-Soldier," *Pennsylvania Magazine of History and Biography*, 38(1914): 271–86.

PECK, ORRIN M. (1860–1921)
approximately 3000 pieces, 1878–ca.1948

Orrin M. Peck, California artist, was born in New York and in 1862 came to San Francisco with his family. His mother had met Phoebe (Apperson) Hearst on the boat trip to California, and Orrin became a close friend of her son, William Randolph Hearst. Peck studied art in Munich, where he became an accomplished portrait and landscape painter. He later painted portraits of Mrs. Hearst and William Randolph Hearst. Peck returned to San Francisco from Munich periodically, then stayed permanently after the outbreak of World War I. He was with Hearst in New York and Florida before being hired to design the landscaping for the San Simeon home of Hearst in California in 1920. Peck died suddenly in Los Angeles in 1921.

Subject matter: letters, etc., of Orrin Peck and his sister, Miss Janet Peck, many relating to Phoebe (Apperson) Hearst and her endeavors in the field of art and in philanthropy, William Randolph Hearst, and San Francisco and national politics, as well as references to artists, authors and musicians.

Significant persons: Phoebe (Apperson) HEARST (ca.100), William Randolph HEARST (6), John Singer SARGENT (19).

Physical description: letters, documents, manuscripts, and photographs.

Source: purchased from William P. Wreden, October, 1961.

PESHINE, JOHN HENRY HOBART (1847–1928)
approximately 850 pieces, 1849–1903

John H. H. Peshine, U.S. military officer, was born in New York. He was appointed midshipman at the U.S. Naval Academy at the age of fifteen, but resigned in 1864 to accept a commission in the army. In 1893, he was sent to the court of King Alfonso XIII as military attaché from the U.S., in which capacity he rendered valuable service during the four years preceding the Spanish-American War by furnishing the Department of State with detailed information on the Spanish military establishment. Peshine served in the Philippines during and after the war with Spain, retiring from active duty in 1903 because of ill health. He died at Santa Barbara, California, in 1928.

Subject matter: information about the Spanish army and navy, Spanish diplomatic and military affairs, and Cuba and the Philippines as reflected in Peshine's dispatches from Madrid to Washington. Strongest for the period from 1893 to 1903. Also includes a few California land papers relating to the affairs of Peshine's father-in-law, Dr. James L. Ord.

Physical description: letters, manuscripts, and documents (in English and Spanish).

Source: gift of Mrs. Mary D. Anchordoquy, November, 1938.

PHELPS, WILLIAM WALTER (1839–94)
199 pieces, 1800–1925

William Walter Phelps, lawyer and diplomat, was born in New York in 1838, practiced law until 1868, and moved to New Jersey, where he represented the state in Congress from 1873 to 1875. Active in Republican politics and a good friend of James G. Blaine, Phelps was appointed U.S. minister to Austria-Hungary in 1881 and to Germany in 1889–93, and was a commissioner to the Berlin Conference on Samoan Affairs in 1889. After an active diplomatic and social life in Berlin (where his daughter Marian married the German under-secretary of the interior, Dr. Franz von Rottenburg), Phelps returned to New Jersey in 1893 to accept an appointment as judge in the Court of Errors and Appeals. He was also active in business, serving on the boards of directors of several eastern banks and railroads, and purchasing a newspaper. Phelps died in 1894.

Subject matter: Phelps's social and diplomatic life while minister in Berlin, including the Samoan Conference and Samoan affairs, American politics and the Republican party, and Phelps's social life and correspondence with several leading American literary figures. Also includes papers concerning John C. Eno's embezzlement of three million dollars from the Second National Bank of New York (of which Phelps was a director), and of Phelps's negotiations with Eno's millionaire father to make good the loss. Strongest for the period 1876–93.

Significant people: Herbert Nikolaus von BISMARCK (10), James Gillespie BLAINE (30), Samuel Langhorne CLEMENS (7), Eugene FIELD (4, including a poem dedicated to Phelps), Benjamin HARRISON (5), and Joseph PULITZER (4).

Physical description: letters, documents, manuscripts, and many newspaper clippings, with some photographs.

Source: purchased from Mrs. Frances Phelps Penry, December, 1963.

PHILLIPS, GEORGE S. (1818–65)
205 pieces, 1840–81

George S. Phillips, Methodist minister and Civil War chaplain, was born in Philadelphia but moved with his parents to Ohio, where the family settled near Wooster. In 1841 he entered the ministry of the Methodist Episcopal Church on the Richwood Circuit of the North Ohio Conference. In 1843 he married Elizabeth Kauffman. Phillips was transferred to the California Mission Conference in 1851, and served in San Francisco, Sacramento, San Jose, and Santa Clara for the following ten years, after which time he and his family returned to Ohio. During 1863 and 1864 Phillips was a chaplain with the 49th regiment of Ohio Volunteer Infantry, but intermittent ill health forced his resignation from this post, and from a subsequent appointment as president of the Colorado Seminary.

Phillips returned again to Ohio in 1865 and died there in March of that year.

Subject matter: everyday life and family matters, Phillips' activities as an itinerant Methodist minister in Ohio and California and as a chaplain during the war; there are a few scattered papers of Addison S. McClure, of Wooster, in Ohio, whose firm of Howard & McClure acted as government beef contractors during the Civil War, and who represented his state in Congress in 1881–83 and 1895–97.

Significant persons: John SHERMAN (6).

Physical description: chiefly letters, with some manuscripts (including 3 volumes of Phillips' journals, 1841–46), documents, and ephemera.

Source: purchased from Dawson's Book Shop, 1956.

PICKENS, ANDREW (1739–1817)
51 pieces, 1785–1835

Andrew Pickens, soldier, was born in Pennsylvania in 1739 but early moved to South Carolina and served with distinction in both the Cherokee War and the American Revolution. Pickens served as a member of the South Carolina legislature, and represented his state in Congress. From 1785 to 1801 he was active on the frontier as a U.S. commissioner to treat with the Southern Indian tribes. Pickens then retired to private life, except for a brief interval during the War of 1812, and died in South Carolina in 1817.

Subject matter: Pickens' activities while he was serving as Indian commissioner, and other information pertaining to Indian affairs in the Carolinas and Georgia from 1785 to 1820, particularly negotiations with the Cherokee and Creek nations and the problem of boundary establishment.

in the Huntington Library

Physical description: letters and documents.

Source: acquired from Walter C. Wyman, 1920.

PITKIN, TIMOTHY (1766–1847)
336 pieces, 1681–1847

Timothy Pitkin, statesman, economist, and historian, was born in Connecticut in 1766, the grandson of governor William Pitkin and of Thomas Clap, rector of Yale. Pitkin graduated from Yale in 1785, was admitted to the bar in 1788, and elected to the Connecticut General Assembly in 1790, where he served until his election to Congress in 1805 as a Federalist. Pitkin was particularly interested in the economy of the young nation, and in 1816 published *A Statistical View of the Commerce of the United States of America.* After the defeat of the Federalists in 1819 Pitkin left Congress to return to the Connecticut legislature, where he served until 1830. In 1828 he published *A Political and Civil History of the United States,* and after his retirement from politics continued to study history, economics, and theology. He died in New Haven, Connecticut, in 1847.

Subject matter: the politics and economy of the U.S. in the early nineteenth century: U.S. diplomatic relations with France and England (1801 Convention with France, the proposed treaty with England in 1807, and events leading to the War of 1812); American economic conditions (commerce, banking, internal revenue, patents); politics and current events (the Jefferson-Burr election, the impeachment of Samuel Chase, the Hartford Convention, and the conduct of the war); Louisiana; and the writing of history. Strongest for the period from 1800 to 1830, but also includes a few scattered papers from Connecticut's colonial period.

Significant persons: John Quincy ADAMS (5), Simeon BALD-
WIN (15), Theodore DWIGHT (27), Chauncey GOODRICH
(8), and Eli WHITNEY (7).

Physical description: primarily letters, with a very few documents.

Source: purchased from Walter C. Wyman in October, 1922.

Bibliography: this collection should not be confused with the
papers of the same name published by the Connecticut Historical Society in its *Collections*, vol. 19 (1921).

PIZARRO, PEDRO (ca.1515–ca.1600)
Relacion Del descubrimiento y conquista Delos Reinos d[e]l
Piru, y Del govierno y horden q[u]e los naturales tenian y
tesoros que Enellos sehallaron y delas de mas cosas q[ue] enel
an cubçedido hasta el Dia Desu f[ec]ha—H[ec]ha Por Pedro
piçarro Conquistador y Poblador Destos d[ic]hos rreynos y
V[e]z[in]o Dela çiudad de arequipa. (February 7, 1571)
MS. 1 volume 166 leaves

Text in Spanish.

PIZARRO-LA GASCA COLLECTION
approximately 1,000 pieces, 1537–80

Francisco Pizarro (1475?–1541) and Diego de Almagro (1475–
1538), who together conquered Peru for the Spanish crown
in 1531–33, were divided by frictions and jealousies which
finally led to the execution of Almagro by Pizarro in 1538 and
the murder of Pizarro by Almagro's followers in 1541. After
Pizarro's death, his brother Gonzalo (1502?–48) seized control of the government from the new viceroy who had been
sent to Peru to put into effect the "New Laws of the Indies"

enacted by Spain for the protection of the Indians by abolishing the *encomienda* system of enforced labor. The colonists, who were mainly opposed to these laws, supported Gonzalo Pizarro, and a period of disorder ensued until Charles V sent his own emissary, Pedro de la Gasca (1485–1567), a leading prelate, to Peru to settle the disputes and quiet the rebellion. La Gasca brought repeal of the "New Laws", and by offering liberal pardons won support for the Crown, executed Gonzalo Pizarro, and established civil government in Peru. Thereafter La Gasca returned to Spain and became, successively, bishop of Sigüenza and of Palencia.

Subject matter: early history of Peru, from Francisco Pizarro's civil war with Almagro to the pacification of the country by La Gasca, including material pertaining to the Catholic Church in Peru, missionaries, the conquest of Chile, Indians of Peru, and Indian slavery. Includes letters and decrees of Charles V and Philip II, letters of the Pizarros, reports of La Gasca, and Pedro de Valdivia's account of the conquest of Chile.

Significant persons: Juan de ACOSTA (7), Hernando BACHICAO (9), Francisco de CARVAJAL (20), CHARLES V (30), Luis GARCÍA SAMAMES (8), Pedro de la GASCA (66), Pedro Alonso de HINOJOSA (6), Alonso de MEDINA (9), Diego de MORA (10), Pedro MUÑOZ (11), PHILIP II (27), Gonzalo PIZARRO (65), Pedro de PUELLES (6), Antonio de QUIÑONES (10), Juan de SAAVEDRA (7), Diego de SILVA (9), Pedro de SORIA (6), Francisco de VILLACASTÍN (7), and Bartolomé de VILLALOBOS (16).

Physical description: letters, manuscripts, and documents (in Spanish).

Source: purchased from Maggs Bros., January, 1926.

POLK, JAMES KNOX (1795–1849)
43 pieces, 1790–1889

James Knox Polk, eleventh president of the United States, was born in 1795, admitted to the Tennessee bar in 1820, and elected to the state legislature three years later. In 1824 he married Sarah Childress of Murfreesboro, Tennessee. A strong supporter of Andrew Jackson, Polk was elected to Congress in 1825 and served until his election as governor of Tennessee in 1839. In 1844, with Jackson's backing, he was nominated as the Democratic party's candidate for president, and defeated Henry Clay for the office. Polk's goals as president were to reduce the tariff, create an independent treasury system, settle the Oregon boundary dispute with Great Britain, and acquire California. He also supported the annexation of Texas. Ill health forced his retirement from politics in 1849, and he died later that year.

Subject matter: the collection falls into two main divisions. The first, covering the years from 1845 to 1849, deals with political matters, the president's comments on newspaper clippings, a certified copy of his will, and Senator Arthur Bagby's open letter to the people of Alabama (1845) concerning the annexation of Texas. Other topics include the Oregon boundary dispute and Polk's efforts to dissuade cabinet members from running for elected office. The second division, from 1883 to 1889, concerns the president's widow and projected biographical sketches of herself and her husband.

Significant persons: George BANCROFT (6).

Physical description: chiefly letters, with a few documents and many newspaper clippings.

Source: acquired from Mrs. James W. Fertig, 1949.

POOR, ENOCH (fl. 1759–60)
Enoch Poor His Book 1759: A Journal from Newbury to Saint Johns (1759–60)
Autograph MS.S. volume 109 pp.

Incomplete. A military journal concerning garrison life and minor clashes with French troops around Fort Frederick at St.

Johns, N.B., April 6, 1759 to May 12, 1760. Also includes a list of the soldiers manning the fort.

POPE, RICHARD (fl. 1775–79)
Richard Pope's Book (1775–79)
Autograph MS.S. volume 218 pp.

Incomplete. A military journal and commonplace book concerning the activities of the British 47th Regiment at Boston, Ticonderoga, and Saratoga. Covers the period from April 18, 1775 to January 10, 1779.

PORTER, CLYDE H. AND MAE (REED)
approximately 4000 pieces, 1928–56

Clyde H. Porter and his wife Mae, of Kansas City, Missouri, and Santa Ana, California, studied and wrote about the early exploration, development, and fur trade of the Far West, particularly the Rocky Mountain area.

Subject matter: research notes for the book *Ruxton of the Rockies* and other books concerning the Rocky Mountain region. Also includes secondary source material pertaining to German immigration to Texas and to various fur traders and adventurers, including Toussaint Charbonneau, August Chouteau, and George Ruxton.

Physical description: letters and manuscripts.

Source: gift of Mae Reed Porter, March, 1959.

PORTER, DAVID DIXON (1813–91)
801 pieces, 1861–70

David Dixon Porter, Union admiral, was born in 1813 and began his career in the Mexican Navy, but was accepted into the U.S. Navy as a midshipman in 1829. He thereafter served in coastal survey work, in the Mexican war, in merchant shipping, and in the Portsmouth Naval Yard until the outbreak of the Civil War, when (during 1861 and 1862) he saw active service off Florida and the Mississippi River. In October 1862 Porter was appointed acting rear admiral, and given command of the Mississippi Squadron, where he was instrumental in keeping the river open to Union shipping and in assisting the army in the reduction of Vicksburg. In the spring of 1864 he was transferred to the North Atlantic Blockade Squadron, where he captured Fort Fisher (at Wilmington, North Carolina), and where he served until the end of the war. Porter was then named superintendent of the U.S. Naval Academy for a term of four years, and spent the remainder of his life in naval administration and historical research. He was promoted to the rank of admiral in 1870, and died in Washington in 1891.

Subject matter: Porter's command (from November 1862 to April 1864) of the Mississippi Squadron, including information on naval administration (recruitment, supplies, personnel, discipline, etc.) and operations (including the disposition and condition of ships under his command and relations with General Grant and the army). Also includes telegrams to and from Secretary of the Navy Gideon Welles and his assistant, Gustavus Vasa Fox, on a wide variety of naval matters (not necessarily concerning Porter), and a few postwar documents concerning naval affairs.

Significant persons: Kidder Randolph BREESE (18), John Adolphus Barnard DAHLGREN (13), Gustavus Vasa FOX (61), James Augustin GREER (14), Samuel Phillips LEE (27), Lewis Baldwin PARSONS (7), Alexander Mosely PENNOCK (29), Robert TOWNSEND (8), Gideon WELLES (144).

Physical description: chiefly letters (including telegrams), with some documents.

Source: purchased from Charles Baker, 1912.

POSTLETHWAITE FAMILY COLLECTION
68 pieces, 1806–63; 1924; 1938

William Dunbar Postlethwaite (ca.1809–63), the son of Samuel Postlethwaite and Ann (Dunbar) Postlethwaite, grew up near Natchez, Mississippi, attended school in Philadelphia from 1821 to 1825, married Sophie Carter (?) in 1838, and settled at Westmoreland, Louisiana, where he died in 1863.

Subject matter: social life and family affairs in plantation society. A series of letters from Samuel to his son William Postlethwaite concern the latter's school years in Philadelphia. Also includes three small travel journals of Samuel Postlethwaite in Mississippi and Louisiana, from 1810 to 1813, and two modern pieces. Strongest for the period from 1821 to 1838.

Physical description: chiefly letters, with a few manuscripts and some ephemera (including a photograph of a painting of a Dunbar ancestor).

Source: acquired from Lenore Green, February, 1957.

POTTER, CHARLES F. AND ISAAC B.
approximately 5,000 pieces, 1905–40

Charles F. Potter and his brother, Isaac B. Potter, were lawyers with offices in Los Angeles and San Francisco. Their clients were chiefly water and power companies in the southwestern U.S. Charles Potter was a director of the Mono Power Company in 1920.

Subject matter: engineering reports, agreements, and surveys for California, Nevada, and Arizona, mainly related to water and power; the Mono Power Company and its legal problems with the City of Los Angeles (1905–23) over Owens Valley water rights, and a few reports on geo-thermal power.

Physical description: letters, manuscripts, documents, and photographs.

Source: purchased from N. A. Kovach, February, 1945.

POTTER, WILLIAM JAMES (1829–93)
489 pieces, 1847–81

William James Potter, New England clergyman and grand-father of the author Conrad Aiken, was born in North Dartmouth, Massachusetts, in 1829 and educated in public schools there, at Harvard, and in Berlin. After some teaching and European travel, he was ordained a Unitarian minister in New Bedford, Massachusetts, in 1859. In 1863, the year of his marriage to Elizabeth Claghorn Babcock, Potter was drafted into the Union army as an inspector of military hospitals and eventually appointed chaplain to a convalescent camp at Alexandria, Virginia. After the war, increasingly dissatisfied with sectarian religions, he joined with Ralph Waldo Emerson and others in founding, in 1868, the Free Religious Association to realize his goal of a universal religious fellowship. Potter continued to preach and work for the Association until his death in Boston in 1893.

Subject matter: family and domestic matters, Potter's education (at Harvard and elsewhere) and early career, travel (in Europe and while preaching in the U.S.), and the Civil War.

Physical description: letters, a few manuscripts (including 7 volumes of Potter's diaries and 4 journals belonging to his wife), and ephemera (including a small ambrotype of Potter's daughter Anna Aiken [Potter] Aiken).

Source: gift of Mrs. Stedman Hoar, 1969 and 1976.

Bibliography: additional material on William James Potter may be found in the Conrad Aiken papers, described in *Guide to Literary Manuscripts in the Huntington Library.*

POWNALL, JOSEPH (1818–90)
approximately 1775 pieces, 1840–1926

Dr. Joseph Pownall, a native of New Jersey, graduated from the University of the City of New York, practiced in Lousiana, and made an overland journey to California seeking gold in 1849. After working the Mariposa diggings, he went to Columbia in 1852 and bought stock in the Tuolomne County Water Company, where he served as a company officer until his death. Dr. Pownall married the widow of William Henry Newell, who had been one of the founders of the Tuolomne County Water Company in 1851. The Pownalls' children attended school in San Francisco. Their son, Joseph Benjamin, after graduation from the University of California, returned to the town of Columbia to work for the Tuolomne County Water Company, and their daughter married Henry Senger, a University of California professor.

Subject matter: material concerning Columbia (California) and the Southern mines; business papers of the Tuolomne County Water Company; a narrative of an overland journey from Louisiana to Mariposa, California, in 1849; and information about the University of California in the 1880s.

Physical description: letters, manuscripts (including 5 journals), documents (including 30 volumes), and 4 maps.

Source: purchased from Edwin Grabhorn, January, 1945.

Bibliography: a portion of Dr. Joseph Pownall's 1849 overland diary has been published: Joseph Pownall, "From Louisiana to Mariposa," ed. Robert G. Cleland, *Pacific Historical Review,* 18 (1949):24–32.

PREBLE, EDWARD (1761–1807)
Commodore Edward Preble's Internal Rules and Regulations
[for the] U.S. Frigate "Constitution," 1803–04 (1803–04)
MS. volume 89 leaves

PRICE, RODMAN McCAMLEY (1816–94)
256 pieces, 1842–ca.1890

Rodman McCamley Price, naval officer, governor of New Jersey, and businessman, was born in New York, attended the College of New Jersey, and studied law. He was appointed a naval purser in 1840, serving first on the frigates "Fulton" and "Missouri." In 1846 he was sent to California aboard the ship "Cyane," landing in Monterey with the American occupation forces. He served as alcalde of Monterey, was a member of San Francisco's first municipal council, and of the first California Constitutional Convention in 1849. Price invested heavily in San Francisco real estate. He returned to New Jersey in 1850, and with his partner, Samuel Ward, established the New York office of Ward & Price, Bankers and Agents for California. In New Jersey he served as congressman (1851–53) and governor (1854–57), and helped establish the state's public school system.

Subject matter: naval affairs, mostly before 1864, discussion of national politics, and news of the business affairs of the firm of Ward & Price and of San Francisco property values and land titles.

Physical description: letters, manuscripts, and documents.

Source: purchased from Edwin Grabhorn, January, 1945.

PRINCE, WILLIAM ROBERT (1795–1869)
65 pieces, 1848–54

William R. Prince, horticulturalist, was born in Flushing, New York, and educated at Jamaica Academy and in Canada. He followed after his horticulturalist father and grandfather of the same name, becoming associated with the Linnaean Botanic Garden & Nurseries at Flushing. He collaborated with his father to write *A Treatise on the Vine* (1830) and *The Pomological Manual* (1831). In 1837, Prince's interest in silk culture caused him to invest heavily in the venture, and he lost his fortune and the mortgaged nursery. He went to California in 1849 to seek gold, and engaged in the horticultural and mercantile business in Sacramento. In 1851, Prince left the business in the hands of Thomas H. Jackson, traveled through Mexico, then returned to Flushing.

Subject matter: the horticultural and mercantile business in Sacramento, California, and the mining interests of William R. Prince and his associates near Marysville; news and descriptions of the city of Sacramento.

Physical description: letters and documents.

Source: purchased from Morris H. Briggs, January, 1926.

PUMPELLY, RAPHAEL (1837–1923)
approximately 3500 pieces, 1839–1916

Raphael Pumpelly, geologist and explorer, was born in Owego, New York, in 1837 and educated as a mining engineer at the Royal School of Mines in Freiberg. After a year's work in an Arizona silver mine, he accepted a post in 1861 as geologist for the Japanese government, and served two years in that country before traveling on through China, Mongolia, and Russia. Pumpelly then returned to the U.S. to study iron and copper deposits in Michigan and the Lake Superior district, lectured for a term at Harvard, and in 1869 married Eliza Frances Shepard. He continued research on national mineral resources and on the problem of water pollution, worked on a geological survey for a projected northwestern railway, and from 1884 to 1889 served as head of the New England division of the U.S. Geological Survey, where he concentrated on a study of the Green Mountains of Massachusetts. Thereafter Pumpelly traveled abroad with his family, continued his work in the Lake Superior region, and in 1903 and 1904 led expeditions to Turkestan under the auspices of the Carnegie Institution of Washington. Mrs. Pumpelly died in 1915, and Pumpelly spent the final years of his life in New England and Georgia. He died in Newport, Rhode Island, in 1923. Among the numerous books and articles resulting from his research, Pumpelly is best known for his study of the loess of China and of copper deposits in the Lake Superior region.

Subject matter: primarily information on the life and family affairs of Eliza (Shepard) Pumpelly, descriptions of travel in Europe and Asia, the expeditions to Turkestan in 1903 and 1904. Also includes a few professional papers, and some personal correspondence, of Raphael Pumpelly, (along with geological notes and descriptions of people and places) covering expeditions to Japan, China, Mongolia, Russia, Turkestan, and various places in the U.S.; a few business papers and personal letters of Pumpelly's parents, William and Mary Wells Pumpelly, and their family.

Physical description: chiefly letters, with some documents and manuscripts (including 29 volumes of notebooks and diaries).

Source: acquired from Raphael Pumpelly (grandson of the geologist), January, 1960.

Q

QUERENET DE LA COMBE ? (fl. 1780–82)
Précis des Operation et des Marches de l'armée Combinée
Français et Americaine . . . Journal du Siege d'York (1780–
82)
Autograph MS. volume 67 leaves illus.

Text in French
Contains 69 pencil, ink, and color sketches showing positions
of the troops at various stops along the route of march from
Boston to Head of Elk on the Chesapeake Bay.

R

RAILROADIANA (WESTERN U.S.A.)
41 pieces, 1860–79

The collection of Railroadiana is composed of material concerning the Central Pacific and the Southern Pacific Railroads and the smaller lines (the California Pacific, the California Pacific Extension, the Northern, and the Western Pacific railroad companies) eventually acquired by the two larger railroads. The owners of the Central Pacific, which was completed as a cross-country route in 1869, had chartered the Southern Pacific Railroad Company in 1865. Through acquisition of smaller branch lines, the construction of several new ones, and the consolidation of their enterprises, the "Big Four," Collis P. Huntington, Leland Stanford, Mark Hopkins, and Charles Crocker, created a vast transportation monopoly, serving a large portion of the western United States. Alfred Andrew Cohen (1829–87), a lawyer who figures prominently in this collection, sold his interests in several small California railroads to the Central Pacific Railroad in 1869. He served as an attorney for the Central Pacific, but resigned in 1876 in protest against the railroad policies. The companies brought litigation against him in retaliation for his efforts to introduce legislation to regulate railroad fares and rates in California. Eventually cordial relations were once more restored and the influential lawyer again defended the interests of the Central Pacific.

Subject matter: mainly court cases concerning the Central Pacific, Southern Pacific, California Pacific, California Pacific

Extension, Northern, and Western Pacific railroad companies.

Physical description: documents, including 14 volumes of the transcript of the *Central Pacific Railroad Company* v. *Alfred A. Cohen* case in 1876.

Source: purchased from Grahame H. Hardy, 1944 and 1945.

RANDALL-GRIGSBY CORRESPONDENCE
81 pieces, 1856–61

Henry Stephens Randall (1811–76), educator and historian, was born in New York in 1811. In addition to work in public education and in the study of agriculture, Randall published in 1858 a three-volume biography of Thomas Jefferson, in the preparation of which he had access to voluminous Jefferson family manuscripts. Hugh Blair Grigsby (1806–81), newspaper editor, man of letters, and Virginia historian, became interested in Randall's work and corresponded with him on the subject of Jefferson and other aspects of Virginia history.

Subject matter: the life and times of Jefferson, the Mecklenburg Declaration of Independence, miscellaneous aspects of Virginia history, the progress of Randall's work, and early critical reaction to the publication of his biography.

Physical description: with the exception of a few newspaper clippings, the collection consists entirely of letters, particularly between 1856 and 1859.

Source: unknown.

RAY, CHARLES HENRY (1821–70)
437 pieces, 1826–1904

Charles Henry Ray, physician and journalist, was born in Norwich, N.Y., in 1821, trained as a physician, and signed on as ship's doctor on a New Bedford whaler in 1841. Thereafter

303

Ray practiced medicine in Michigan, Iowa, and Illinois, but abandoned his practice in 1851 for journalism. He acquired part interest of the Democratic *Jeffersonian* of Galena, Illinois, but switched to the Republican party and moved, about 1855, to Chicago where, with John C. Vaughan and Joseph Medill, Ray purchased controlling interest in the Chicago *Tribune,* which he edited until the middle years of the Civil War. Thereafter Ray unsuccessfully speculated in several business ventures, left the *Tribune,* and worked for some years for the Chicago *Evening Post.*

Subject matter: chiefly Ray's correspondence with his family (including his first wife Jane Yates [Per Lee] Ray and his second wife Julia Annah [Clarke] Ray) and with his business colleagues. Topics include Ray's family life and early career, journalism, the Chicago *Tribune,* the Republican party, and the politics of the years immediately before and during the Civil War (including information on Abraham Lincoln, Winfield Scott, John C. Frémont, and George B. McClellan).

Significant persons: James Wilson GRIMES (9), Joseph MEDILL (6), Lyman TRUMBULL (9), Elihu Benjamin WASHBURNE (8), Horace WHITE (12).

Physical description: chiefly letters (including some typewritten transcripts of letters), with some documents. Among the ephemera are newspaper clippings and a few early photographs of Ray.

Source: gift of Mrs. Julia Ray Andrews (Charles Henry Ray's daughter), 1943 and of Mr. Paul Ray and Mrs. James P. Andrews, 1954.

REDFIELD, LEONARD G. (fl. 1850s)
99 pieces, 1853–58

Leonard Redfield, California emigrant and miner, journeyed overland from Jefferson County, New York, in 1853. He lived in San Jose, where his relatives, including cousins Aldin E., Charles, and Volney D. Moody, had settled, some as early as 1849. The Moodys were prominent businessmen and politicians in San Jose. Redfield also engaged in mining at Moore's Flat, Nevada County.

Subject matter: mining in Nevada County (California), and life in San Jose and San Francisco (1855–56), and the development of Poweshiek County, Iowa.

Physical description: letters.

Source: purchased from Edwin Grabhorn, January, 1945.

REQUA, ISAAC LAWRENCE (1828–1905)
381 pieces, 1819; 1859–1935

Isaac L. Requa, mining engineer, a native of Tarrytown, New York, came to California in 1850. He engaged in mining in California until 1860, when he moved to Virginia City, Nevada. Requa became superintendent of the Chollar-Potosi Mining Co., the Savage, Hale and Norcross Mines, and the Union Mill and Mining Co. Although he continued his business interests in Nevada, he built his family home in Oakland, California, in 1880, where he became president of the Oakland Bank of Savings. He was active in Republican politics and in 1894 was made president of the Central Pacific Railroad. Requa's daughter Amy (1876–?) married General Oscar Fitzalan Long. His son, Mark Lawrence Requa (1865–1937), born in Virginia City, Nevada, engaged in mining in California and Nevada, helped organize the Nevada Consolidated Copper Co. of Ely, Nevada, and built the Nevada Northern Railroad. Mark Requa also served as head of the oil division of the U.S. Fuel Administration in 1918–19, and helped manage the presidential campaigns of Herbert Hoover in 1928 and 1932.

Subject matter: family matters (1877–1901), vouchers of the Chollar Norcross Savage Shaft Co. and the Chollar Potosi

Mining Co. (1876–79), a few manuscripts by Mark L. Requa including his memoirs of January 10, 1918 to June 30, 1919 while director of the Oil Division of the U.S. Fuel Administration.

Physical description: letters, documents, manuscripts, scrapbook, and 2 photographs.

Source: gift of Mrs. John Henry Russell and Mrs. Mark L. Requa, 1934–59, and by purchase from the Argonaut Book Co., 1961.

RHEES, WILLIAM JONES (1830–1907)
approximately 4700 pieces, 1744–1906

William Jones Rhees, bibliographer, collector, and chief clerk of the Smithsonian Institution, was born and educated in Philadelphia and moved to Washington, D.C., shortly after 1847. In July, 1852, he became chief clerk of the Smithsonian and served thereafter as chief executive officer under the secretary, with particular authority in the publications program. In 1891 Rhees was placed in charge of the Smithsonian's archives and continued his association with the Institution until his death in 1907. As an enthusiastic autograph collector, Rhees accumulated numerous unrelated letters and papers of prominent men as well as more coherent groups of manuscripts relating to his official position.

Subject matter: in addition to the four main sub-collections described below, the collection contains Rhees's personal correspondence and autograph collection, and includes letters and papers relating to his private life, to the Sons of the American Revolution (particularly its Washington, D.C., chapter), to Indian affairs in the first half of the 19th century, and to the U.S. Pension Bureau. Also included are numerous receipts for Smithsonian publications.

Sub-collections of the Rhees papers include letters and papers of:

1. ALEXANDER DALLAS BACHE (1806–67), physicist and educator, including information about the U.S. Coast Survey (of which Bache was superintendent from 1843 until his death), Girard College in Philadelphia (of which he was president from 1836 to 1842), about the Civil War, and about mid-19th century science and scientists (particularly in Bache's own field of terrestrial magnetism). *1898 pieces, 1827–67.*

2. HENRY ROWE SCHOOLCRAFT (1793–1864), Indian agent and ethnologist, including information about his family and private affairs, about the publication of his writings on travel and on Indian ethnology, and about his death (including letters of condolence to his wife, Mary Howard Schoolcarft). *129 pieces, 1815–74.*

3. SMITHSONIAN INSTITUTION and its executive officers, including information about the routine activities and administration of the Smithsonian under its first two secretaries, Joseph Henry (1787–1878) and Spencer Fullerton Baird (1823–87), about Smithsonian publications and reports, and about Joseph Henry's life and interests (in physics, in Princeton University, in the U.S. Lighthouse Board, and in the National Academy of Sciences). There is little information about James Smithson, the founder of the institution which bears his name. *1624 pieces, 1831–1906.*

4. THE NATIONAL INSTITUTE FOR THE PROMOTION OF SCIENCE (now the National Institution) of Washington, D.C., including information about the forerunners of the Institute, its organization, membership and activities, its museum, and its collection of specimens from the U.S. Exploring Expedition commanded by Charles Wilkes from 1838 to 1842. *313 pieces, 1816–58.*

Significant persons: Louis AGASSIZ (41), James ALDEN (11), John Henry ALEXANDER (9), Stephen ALEXANDER (10), Alexander Dallas BACHE (61), Frederick Augustus Peter BARNARD (12), Lewis CASS (12), Alexis CASWELL (7), Salmon Portland CHASE (10), William CHAUVENET (7), Howell COBB (9), Schuyler COLFAX (16), Tunis Augustus CRAVEN (7), Charles Anderson DANA (6), James Dwight DANA (39), Charles Henry DAVIS (20), Dorothea Lynde DIX (25), Samuel Francis DuPONT (11), William Hemsley EMORY (5), William Pitt FESSENDEN (5), Cyrus West FIELD (6), Peter FORCE (13), Oliver Wolcott GIBBS (28), Samuel Augustus GILBERT (12), James Melville GILLISS (36), Benjamin Apthorp GOULD (30), Asa GRAY (17), Arnold GUYOT (6), Hannibal HAMLIN (10), Robert HARE (6), Isaac Israel HAYES (6), Joseph HENRY (78), Julius Erasmus HILGARD (13), Ambrose Powell HILL (6), Andrew Atkinson HUMPHREYS (15), Thornton Alexander JENKINS (13), Joseph Camp Griffith KENNEDY (7), John LeCONTE (5), John Lawrence LeCONTE (7), Sir John Henry LeFROY (11), J. Peter LESLEY (5), Francis LIEBER (32), Humphrey LLOYD (7), James McCOSH (6), John MACLEAN (40), Francis MARKOE (9), Matthew Fontaine MAURY (8), Montgomery Cunningham MEIGS (9), Henry MITCHELL (7), Simon NEWCOMB (7), Peter PARKER (9), Carlile Pollock PATTERSON (10), James Alfred PEARCE (24), Benjamin PEIRCE (38), Thomas Stowell PHELPS (10), Orlando Metcalfe POE (5), Joel Roberts POINSETT (5), David Dixon PORTER (10), Noah PORTER (10), Alonzo POTTER (8), George Henry PREBLE (5), Lambert Adolphe Jacques QUETELET (8), Christopher Raymond Perry RODGERS (8), John RODGERS (5), Fairman ROGERS (28), Sir Edward SABINE (30), Henry Rowe SCHOOLCRAFT (11), William Henry SEWARD (7), Benjamin SILLIMAN, Jr. (31), James Hervey SIMPSON (9), Gerrit SMITH (7), Isaac Ingalls STEVENS (18), Joseph Gilbert TOTTEN (26), Stephen Decatur TRENCHARD (16), William Petit TROWBRIDGE (23), Hector TYNDALE (11), John TYNDALL (16), Morrison Remick WAITE (35), Charles WILKES (26).

Physical description: primarily letters, with documents and a very few pieces of ephemera.

Source: purchased from Mrs. Romenia Rhees, 1922.

RICHARDSON, AUGUSTUS G. (fl. 1860s)
67 pieces, 1860–66

Augustus G. Richardson, officer of the California Stage Company, was a resident of Sacramento, California. The California Stage Company was formed in 1854, with headquarters at Sacramento, when several stage-line owners consolidated the major lines in northern California. James E. Birch, who had operated one of the first stage lines in California, was elected president and Frank Shaw Stevens, long active in the stage business and founder of the Pioneer Stage Line in 1851, was elected vice-president. In 1855, the company extended its lines into territory south of San Francisco. James Haworth replaced Birch as president in 1856, and promoted northward expansion of the lines. By 1860, the company had disposed of its southern lines and, operating mainly from Sacramento, Folsom, and Marysville, concentrated on their government contract for mail service from Sacramento, California, to Portland, Oregon. The contract expired in 1864 and was not renewed.

Subject matter: business affairs of the California Stage Company (with references to James E. Birch, James Haworth, Isaiah C. Woods, and others), the Butterfield Overland Mail, the Pony Express, state and national politics (including secession), and local news.

Physical description: letters and 1 document.

Source: purchased from Mrs. Frank H. Stevens, March, 1955.

RIESENBERG, FELIX, SR. (1879–1939)
approximately 750 pieces, 1939–60

Felix Riesenberg, Sr., civil engineer and author, was born in Wisconsin, attended school in Chicago and New York City, and went to sea in 1895 for twelve years. He joined the U.S. Coast and Geodetic Survey in 1901, and from 1906 to 1907 went with a private expedition to the North Pole. Riesenberg returned to the U.S. and graduated in civil engineering from Columbia University in 1911. He served as a naval officer in World War I and practiced as a consulting engineer until his death in 1922. He wrote technical and historical works and novels. His son, Felix Riesenberg, Jr. (1913–65), newspaper editor, traveler, reviewer and historian, began his writing career as a reporter for Scripps-Howard's *News* in San Francisco in 1936. He was appointed radio news editor with the U.S. coordinator of information at the beginning of World War II, then served in public relations with the U.S. Maritime Service, mainly as liaison with the motion picture industry. He wrote books on California and teen-age adventure stories.

Subject matter: drafts, typescripts, galley proofs, etc. of books written by Felix Riesenberg, Jr., and two by Felix Riesenberg, Sr.; secondary source material relating to California and Spanish galleons, and some correspondence of, and biographical notes on, Felix Riesenberg, Jr.

Physical description: letters and manuscripts.

Source: purchased from Mrs. Felix Riesenberg, October, 1966.

RITCH, WILLIAM GILLET (1830–1904)
2274 pieces, 1539–1890

William G. Ritch was territorial secretary of New Mexico from 1873 to 1885 and author of books on New Mexico history. He was a native of New York who had moved to Michigan in 1855, then settled in Wisconsin. After serving with the 46th Wisconsin Cavalry in the Civil War, Ritch returned to Wisconsin where he was elected state senator. He was later proprietor and editor of the *Winnebago County Press*. Failing health forced Ritch to seek a better climate, and in 1873 he was appointed secretary of the Territory of New Mexico. He served in this capacity until 1885, with the added responsibility of serving as acting territorial governor in 1875. He was active in the establishment of a public school system in the Territory and became a regent of the State Normal School. He developed a great interest in the history of New Mexico and began collecting historical documents to prevent their destruction or dispersal. He was elected the first president of the New Mexico Historical Society in 1880, and wrote many books and articles relating to New Mexico.

Subject matter: early New Mexican history. The very early portion of the collection (1539–1700) contains original manuscripts, contemporary copies, and later translations of journals of explorers and official documents. The period from 1700 to 1846 contains official documents, correspondence and papers of the governors, court records, church inventories, passport lists of American traders, etc. The papers for the years 1846 to 1873 cover the American military occupation, New Mexico politics and government, New Mexico during the Civil War, and Indian affairs (particularly relating to the Navajo, Apache, Comanche, and Pecos tribes). Items after 1873 tend to be the personal papers of William G. Ritch: his biographical sketches of significant New Mexicans, drafts of articles, and notebooks of research material (including the biography of Father Antonio José Martínez by Santiago Valdez).

Significant persons: Manuel ARMIJO (18), William Frederick Milton ARNY (55), James Henry CARLETON (30), Philip St. George COOKE (5), William S. MESSERVY (11), Miguel Antonio OTERO (16), Ceran ST. VRAIN (5), Diego de VARGAS ZAPATA LUJÁN PONCE DE LEÓN (3 originals and 10 later copies), Donaciano VIGIL (14).

Physical description: letters, manuscripts (including 17 volumes), documents, and maps (in English and Spanish).

Source: acquired from Watson L. Ritch, May, 1923.

ROCKWELL, JOHN ARNOLD (1803–61)
approximately 3000 pieces, 1791–1871

John Arnold Rockwell, jurist and land developer, was born in Norwich, Conn., in 1803, graduated from Yale in 1822, and practiced law in Norwich. He entered public life as state senator in 1838, was appointed judge of the New London (Conn.) County Court in 1840, and in 1845 was elected to Congress where he served two terms and acted as chairman of the Committee on Claims. At the close of the Mexican War, Rockwell established his headquarters in Washington, D.C. and resumed his legal practice, acting especially before the U.S. Court of Claims (approved by Congress in 1855), of which he was the chief originator. Rockwell was also active in various enterprises concerning western expansion, such as land development, railroads and other transportation, banking, and mining operations. He had interests in Illinois as early as 1836, when the Rockwell Land Company was founded at Chicago to develop lands in La Salle County. His treatise on *Spanish and Mexican Law in Relation to Mines & Titles to Real Estate* was published in 1851. Rockwell died in Washington in 1861.

Subject matter: Rockwell's law practice and the development of the U.S. Court of Claims, politics and the Constitutional Union Party of 1860, land development (particularly in Illinois, Indiana, Ohio, and Michigan), transportation (including land grants in aid of canals and railroads such as the Illinois Central RR and the projected Pacific Railroad), mining (including the New Almaden Quicksilver Mine), and banking. Also two subcollections: correspondence of the Tisdale family of Connecticut (1802–32), and papers of the Perkins, Kinsman, and other families relating to the Western Reserve (1791–1832).

Significant persons: Frederick BILLINGS (11), William W. CAMPBELL (10), Reverdy JOHNSON (48), William Butler

OGDEN (18), William H. OSBORN (19), John Osborne SARGENT (10).

Physical description: letters and documents.

Source: purchased from George D. Smith Book Company, 1925. Printed materials acquired with the collection are in the Rare Book Department of the Huntington Library.

ROPER, SAMUEL (1839– ?)
68 pieces, 1862–65

Samuel Roper of Colcanda, Illinois, Union soldier, entered the 56th Regiment of Illinois Volunteer Infantry as a lieutenant in February, 1862. He saw action in the Franklin and Nashville Campaigns, in the Vicksburg Campaign, at Missionary Ridge, and in various minor battles. Roper was promoted to captain of Company K, and was discharged as a major in August, 1865.

Subject matter: the Battle of Vicksburg, the Chattanooga Campaign, Sherman's victory march to Washington, D.C., and family affairs; a few documents related to Roper's military activities.

Physical description: letters and documents.

Source: unknown.

ROST, ERNEST CHRISTIAN (1867–1940)
140 pieces, 1918–37

Ernest C. Rost, cactus specialist, was born in New York and studied geology at Harvard and Yale, where he was awarded an honorary Ph.D. He became interested in horticulture and was elected to the German Horticultural Society for his scientific studies of cactus species. He served as a photographer for the U.S. War Department, making pictures in the Philippines and Cuba for an official pictorial history of the Spanish-American War, and published articles with photographs of his travels in *Scientific American, Harper's,* and other periodicals. Rost lived in Alhambra, California, and with his wife, Etta contributed to *Desert,* the official publication of the California Cactus Society.

Subject matter: Ernest C. Rost, and fellow botanists Joseph Nelson Rose of the Smithsonian Institution and Nathaniel Lord Britton, director of the New York Botanical Garden. Also includes the typewritten draft of an unpublished manuscript, *Something About Cacti,* by Ernest C. Rost, a translation of Alwin Berger's *Kakteen,* and articles by Etta N. Rost (using the pseudonym Esther Norton).

Significant persons: Nathaniel Lord BRITTON (10), Joseph Nelson ROSE (69).

Physical description: letters, manuscripts, documents, and photographs.

Source: purchased from Mrs. Miles E. Rost, August, 1968.

RUSSELL, MAJORS & WADDELL
508 pieces, 1839–68

The firm of Russell, Majors & Waddell, freighters, stagecoach operators and originators of the Pony Express, was established in 1854. The principals of the company, William Hepburn Russell (1828–72), William Bradford Waddell (1807–72), and Alexander Majors (1814–1900), had been active in many business ventures together before consolidating their firm. All three had been involved in retailing. Russell and Majors were in the Santa Fe trade and Waddell had helped organize small railroads. The company received a government contract to supply the Army of Utah, a force sent to suppress Mormon rebellion. In 1859, they organized the Leavenworth & Pike's Peak Express Company, which, in 1860, became the Central Overland California & Pike's Peak Express Company, chartered to carry mail from St. Joseph, Missouri, to San Francisco. In 1860, urged chiefly by Russell, the company began operation of the Pony Express, which carried mail by the central route for eighteen months until its demise was brought on by the completion of a transcontinental telegraph service. The firm of Russell, Majors, & Waddell collapsed in 1861, following a financial scandal, and declared bankruptcy. After the partners surrendered their personal fortunes, the company was purchased at auction by Ben Holladay in 1862.

Subject matter: business and legal papers of Russell, Majors & Waddell, freighting operations, the mercantile business, land transactions, and the Pony Express.

Significant persons: Alexander MAJORS (6), William Hepburn RUSSELL (60).

Physical description: letters and documents.

Source: purchased from Mrs. William B. Waddell, June, 1946.

RUST, HORATIO NELSON (1828–1906)
1229 pieces, 1799–1906

Horatio N. Rust was a U.S. Indian Agent and a horticulturalist in California. He was born in Amherst, Massachusetts, and as a young man was influenced by the early abolitionists of New England. In Connecticut, he became acquainted with John Brown, leader of the Harper's Ferry raid, whose descendents Rust later aided. Rust's early interest in archaeology led to his exploration and investigation of North American Indian antiquities, and he served as U.S. Indian Agent to the Mission Indians of Southern California from 1890 to 1892, taught agriculture to the Indians, and helped establish an Indian school at Perris, California. He settled in Pasadena, California, in 1881, engaged in the nursery business, and became influential in civic affairs there and in South Pasadena.

Subject matter: Indian culture in the Southwest, horticulture in Southern California, and the Freedmen's Bureau, mainly the period 1870–1906; abolitionist John Brown's family affairs and Rust's efforts to raise funds for their relief.

Significant persons: Jessie (Benton) FRÉMONT (8), Frederick Webb HODGE (6), Charles Fletcher LUMMIS (8), Horatio Nelson RUST (165, including 45 diaries).

Physical description: letters, manuscripts (including 45 diaries), 2 scrapbooks (ca.1864–ca.1919) (in Rare Book Department), and 5 photograph albums (in Rare Book Department).

Source: gift of Mrs. Nellie Rust Lockwood and Edward A. Rust, June, 1943.

S

SAMSON, WILLIAM HOLLAND (1860–1917)
59 pieces, 1755–1810 and 1880–1910

William Holland Samson, journalist and historian, was born in 1860 in Le Roy, Genesee County, New York. Although most of his career was spent in the newspaper business, notably as writer and managing editor of the *Rochester Post-Express*, Samson's greatest interest was in the early history of western New York State and the Seneca Indians. He edited the *Private Journal of Aaron Burr*, the letters of George Washington to Tobias Lear, and the letters of Zachary Taylor.

Subject matter: research into the early history of western New York and the Seneca Indians. Also includes some of Samson's research notes and copies of earlier letters and papers relating to the Senecas, including a manuscript of biographical sketches of early Indian traders in western New York and a geographical glossary of early Indian settlements.

Significant persons: John S. CLARK (19), George Stillwell CONOVER (6).

Physical description: letters and manuscripts. All of the items in the period from 1755 to 1810 are later copies.

Source: purchased from the Anderson Galleries, 1918, along with numerous printed books and pamphlets now in the Library's Rare Book Department.

SAN FRANCISCO COMMITTEE OF VIGILANCE, 1856
approximately 3750 pieces, 1853–58

The San Francisco Committees of Vigilance of 1851 and 1856 were formed when crime became widespread in the city of San Francisco in the wake of the Gold Rush. The city was without adequate processes of law, and the courts were a public scandal. As a means to preserve social order, a vigilance committee was formed for the administration of summary justice. The original committee, organized in the spring of 1851, disbanded after four months of vigorous activity served to accomplish its purpose. The reform was not a lasting one, however, and in 1856 renewed abuses by corrupt officials brought about a revival of the movement on a greatly augmented scale. The murder of James King of William sparked the reactivation of vigilante activities. King, a crusading San Francisco newspaper editor, was shot by James P. Casey, a corrupt official, after King attacked Casey in the columns of his paper. Immediately 10,000 men hastened to join the vigilantes, including many veterans of the earlier committee. William T. Coleman was again chosen as leader, and the members were organized into companies and regiments. Opposition to the vigilance committee was led by California Supreme Court Justice David S. Terry, but the efforts of his group were largely ineffective. The "Great Committee" of the vigilantes functioned for five months, then surrendered its powers to a regularly constituted civil authority.

Subject matter: individuals making charges or giving information about suspects or prisoners to the San Francisco Committee of Vigilance of 1856, applications for membership, lists of members and members of the executive committee, and financial documents.

Significant persons: James P. CASEY (24), David Smith TERRY (16).

Physical description: letters and documents.

Source: purchased from A. S. McDonald, 1916, and Sigurd Frederickson, 1931.

Bibliography: the collection is described in the *Huntington Library Bulletin,* no. 7 (1935): 50–53.

SAN RAFAEL RANCH COMPANY
41 pieces, 1871–1923

The San Rafael Ranch was created in 1883, when Mr. and Mrs. Alexander Robert Campbell-Johnston visited the small town of Garvanza, California (near present-day Pasadena), and purchased 2000 acres of the former Rancho San Rafael from Victor Beaudry. They left the ranch in the hands of their sons and went back to England, but returned to the ranch in 1888. The senior Campbell-Johnston died soon thereafter and the sons continued to run the ranch until about 1920. The ranch was used for cattle grazing and many buildings were constructed, including the Church of the Angels, erected in 1889 by Mrs. Campbell-Johnston in memory of her late husband. The land was subdivided after 1920.

Subject matter: business affairs (1898–1923) of Conway S. Campbell-Johnston and A. Campbell-Johnston, the sons of Alexander Robert Campbell-Johnston, including property titles, cattle records, property annexation agreements with the City of Pasadena, right-of-way agreements with the Pacific Electric Railway Company, and records of the Church of the Angels in Highland Park.

Physical description: letters, documents, and maps, including 14 bound volumes.

Source: gift of Lawrence Cook, February, 1955, and Nicholas Brandt, June, 1972.

SAUNDERS, CHARLES FRANCIS (1859–1941)
approximately 1500 pieces, 1901–41

Charles F. Saunders, horticulturalist and author, was born in Pennsylvania of Quaker ancestry. He was educated at the Friends Central School in Philadelphia, where he edited *The United Friend* (1894–97), engaged in commerce from 1875 to 1903, and studied botany as a hobby. In 1902, after his marriage to Elisabeth Moore Hallowell, the couple traveled throughout the West into New Mexico, Arizona, and California. Shortly afterward they settled in Pasadena, and subsequently collaborated on a number of books, mainly about the plants, gardens, Indians, the missions of California, and the West in general, including *The Indians of the Terraced Houses* (1912), published after Elizabeth Saunders' death in 1910, and *Under the Sky in California* (1913). After his first wife's death, Saunders continued to write and in 1921 married Mira Barrett Culin, a writer herself, who shared his interests.

Subject matter: mainly the concerns of Charles Francis and Mira B. (Culin) Saunders with horticulture, Indians, and missions of California and the Southwest. Includes a small group of letters dealing with world peace movements, and letters from Mary (Ritter) Beard, the historian, while she was chairman of the World Center for Women's Archives, Inc.

Significant persons: Mary (Ritter) BEARD (24).

Physical description: letters, manuscripts, 28 notebooks, and photographs.

Source: gift of Mrs. Mira C. Saunders, 1952, 1956.

SAXTON FAMILY COLLECTION
61 pieces, 1860–65

The Saxton, Buck, and Carroll families lived in central New York state during the time of the Civil War, and were related by the marriages of Ann Carroll to a Buck and Clarissa Carroll to a Saxton.

Subject matter: William Carroll's life as an itinerant schoolteacher in California, Americus D. Buck's service in Virginia during and immediately after the war, and Edward H. Spencer's service as a Union soldier in South Carolina and elsewhere during the war. Topics include family matters and soldiers' everyday lives.

Physical description: letters, with a few documents and ephemera.

Source: acquired from Harriette Saxton, 1955 and 1959.

SCHUYLER, PHILIP JOHN 1733–1804)
[Letterbook Containing Copies of 182 Letters] (ca.1850)
MS. volume 181 pp.

The letters were written between June 4 and Aug. 13, 1777 and concern the War for Independence.

SCHUYLER, WALTER SCRIBNER (1850–1932)
152 pieces, 1871–1932

Walter S. Schuyler, U.S. Army officer, was born in New York and graduated from West Point in 1870. He was assigned to the 5th Cavalry and participated in many Indian campaigns, serving with General Crook during the Apache hostilities (1872–75), and as Crook's aide-de-camp in the Big Horn, Yellowstone, and Powder River Expeditions (1876–77). Schuyler served at many Army posts in the West during his career, and was commissioned a brigadier-general in 1911 following duty in Russia, the Philippine Islands, Cuba, Manchuria, and Hawaii. He also was interested in mining, promoted the

Murchie Mine in Nevada City, California (1880–81), and became president of the Sierra-Alaska Mining Company of California.

Subject matter: Indian campaigns (1872–79), mainly in Arizona and Wyoming; general aspects of army life from 1872 to 1912; the Philippine Insurrection (1899–1901); the American occupation of Puerto Rico (1899) and of Cuba (1901–02); Manchuria during the Russo-Japanese War (1904); and mines and mining in California (1880–81; 1913–32).

Significant persons: George CROOK (31), Walter Scribner SCHUYLER (86).

Physical description: letters, manuscripts (including 46 of Schuyler's diaries, and 8 other volumes), documents.

Source: gift of Mrs. John Dunlop and George S. Schaeffer, May, 1943.

SCOTT, JAMES (fl. 1764–66)
Transaction on Board the Brig[anti]ne Lydia Myself Master [During Seven Trips between Boston and London] (1764–66) Autograph MS.S. volume 50 leaves

The vessel was owned by John Hancock.

SCRIBNER, BENJAMIN FRANKLIN (1825–1900)
approximately 1100 pieces, 1838–1911

Benjamin Franklin Scribner, Union officer, was born in 1825 and educated in New Albany, Indiana. During the Mexican War he served as a private in the 2nd Indiana Regiment, and in the Civil War he was commissioned colonel of the 38th Indiana Infantry Regiment, fighting with the Army of the Cumberland. After the war Scribner returned to private life and his pharmacy business, and from 1868 to 1880 was an agent and collector for the U.S. Treasury. He died in 1900.

Subject matter: Scribner's command and the administration of his regiment, including numerous general and special field orders, returns and final statements of deceased soldiers, personnel records, circulars, duty rosters, and requisitions and receipts for supplies; also a few postwar documents relating to Scribner's Treasury work and to veterans organizations and activities; a childhood composition book (1838); and a four-volume journal of his activities during the Mexican War. (1846). Strongest for the period from 1861 to 1865.

Physical description: chiefly documents (including many printed forms, filled in), with letters and a few manuscripts (including 6 bound volumes).

Source: purchased from John Howell, 1923.

SEARING FAMILY COLLECTION
2245 pieces, 1810–1941

The Searing family was socially prominent in Long Island, New York, during the later nineteenth century, and was related by marriage to William E. Valentine (1820–96?), a farmer with extensive property holdings in Brooklyn and Flushing, New York.

Subject matter: a little concerning the Searing family (including material on the U.S. Sanitary Commission), the vast majority of the papers in the collection pertain to Valentine and his financial and real estate affairs, and consist chiefly of bills, accounts, deeds, tax records, and banking papers. A few items refer to other members of the Valentine family.

Physical description: chiefly documents, with a few letters, one map of building sites located in Long Island in 1872, and 26 photographs.

Source: acquired from Mrs. Ruth Knowlton, 1972.

SERLE, AMBROSE (1742–1812)
[Military Journal] (1776–78)
Autograph MS. volume 180 leaves

Kept while Serle was secretary to General William Howe, May 2, 1776 to July 22, 1778. Published in *The American Journal of Ambrose Serle, Secretary to Lord Howe, 1776–1778*, ed. Edward H. Tatum (San Marino: Huntington Library, 1940).

SEVERANCE, CAROLINE MARIA (SEYMOUR) (1820–1914)
8400 pieces, 1875–1919

Caroline M. Severance, women's rights leader and founder of women's clubs, was born in New York and graduated from Record Female Seminary at the age of fifteen. In 1840 she married Theodore C. Severance, a banker, and they became the parents of five children. During their residence in Cleveland and Boston, Mrs. Severance was active in civic affairs. She helped found the first women's club in the U.S. in Boston in 1868. In 1875, the Severances moved to California. In Los Angeles, she became deeply involved in many projects including kindergarten schools, the Friday Morning Club, the Children's Orphan Asylum, and the founding of the Unitarian Church of Los Angeles and the Ebell Club of Los Angeles.

Subject matter: family business affairs, Caroline Severance's work with women's organizations. The variety of material in the collection contributes to the description of feminist involvement about the year 1900.

Significant persons: Jessie (Benton) FRÉMONT (34), Lucretia (Rudolph) GARFIELD (15), Francis Jackson GARRISON

(14), Elizabeth Morrisson (Boynton) HARBERT (15), Charles Fletcher LUMMIS (37), Helena (Opid) MODJESKA (8), Harriet (Mann) MILLER (14), Louis PRANG (11), Mary Dana (Hicks) PRANG (6), Caroline Maria (Seymour) SEVERANCE (125), and Marie Elizabeth ZAKRZEWSKA (14).

Physical description: letters, manuscripts (including notebooks and diaries), documents, and photographs.

Source: gift of The Historical Society of Southern California, September, 1974.

SHERMAN, WILLIAM TECUMSEH (1820–91)
52 pieces, 1862–90

William Tecumseh Sherman, Union general, graduated from West Point in 1840 and served as a career officer until 1853, when he resigned to enter the banking business. At the outbreak of the Civil War he was commissioned a colonel in the 13th Infantry and was soon promoted to brigadier general of volunteers, serving in Kentucky, Missouri, Mississippi, and Tennessee. After his promotion to brigadier general in the regular army following the capture of Vicksburg, Sherman was given command of the Armies of the Cumberland, the Tennessee, and the Ohio for the beginning of the Atlanta Campaign. In August 1864 he was promoted to major general, and in November began his famous "march to the sea" through Georgia, culminating in the capture of Savannah in December. Sherman then campaigned in the Carolinas until the end of the war. Thereafter he commanded the Division of the Mississippi, undertook a diplomatic mission to Mexico, and retired from the army in 1883. The remainder of his life was spent in St. Louis, Missouri, and New York.

Subject matter: strategy and tactics during the Civil War, as seen in Sherman's letters to his fellow commanders in the field (especially to David Dixon Porter [q.v.] concerning operations along the Yazoo River in 1862); the March to the Sea and the occupation of Savannah; Sherman's attempt to avoid post-war political quarrels. Strongest for the period from 1862 to 1865. Also includes a lengthy criticism by General Alpheus Starkey Williams of Sherman's memoirs.

A separate collection of typescript copies of correspondence between Sherman's wife, Ellen Boyle (Ewing) Sherman, and her mother, Maria (Boyle) Ewing, 1840–63, was given to the Library by Allan Nevins in 1959.

Physical description: chiefly letters, with a very few documents and manuscripts.

Source: acquired from various sources, including G. D. Smith, William K. Bixby, and others, beginning about 1918.

SHIMMIN, WILLIAM HENRY (fl. 1885–1916)
82 pieces, 1882–1915
William H. Shimmin was a mining prospector in Goldfield, Nevada, who helped develop the mining camp of Jamestown, Nevada, about twenty miles southeast of Goldfield. Goldfield developed after the discovery of gold in 1903 and grew into a town of over a thousand within a year. It continued to flourish with the discovery of rich ore in the Mohawk Mine, and reached a population of 20,000 in 1907–08. In 1910, over $10,000,000 worth of ore was removed, but by 1918 it was exhausted and the mine closed its mill.

Subject matter: business and mining matters, dealing chiefly with mining claims in Nevada, mainly at Goldfield, and with the Jamestown Townsite Co.

Physical description: letters, documents, and 1 map.

Source: gift of Thomas and James Watterson, September, 1934.

SHIRLEY, WILLIAM (1694–1771)
[Journal of the Siege of Louisbourg] (1745)
MS. volume 10 pp.

A contemporary copy covering April 22 to June 16, 1745. Published as *A Letter . . . to His Grace the Duke of Newcastle . . . with a Journal of the Siege of Louisbourg* (London, 1746).

SHORB, JAMES de BARTH (1842–96)
approximately 10,600 pieces, 1816–1931

James de Barth Shorb, an attorney and civil engineer from Maryland, came to California in 1864 to represent the Philadelphia and California Petroleum Company. He was later an engineer with the United States Army. After his marriage to Maria de Jesus Wilson in 1867, Shorb joined his father-in-law, Benjamin Davis Wilson, in the development of their extensive land holdings and in the founding of the San Gabriel Winery. Shorb constructed and was president of the San Gabriel Valley Railroad and the Alhambra Railroad. He was active in many business ventures and served as Los Angeles County treasurer in 1892.

Subject matter: personal and business affairs of James de Barth Shorb: the San Marino Ranch (now the city of San Marino, California), land development in Southern California, the citrus and wine industries in California (especially the San Gabriel Winery owned by Benjamin Davis Wilson and managed by James de Barth Shorb), and California politics.

Significant persons: Phineas BANNING (15), Thomas Robert BARD (13), Stephen Johnson FIELD (5), William McKendree GWIN (8), George HEARST (9), Isaias William HELL-

MAN (25), Abbot KINNEY (7), William W. MORROW (7), Francis Griffith NEWLANDS (24), Harrison Gray OTIS (10), Leland STANFORD (5), Harriet Williams (Russell) STRONG (5), Benjamin Cummings TRUMAN (5), Stephen Mallory WHITE (30), Charles Dwight WILLARD (10), Benjamin Davis WILSON (109).

Physical description: letters (including 22 letterbooks), manuscripts (including 3 diaries), documents (including 9 record books), and maps.

Source: gift of Mrs. Edith Shorb Steele, 1934–50, and Miss Ethel R. Shorb, 1959.

SIERRA NEVADA SILVER MINING COMPANY
53 pieces, 1860–80

The Sierra Nevada Silver Mining Company, one of the mines of the Comstock Lode at Virginia City, Nevada, was actively worked during the boom years of the 1860s and 1870s, but never produced great yields. George Hearst was one of the investors in the Sierra Nevada company. Another was William Morris Stewart, a prominent lawyer in Comstock mining cases and U.S. senator from Nevada (1864–75; 1887–1905). As attorney for the Sierra Nevada Silver Mining Company in 1862–63, Stewart represented them in a suit against the American Mining Company involving title rights. The case took a remarkable turn when Stewart made the discovery that George D. Whitney, president of the Sierra Nevada Silver Mining Company, had secretly sided with the American Mining Company in return for a large amount of stock (as it was later ascertained). Stewart's legal expertise in his courtroom interrogation of Whitney, however, won the verdict for the plaintiff. The Sierra Nevada Silver Mining Company continued producing ore until 1881, but its last dividend was paid in 1871.

Subject matter: business affairs of the Sierra Nevada Silver Mining Company, chiefly from the period 1860–63, as well as the court case of the *Sierra Nevada Silver Mining Company v. the American Mining Company* (1862–63).

Significant persons: William Morris STEWART (7).

Physical description: letters and documents.

Source: purchased from Grahame H. Hardy, March, 1950.

SILL, HARLEY A. (fl. 1930–64)
approximately 1445 pieces, 1901–64

Harley A. Sill, Los Angeles mining engineer, was a consultant who visited and made reports on various types of mines throughout the western hemisphere, but particularly in California and the American West.

Subject matter: reports on ores and mines, and technical data, chiefly from California, Arizona, Nevada, Canada and Mexico, but also including some reports on mines in other parts of the U.S. and in South and Central America.

Physical description: letters, documents, and maps.

Source: gift of Mrs. Harley A. Sill, October, 1973.

SIMCOE, JOHN GRAVES (1752–1806)
[Journal of Operations of the Queen's Rangers] (1777–83)
Autograph MS. volume 55 pp.

Comprises the introduction to and a variant part of the text printed in John Graves Simcoe, *Journal of the Operation of the Queen's Rangers* (Exeter, Eng., [1787]).

———

[Letterbook] (1791–93)
MS. volume 283 pp.

Kept while Simcoe was lieutenant governor of Upper Canada.

SIMSBURY (CONN.) UNION LIBRARY
[Constitution, By-laws, Accounts, Minutes, and Catalogue of
Books Belonging to the Simsbury Union Library] (1797–1813)
MS. volume 180 pp.

SINCLAIR, HENRY HARBINSON (?–1914)
approximately 1300 pieces, 1819–1937

Henry H. Sinclair, Southern California hydro-electrical engineer, settled in Redlands, California, for his health in 1887.
There he was active in community affairs, and served as one
of the first city trustees in 1888. Sinclair was instrumental in
the development of hydro-electric power in Southern California and helped organize the Redlands Electric Light and
Power Company, which was franchised in 1892. Working with
A. W. Decker, developer of electrical power for Mt. Lowe,
Sinclair was responsible for the building of the first three-
phase long distance transmission power plant in the world,
from Mill Creek, near Redlands, to Los Angeles. He became
director of the California Power Company (formed to build
an electric plant on the Kern River), general manager of
the Edison Electric Company, and a director of the Southern
California Edison Company and various other corporations.
Sinclair later moved to Pasadena where he was active in the
Tournament of Roses Association.

Subject matter: mostly business matters (1909–14) dealing
with the Great Western Power Company, Palmer Oil Company, Mt. Hood Railway and Power Company, etc.; diaries
(1896–1907), and notebooks (1893–1909) concerning power
plant inspection trips, mostly to the Kern River in California;
the Pasadena Tournament of Roses Association (1911–14);
the California to Honolulu Yacht Races (1905–08). Also includes his son's papers pertaining to California Delta Farms,
Incorporated (1920–29).

Physical description: letters, manuscripts (including 9 diaries and 17 notebooks), and documents.

Source: gift of Arthur W. and Marjorie Sinclair, February, 1936.

SLAUGHTER, MONTGOMERY (fl. 1862–67)
50 pieces, 1862–66

Montgomery Slaughter, Fredericksburg merchant and civic leader, served as mayor of the city during and immediately after the Civil War. During the Union occupation in the summer of 1862, Slaughter and other civic leaders were temporarily imprisoned, although relations between municipal and military authorities were generally good. After the defeat of the Union forces under Burnside in the battle of December 13, 1862, Slaughter organized the rehabilitation of the war-torn city and its population of wounded, refugees, and regular citizens. After the war he returned to mercantile affairs for a brief while, but was elected judge of the Corporation Court of Fredericksburg, in which post he continued until his retirement.

Subject matter: chiefly letters: (1) to Slaughter from military authorities concerning relations between the army and the civilian population in 1862, including Sumner's request for surrender dated November 21, 1862, and Slaughter's answer; and (2) to Slaughter after the battle from contributors to a relief fund for the city.

Significant persons: Rufus KING (1814–76) (8).

Physical description: letters, mounted into a one-volume scrapbook which also includes some ephemera, such as etchings of several Civil War generals.

Sources: purchased from Walter C. Wyman, ca.1925.

SMITH, LURA (CASE) (fl. 1854–60)
80 pieces, 1852–65

Lura (Case) Smith arrived in California in 1853, joining her husband Jesse R. Smith, who, in 1851, had left their home on Long Island, New York, to engage in mining in California. The family settled in San Francisco where Jesse worked as a contractor until 1855, when they moved to Vallejo, California, where he worked at the U.S. Naval Shipyard at Mare Island. They returned to San Francisco six months later and lived there, where Jesse was employed in the lumber business until 1867.

Subject matter: incidents of daily life in San Francisco (1854–65) and the 6 month stay at the Mare Island Naval Shipyard in Vallejo, California (June–November, 1855), mainly as seen by Lura (Case) Smith; a small amount of information on mining near Columbia, California (1852).

Physical description: letters.

Source: purchased from Edwin Grabhorn, January, 1945.

SMITH, SAMUEL FRANCIS (1808–95)
129 pieces, 1822–94

Samuel F. Smith, Baptist clergyman, editor, and poet, was born in Boston and graduated from Harvard University in 1829 and from Andover Theological Seminary in 1832. He wrote the words for the patriotic hymn "America" while he was a student at the Seminary. After becoming ordained as a Baptist minister in 1834, he served as a pastor in Maine from 1833 to 1842, (where he was also professor of modern languages at Waterville, now Colby, College) and at Newton Center, Massachusetts, from 1842 to 1848. He also edited *The*

Christian Review, and in 1854 became editorial secretary of the American Baptist Missionary Union. Smith wrote many poems, hymns, and prose works.

Subject matter: the family, social, and religious life of New England Baptists, mainly in the years 1834 to 1840, as seen in the letters of Samuel F. Smith to members of his family, also some critical letters regarding Andover Theological Seminary (1829–32) and descriptions of travel in Europe (1875–76).

Physical description: letters and 1 manuscript

Source: gift of Mrs. Bess Hathaway, 1966 and purchase from Scribner's, 1967.

SMITH, THOMAS KILBY (1820–87)
434 pieces, 1848–87

Thomas Kilby Smith, Union general, was prominent in the western campaigns of the Civil War. He was born in Boston, then moved with his family to Cincinnati in 1820. Smith was educated in Cincinnati, and after legal training in the office of Salmon P. Chase, was admitted to the bar in 1843. He practiced law until 1853, then served in the Post Office Department in Washington, D.C. and as a United States marshal in Ohio. In 1861, Smith became a lieutenant colonel in the 45th Ohio Infantry. He commanded several campaigns in the Civil War, and was assigned to staff duty with General Ulysses S. Grant in 1863. Soon after, he was commissioned brigadier general of volunteers, and continued to lead troops in many Civil War encounters. Failing health caused him to retire from active duty in 1864. He became United States consul at Panama in 1866, and later worked for the New York *Star* until his death in 1887.

Subject matter: mainly Civil War, concentrated in the years 1861–65, dealing with Smith's recruitment of the 54th Regiment in Ohio, his involvement in the battles of Shiloh and Corinth, the Tallahatchie and Arkansas Post Expeditions, the Chickasaw Bluffs attack, the Vicksburg assault and seige, the Red River campaign with General Banks, and other battles; also material concerning Smith's pre-Civil War service with the federal government in Washington, D.C., and in Cincinnati, Ohio, and, after the Civil War, his career as United States consul in Panama and other activities.

Physical description: letters and 1 manuscript.

Source: purchased from Peter Decker, 1959.

Bibliography: about half of the letters have been published in Walter George Smith, *Life and Letters of Thomas Kilby Smith, Brevet-Major General, United States Volunteers, 1820– 1887* . . . , (New York: G. P. Putnam & Sons, 1898).

SMITH-SPOONER COLLECTION
899 pieces, 1819–1916

Caleb Blood Smith (1808–64), lawyer, congressman, and cabinet officer, was born in Boston and went to Cincinnati with his family in 1814. After attending college, he studied law and was admitted to the bar in 1828. He purchased a newspaper, renamed it the *Indiana Sentinel,* and used it to promote his Whig views. He was elected to the Indiana House of Representatives, where he served during the years 1833–37 and 1840–41, and to the United States congress as a Whig from 1843 to 1849. Smith returned to law practice in Cincinnati in 1851. He became president of the Cincinnati and Chicago Railroad Company in 1854, but following financial problems he moved to Indianapolis. In 1860, Smith was active in Lincoln's campaign for the presidency and was in turn appointed secretary of the interior in 1861. His failing health caused him to resign the next year and he became a United States district court judge for Indiana.

Charles William Spooner (fl. 1864–1900), was a Union naval officer, European traveler (1871–72), and New York City attorney, whose father had studied law with Caleb Blood Smith in 1843–44.

Subject matter: politics, railroad lands, and alleged irregularities in the Bureau of Indian Affairs, as reflected in the papers of Caleb Blood Smith, especially in correspondence with many prominent persons in the military, the Whig Party, and the abolition movement; also material concerning Charles William Spooner and his service as an ensign aboard the gunboat U.S.S. "Reindeer" in the Civil War, and his travels in Europe.

Significant persons: Cassius Marcellus CLAY (10).

Physical description: letters (including 1 letter book), manuscripts (including 1 copy book), documents, 2 maps, and 1 scrapbook.

Source: purchased from Mrs. Caleb Blood Smith, June, 1958.

SOCIETY OF FRIENDS IN OHIO
75 pieces, 1798–1869

A collection of correspondence and other papers relating to the Society of Friends in Ohio, including minutes and other reports of Monthly, Quarterly, and Yearly Meetings, letters to Quakers in other states, and accounts of the daily religious and social life of various Ohio communities. Included is a journal-letterbook of Rachel Patterson, a Quaker minister active in the 1840s and 1850s.

Physical description: letters, documents (including two volumes of minutes) and manuscripts, with ephemera.

Source: acquired from Mrs. Howard H. Carpenter, 1953 and Daniel J. Jaeger, 1965.

SOLANO-REEVE COLLECTION
approximately 1400 pieces, 1849–1900

In 1875 Alfred Solano became associated with surveyor George Hansen (1824–97), assisting him in the making of surveys of various tracts in Los Angeles County and in other parts of Southern California. Hansen, a native of Austria, had come to California around the Horn in 1850 to seek gold, and unsuccessful in this, came to Los Angeles in 1853. In 1857, he was elected superintendent of the Los Angeles Vineyard Society of San Francisco, for whom he laid out the colony of Anaheim. He served as Los Angeles city surveyor from 1863 to 1868, and in 1883. After Hansen's death in 1897, his records were left to Solano, who became a partner of Sidney B. Reeve, also a surveyor, with an office in Los Angeles. Following the death of Reeve, the material in the office concerning surveys was gathered together by his widow and Solano, and subsequently formed this collection.

Subject matter: maps (approximately 1000) and surveys made by George Hansen, Alfred Solano, and others, of the city of Los Angeles, Southern California ranchos, and subdivisions of the city of Los Angeles and neighboring towns.

Physical description: maps and documents (including 302 volumes of field books, 1854–98, and daily record books).

Source: purchased from Alfred Solano and Anna B. Reeve, May, 1933.

SPALDING, WILLIAM ANDREW (1852–1941)
1493 pieces, 1861–1941

William A. Spalding, Los Angeles journalist and civic leader, attended the University of Michigan in 1871 and came to Los

Angeles in 1874. He was business manager of the *Daily Herald* and city editor of both the *Evening Express* and the *Los Angeles Times* (1886). He became a vice-president of the Times-Mirror Company, which owned the *Los Angeles Times*. Spalding engaged in fruit growing for several years, wrote *The Orange and its Culture in California* (1885), and was one of the organizers of the California Fruit-Growers Exchange. He served on several municipal commissions, was a founder and board member of the Los Angeles Museum of Natural History, and president of the Southern California Academy of Sciences. Spalding wrote *History and Reminiscences, Los Angeles City and County* in 1931.

Subject matter: Spalding's life and interest in Los Angeles civic affairs, as reflected in correspondence (1861–1941), business papers (1883–1929), and drafts of speeches (mainly given before Los Angeles civic organizations). Also included are Spalding's autobiography and additional biographical material.

Physical description: letters, manuscripts, documents, and photographs.

Source: gift of Mrs. Wilfred L. Cooper, 1943.

Bibliography: the manuscript autobiography of Spalding in this collection has been published in *William Andrew Spalding; Los Angeles Newspaperman; an Autobiographical Account,* ed. Robert V. Hine (San Marino: Huntington Library, 1961).

SPANISH DOCUMENTS
86 pieces, 1783–95

At the close of the American Revolutionary War, preliminary articles of peace between Great Britain and her adversaries the United States, Spain, and France, were signed on January 20, 1783, at Versailles. In the agreement between Spain and Great Britain, the former regained Florida, which it had lost to Great Britain at the end of the Seven Years' War in 1763. Yet Americans were hostile to Spanish control. They began to expand into Florida, first gaining the territory called the Yazoo Strip through the Treaty of San Lorenzo (Pinckney's Treaty) in October, 1795. By 1821 Spain agreed, by the Adams-Onís Treaty, to the cession of Florida to the United States.

Subject matter: the Peace Treaty of 1783 as it affected Spain and its possessions (especially the West Indies), including original notifications of the cessation of hostilities and orders to civil and military authorities, the validity of captures at sea, and the test of 2 articles of the treaty; also papers concerning the invasion of Florida by "the American Abner Hammond, and 62 other vagabonds," in August of 1795.

Physical description: documents (in Spanish).

Source: purchased from Maggs Brothers, 1926.

SPENCE-LOWELL COLLECTION
321 pieces, 1740–>1958

Keith Spence, American naval officer and merchant, left his home and family in Portsmouth, New Hampshire, in 1791 in an attempt to better his fortune in the West Indies. He later served as purser aboard the "Constellation" during the Tripolitan War, was taken prisoner of war in Tripoli, returned to the United States at the close of the war, and spent his final years as a Navy agent in New Orleans. Spence died about 1810. His wife, Mary (Traill) Spence(d.1824), was connected with the prominent Whipple and Lowell families, and their daughter, Harriet Brackett (Spence) Lowell, was the mother of James Russell Lowell.

Subject matter: trade and privateering in the West Indies (1797–1800); the U.S. Navy and the Tripolitan War (1802–05); description of or travel in Malaga, Gibraltar, Malta,

Tunis, Algiers, Sicily, Italy, New England, and New Orleans; Whipple and Lowell families; early history of Portsmouth, New Hampshire. Also includes ninety-eight autograph letters collected by Mary Traill Spence (Lowell) Putnam, sister of James Russell Lowell, and written by various prominent American and European figures of the nineteenth century. Strongest for 1797 to 1810.

Physical description: chiefly letters, with a few manuscripts and documents.

Source: purchased from Mary B. Bigelow, 1960.

SPENCER, CHARLES, 3RD EARL OF SUNDERLAND (1674–1722)
87 pieces, 1704–10

Charles Spencer, 3rd Earl of Sunderland, Whig politician, was appointed secretary of state for the Southern Department in 1706 through the influence of his father-in-law, John Churchill, Duke of Marlborough. Dismissed from office in 1710, Spencer returned to power only with the accession of George I, whom he served as 1st lord of the treasury (1718–21).

Subject matter: Queen Anne's War; politics and war in New York and New Jersey, including Lewis Morris and his "factious party"; the Palatine settlements; Newfoundland fisheries; colonial trade.

Significant persons: Joseph DUDLEY (6), Edmund JENNINGS (12).

Physical description: letters and documents.

Source: purchased from Maggs Brothers, 1926.

Bibliography: some of the pieces in this collection have been published in William A. Whitehead, ed., *Documents Relating*

to the Colonial History of the State of New Jersey (Newark,
1880–86).

SQUIER, EPHRAIM GEORGE (1821–88)
489 pieces, 1852–58

Ephraim G. Squier, archaeologist and author, was a native of
New York. Mainly self-educated, he learned the essentials of
civil engineering. Squier wrote for newspapers and became
editor of the *Hartford Journal*. His investigations of prehistoric
Indians in the U.S. were published in scientific journals. In
1849, he went to Central America as chargé d'affaires, and
returned in 1853 to make surveys for the Honduras Interoceanic Railway, of which he was secretary. He served as
U.S. commissioner to Peru (1863–65) and as consul general
of Honduras in New York in 1868. Squier wrote many books
on Central and South America.

Subject matter: Squier's unrealized project for the Honduras
Interoceanic Railway, explorations and surveys with reference
to the practicability of a ship canal, etc.

Physical description: letters, documents, manuscripts (including 35 notebooks and field books), and maps.

Source: purchased from the American Art Association, January, 1924.

STANTON, EDWIN McMASTERS (1814–69)
46 pieces, 1815–1907

Edwin McMasters Stanton, lawyer and public official, was
born in Steubenville, Ohio, in 1814, the son of the Quaker
physician David Stanton and Lucy (Norman) Stanton. Stan-

ton was admitted to the bar in 1836 and practised law in Ohio and Pennsylvania before moving to Washington, D.C., in 1856. In 1862 he was appointed secretary of war, and served in that office until 1868, when his opposition to the Reconstruction policies of Andrew Johnson forced his dismissal. Stanton died in 1869 before he could take up a position on the U.S. Supreme Court.

Subject matter: chiefly the business and personal correspondence of Stanton's uncle, Dr. Benjamin Stanton of Salem, Ohio, with the latter's son William and their acquaintances. Topics include Stanton family activities and home life, William Stanton's decision to study law, and some information about politics and patronage.

Significant persons: Edwin McMasters STANTON (8).

Physical description: letters, with ephemera.

Sources: acquired from Dr. Lewis Picher of Denver, Colorado, December 1969.

STANTON, PHILIP ACKLEY (1868–1945)
approximately 265 pieces, 1909–29

Philip A. Stanton, Los Angeles realtor and California politician, was born and educated in Ohio. He came to California in 1887, became president of several real estate companies, and was responsible for building the towns of Huntington Beach, Seal Beach, and Stanton. He served in the California assembly (1903–09), as candidate for governor of California in the primary election of 1910, and as a member of the Republican National Committee for California (1912–16).

Subject matter: personal, business, and political matters, dealing in part with land development in Orange County but chiefly with California and national politics, including the

Herbert Hoover campaign of 1920, Hiram Warren Johnson, and William Howard Taft.

Significant persons: Isaias William HELLMAN (11).

Physical description: letters and documents.

Source: purchased from G. F. Hollingsworth, 1956 and 1958.

STEARNS, ABEL (1798–1871)
approximately 12,500 pieces, 1821–>1935

Abel Stearns, pioneer ranch owner and businessman of Los Angeles, left Massachusetts as a young man to engage in the South American and China shipping trade. He went to Mexico in 1826, became a naturalized citizen, and in 1829 moved to Monterey, California, where he went into merchandising. In about 1833 Stearns settled in Los Angeles, joined Juan Bandini in the trading business, and married Bandini's daughter Arcadia. Stearns became involved in almost every type of business, held minor political offices, and was sent as a representative of the Los Angeles district to the state constitutional convention in Monterey in 1849. He began acquiring rancho property and by 1858 was the owner of vast land holdings and cattle herds and the wealthiest man in Los Angeles county. As a member of the state assembly in 1861, he took an active part in promoting the Los Angeles and San Pedro Railroad. Stearns was forced to sell a great deal of his property when he became bankrupt after the drought of 1863–64, which caused the decline of the cattle industry in California. He died in San Francisco in 1871.

Subject matter: life in California during the Mexican and early statehood periods, with cattle raising, trading transactions (especially in hides and tallow), ranchos of Upper and Lower California, land titles and transfers, political and social life, and the gold discoveries in Southern California in 1842.

Also included are diaries written in the Santa Monica area (1879–1905) by Juan Bautista Bandini, son of Juan Bandini. There is a small sub-collection, the Gaffey Papers, assembled by John Tracy Gaffey, who married Arcadia Bandini, niece of Mrs. Abel Stearns. They consist of correspondence, including letters from Stephen Mallory White, papers relating to San Pedro, California, and historical sketches.

Significant persons: Juan Bautista ALVARADO (13), Juan BANDINI (190), Lewis T. BURTON (15), Carlos Antonio de Jesús CARRILLO (21), José Antonio Ezequiel CARRILLO (12), José CASTRO (11), John Bautista Rogers COOPER (10), Cave Johnson COUTS (90), Henry DALTON (12), Tomás Eleuterio ESTÉNAGA (106), Francisco FIGUEROA (27), Henry Delano FITCH (45), John FORSTER (83), John Charles FRÉMONT (11), Thomas Oliver LARKIN (93), Augustín OLVERA (27), Blas ORDAZ (18), Pío PICO (21), Perfecto Hugo REID (116), Alfred ROBINSON (221), Nathan SPEAR (17), David SPENCE (16), Abel STEARNS (169), Alpheus Basil THOMPSON (73), Jonathan Trumbull WARNER (14), Stephen Mallory WHITE (69), Isaac WILLIAMS (11).

Physical Description: letters and documents (including 13 volumes), in Spanish and English.

Source: purchased from Mrs. Margaret Gaffey Kilroy Mel, 1937–39 and 1971. Gift of additional material by Mrs. Susanna B. Dakin, 1939.

STEELE, JAMES KING (1875–1937)
approximately 590 pieces, 1909–36

James King Steele, editor and author, was born in Iowa, received his education there, and went to San Francisco in 1901 to become a publicity man for a chain of merchandising stores. He published the *Del Monte* (Calif.) *Weekly* (1908–11), and was editor and publisher of the *World Traveler* (1911–16) and the travel magazine *Japan* (1917–29). Steele was active in tourist development organizations, including the Philippine Tourist Association (1930–35) and the Japan Tourist Bureau, which he founded. He lectured and wrote articles on Asia and presented radio talks on a variety of subjects. Steele married Edith Shorb, the daughter of James de Barth Shorb (q.v.).

Subject matter: correspondence of James King Steele (1926–37) and Edith (Shorb) Steele (1909–10), business papers mainly relating to the tourist business in the Philippine Islands and Japan, and 8 radio scripts (1934–36).

Physical description: letters, documents, manuscripts, and photographs.

Source: gift of Mrs. James King Steele, March, 1950.

STERN, BERNHARD JOSEPH (1894–1956)
840 pieces, 1926–43

Bernhard Joseph Stern, sociologist, author, and educator, was born in Chicago and studied at the universities of Cincinnati, Michigan, Berlin, and the London School of Economics before receiving, in 1927, a Ph.D. in sociology and anthropology at Columbia University. Following a brief appointment at the University of Washington (1927–30), Stern returned to the New School for Social Research at Columbia, where he continued to teach until his death in 1956. Stern was particularly interested in historical sociology, anthropology, genetics, and medical sociology, and published textbooks and articles as well as founding and editing the quarterly journal *Science and Society.* In 1931 his biography *Lewis Henry Morgan: Social Evolutionist* was published by the University of Chicago Press, and five years later Stern entered into an agreement with the Institute of Anthropology and Ethnography of the Academy of Sciences of the Soviet Union to join their editorial committee for the publication of the complete works of Lewis Henry Morgan.

Subject matter: Stern's research into, and publication of, the life of Lewis Henry Morgan, especially his correspondence with the library of the University of Rochester where much Morgan material was deposited; negotiations with the Soviet Institute and with Soviet scholars concerning their mutual interest in Morgan. Also includes copies of 148 letters or extracts of letters from Morgan written during the period 1862–81, as well as Stern's working notes, outlines, and drafts of articles.

Physical description: letters and manuscripts, with some printed material (including Russian reviews of Stern's book), photographs, and other ephemera. Some of the letters are in Russian, with accompanying translations.

Source: gift of Mrs. Bernhard Stern, April, 1968.

STETSON, AUGUSTA EMMA (SIMMONS) (ca.1842–1928) 610 pieces, 1885–1928

Augusta Emma (Simmons) Stetson, Christian Science leader, was born and educated in Maine, and in 1864 married Frederick J. Stetson, with whom she traveled extensively in the Orient before his poor health forced their return to the United States. Settling in Boston, Mrs. Stetson became a follower of Mary Baker Eddy, and was sent to New York in 1886 to carry the Church to that city. The First Church of Christ, Scientist, New York, was founded by Mrs. Stetson two years later. Increasing differences with Mrs. Eddy, however, led to the excommunication of Mrs. Stetson in 1909. She continued to support the Church and Mrs. Eddy, nevertheless, and wrote favorably about Mrs. Eddy in numerous books and other writings.

Subject matter: Christian Science and the First Church of Christ, Scientist, of New York (including letters to students and the press), Mary Baker Eddy and her relations with Mrs. Stetson, and Mrs. Stetson's publications and other writings. Strongest for the years 1900–15.

Significant persons: Mary Baker EDDY (153), Calvin A. FRYE (36), Laura E. SARGENT (29).

Physical description: letters, documents, and manuscripts, with ephemera (including newspaper clippings and some photographs).

Source: gift of Mrs. Charlotte B. MacLaren, 1956.

Bibliography: some of the Stetson-Eddy correspondence is printed in Augusta E. Stetson, *Reminiscences, Sermons, and Correspondence* (New York: G. P. Putnam's Sons, 1913) and *Vital Issues in Christian Science* (New York: G. P. Putnam's Sons, 1914).

STETSON-HAYES COLLECTION
41 pieces, 1906–25

Augusta Emma (Simmons) Stetson (q.v.), Christian Science leader and sometime associate of Mary Baker Eddy, founded the First Church of Christ, Scientist, in New York City. Among the many people with whom she corresponded were James Henry Hayes and his wife, Florence Belle (Donnelly) Hayes, of Atlantic City, New Jersey.

Subject matter: Augusta Stetson's belief in and philosophy of Christian Science.

Physical description: letters.

Source: gift of Mrs. James H. Hayes, 1957

STIMSON, MARSHALL (1876–1951)
932 pieces, 1893–1951

Marshall Stimson, Los Angeles lawyer, came to Pasadena, California, from Massachusetts with his family in 1887, but returned to Harvard College, where he graduated in 1901, and began to practice law in Boston. In 1903 Stimson moved his practice to Los Angeles, where he became an important figure in civic affairs. He was instrumental in the development of Los Angeles Harbor, director of the Los Angeles Chamber of Commerce, and active in reform movements in state and local governments. Stimson was prominent in Republican politics, and organized the Lincoln-Roosevelt Republican League of California (1907) and the Progressive Party in California (1912). He was also active in supporting the League of Nations and the United Nations.

Subject matter: radio addresses of Marshall Stimson, and the manuscript of his autobiography; California and national politics (including Hiram Johnson and the Progressive Party "Bull Moose" Convention of 1912), General Homer Lea, the League of Nations, and World War II.

Physical description: letters, manuscripts (including 25 diaries and notebooks), documents (including 5 account books), photographs, and 9 scrapbooks.

Source: gift of Mrs. Marshall Stimson, November, 1953, and Gordon Stimson, 1972 and 1973.

STONE, ANDREW J. (fl. 1852–65)
45 pieces, 1852–65

Andrew J. Stone, gold seeker, came to California from Dunbarton, New Hampshire, in 1852. He traveled on the steamship "Northern Light" to Nicaragua, crossed the isthmus, and continued the journey on the steamship "Lewis," arriving in San Francisco after a journey of sixty-three days. Stone worked in the mines in El Dorado and Placer Counties, in a sawmill, and as a steam car engineer for a quartz mine. After his return home, he served in the Union army in the Civil War.

Subject matter: Stone's voyage by ship from New York to San Francisco and life in the California mines; a few letters from friends who stayed in California, written to Stone after his return home.

Physical description: letters.

Source: purchased from Aldini Book Company, November, 1944.

STOW, JOSEPH WASHINGTON (ca.1830–74)
41 pieces, 1865 (July–September)

Joseph W. Stow, early San Francisco businessman and philanthropist, was a native of Vermont who came to California by the Isthmus of Panama. He was associated in several business enterprises with William C. Ralston, president of the Bank of California, which made loans to mines after their appraisal. Stow received the reports and sold mining machinery from his hardware warehouse. Ralston, Edward P. Pringle, and Stow were partners in an unsuccessful venture to treat refractory ores, called the Hagan Process for the Disintegration of Ores. Stow was active in the San Francisco Mercantile Library, the San Francisco Benevolent Society, and other charities, and served as president of the Commercial Association and a trustee of the Chamber of Commerce. His wife, Marietta Lois "Lizzie Bell" (Beers) Stow, was a leader in women's rights causes.

Subject matter: the examination of quartz mines in El Dorado, Calaveras, Amador, and Tuolomne Counties.

Physical description: letters and documents.

Source: purchased from Edwin Grabhorn, January, 1945.

STOWE COLLECTION—AMERICANA
approximately 850 pieces, 1680–1904

The Stowe Collection, consisting of the muniments and family papers of the English Grenville, Temple, Brydges, Nugent, and O'Conor families, numbers well over half a million pieces and ranges in date from the twelfth century to the twentieth. The STOWE AMERICANA is a small sub-collection consisting of the papers of those various members of the five related families who had interest or office in America or the West Indies.

Subject matter: James Brydges, 1st Duke of Chandos (1674–1744), and his interest in trade, the Royal African Company, and "Equivalent Lands" in New York; St. Christopher and the Leeward Islands at the time of Governor William Mathew, 1718–25; Governor Henry Grenville of Barbados and Anglo-French diplomatic negotiations, 1747–52; Jamaica and the administration of the "Hope" and "Middleton" plantations, which came into the possession of the Brydges family with the marriage of the 3rd Duke of Chandos to Anne Eliza (Gamon) Elletson (including information on plantation finance, Negro slaves, cultivation of crops, weather conditions, and livestock), 1743–1904; the Treaty of Paris and peace preliminaries at Fontainebleau, as seen in the papers of British secretary of state George Grenville, 1762–63; British colonial administration (chiefly of possessions acquired by the Treaty of Paris); public revenue in North America, 1764–70, as illustrated in the papers of John Temple, surveyor general of the

349

customs in the colonies (including Temple's dispute with Governor Bernard of Massachusetts and American reaction to the Stamp Act).

Significant persons: James BRYDGES, 1st Duke of Chandos (18 letterbooks, including about 100 letters to American correspondents), Marquis de CAYLUS (6), Duc de CHOISEUL (8), Comte de CHOISEUL (7), Henry GRENVILLE (52), Francis HOLBURNE (8), LE BAILLI SOLAR DE BREILLE (12), John RUSSELL, 4th Duke of Bedford (12), Charles WYNDHAM, 2nd Earl of Egremont (28).

Source: purchased through Frank Marcham and the Museum Bookstore, London, August, 1925.

STOWELL, NATHAN W. (fl. 1903–06)
approximately 150 pieces, 1858–1916

Nathan W. Stowell, Los Angeles businessman and financier, was an early resident of Ontario, California. He was associated with the hydro-electrical engineer George Chaffey in land and water development in the Cucamonga area and in the Imperial Valley. Stowell was vice-president of the California Development Company and president of the Imperial Water Company Number 1 in 1902. Both companies were involved in the development of the Imperial Valley Irrigation Project.

Subject matter: business affairs relating to the Cucamonga area, Los Angeles, and the Imperial Valley; surveys and maps (mostly copies) of Los Angeles by Henry Hancock, George Hansen, and others.

Physical description: letters, field notes and other documents (including 7 volumes), and maps.

Source: purchased from N. Kovach, 1943–45.

STRONG, HARRIET WILLIAMS (RUSSELL) (1844–1926)
1072 pieces, 1815–1939

Harriet W. R. Strong, California businesswoman and social leader, grew up near Quincy, California, and attended the Young Ladies Seminary at Benicia from 1858 to 1860. In 1861 she moved with her family to Carson City, Nevada, where she married Charles Lyman Strong, a graduate of Amherst College and superintendent of the Gould and Curry Mine in Virginia City. The couple lived in Virginia City until Strong's failing health forced him to resign his position with Gould and Curry; they then moved to Oakland, California. In the 1860s Strong purchased part of Pío Pico's Ranch near Whittier, California, but left to engage in mining ventures in Hardyville and La Paz, Arizona (1866–67), Kernville, California (1872–76), and Galena, Nevada (1877–80). In 1883, following an unfortunate investment in an Auburn, California, mine, he took his own life. Mrs. Strong had been living in Oakland and Whittier, taking care of their four daughters, but after the death of her husband she took over the active management of their property, devising new types of crops, business methods, and systems of flood control. She became an active clubwoman in Los Angeles, and was influential in both business and cultural circles.

Subject matter: mining in Virginia City (1860–67) and Galena (1877–80), Nevada, and in California and Arizona; California horticulture; Civil War General George Crockett Strong, the brother of Charles Lyman Strong.

Significant persons: Charles Lyman STRONG (416), Harriet Williams (Russell) STRONG (112).

Physical description: letters, manuscripts, documents, and 2 scrapbooks.

Source: gift of Mrs. John R. Mage, 1965.

STUART, JAMES EWELL BROWN (1833–64)
266 pieces, 1855–64

J. E. B. Stuart, Confederate cavalry general, graduated from West Point in 1854 and served in Kansas with the 1st Cavalry (1855–61) before being commissioned, in May, 1861, as a captain of Confederate cavalry and a lieutenant colonel of Virginia infantry. Stuart was promoted to brigadier general in September 1861 and to major general a year later. As one of the most skillful commanders of the war, Stuart saw action in many of the major Civil War battles, including those at Bull Run (1st), Fredericksburg, Gettysburg, and Chancellorsville. He was killed in May, 1864, in the course of opposing Sheridan's drive on Richmond.

Subject matter: J. E. B. Stuart's career and the Confederate cavalry during the Civil War, including orders received by Stuart, reports of military actions, and Stuart's addresses to his troops. Strongest after 1860.

Significant persons: Thomas Jonathan JACKSON (12), Joseph Eggleston JOHNSTON (24), Robert E. LEE (141), James LONGSTREET (11).

Physical description: letters and documents, with some printed material.

Source: purchased from Stan V. Henkels & Son, February, 1925

SUCKLEY, GEORGE (1830–69)
97 pieces, 1846–86

George Suckley, U.S. Army surgeon and naturalist, participated in the Northern Pacific Railroad Route Survey led by Isaac I. Stevens. The party made explorations and scientific investigations from St. Paul, Minnesota, to Puget Sound in

Washington during the years 1853–57. In 1856, Suckley also served as assistant U.S. Army surgeon at Fort Steilacoom, Washington Territory. He resigned his commission in 1857 to join an expedition to China, and returned to spend several years making scientific studies in the western U.S. Suckley collaborated with James G. Cooper on *The Natural History of Washington Territory,* published in 1859.

Subject matter: correspondence and papers of George Suckley's activities and interest in the field of natural history, especially ornithology; some letters relating to the Northern Pacific Railroad Route Survey of 1853–57.

Physical description: letters, manuscripts, and documents.

Source: purchased from M. F. Savage, January, 1923.

SUMMERS, ALFRED B. (fl. 1875–1909)
approximately 330 pieces, ca.1875–1909

Alfred B. Summers, a U.S. deputy mineral surveyor for California, made surveys of mines in northern California.

Subject matter: California mines in Amador, Calaveras, Colusa, El Dorado, Mariposa, Tuolumne and Yuba counties. Also includes a few letters and business papers.

Physical description: letters, documents (including 17 field books and survey notes), and maps.

Source: gift of Egbert Robinson, August, 1937.

SUMNER, CHARLES (1811–74)
204 pieces, 1835–74

Charles Sumner, American senator and statesman, was born in Massachusetts, where he studied law and won fame as an orator. An early opponent of slavery, Sumner was elected to the United States Senate in 1851 and, apart from three years' travel in Europe (1857–59) to recover his health following an assault on the Senate floor by an opponent, served there for the rest of his life. In 1861 he was named chairman of the Senate Foreign Relations Committee, and he was instrumental in maintaining peace between the Union and Great Britain during the Civil War. Sumner opposed Johnson's Reconstruction policies and was a leader in the move to impeach the president. He died suddenly, in Washington, in 1874.

Subject matter: the major part of the collection consists of a series of 124 letters written by Sumner to Elizabeth Georgiana (Leveson-Gower) Campbell, Duchess of Argyll, over the period 1857–73, in an attempt to win her husband, a Liberal politician and a privy councillor, to the side of the Union in the conflicts between North and South. Subjects covered in those letters and in others (notably written by Sumner to William Wetmore Story) include: relations of the United States with Great Britain; British opinion of the Civil War; national politics in the years immediately preceding, during, and after the war; Sumner's opinion of Andrew Johnson; Sumner's travels in England, France, and Italy; law and literature.

Physical description: letters, with two brief manuscript notes.

Source: Sumner-Argyll correspondence acquired from the present Duke of Argyll through the agency of Harry Levinson, December, 1956; other pieces acquired from various sources over several years.

SUTRO, ADOLPH HEINRICH JOSEPH (1830–98)
2786 pieces, 1853–1931

Adolph H. J. Sutro, mining engineer, mayor of San Francisco, and bibliophile, emigrated in 1850 from Prussia to the eastern United States with his widowed mother and family. Very soon Sutro went to San Francisco to sell supplies to miners during the Gold Rush. Here he established his home and began acquiring property. In 1860 he was attracted by the discovery of silver on the Comstock Lode in Nevada. He established the Sutro Metallurgical Works at Dayton, Nevada, in 1861, utilizing the invention he and John Randohr had made for a metal extracting process. He had constructed a ten-stamp mill in 1862, when he conceived the idea of a tunnel to relieve the problems of floods, high temperatures, and noxious gases in the mines of the Comstock Lode. Procuring a franchise from the first Nevada legislature, he contracted with adjoining mining companies in 1865 to undertake the work for a royalty. The tunnel was completed in 1868 and the town of Sutro grew up at the base of operations. He sold his interest in the tunnel in 1880, and returned to San Francisco, where he increased his land holdings, took part in city affairs, and served as mayor from 1894 to 1896. Sutro's large collection of books became the foundation of the Sutro branch of the California State Library in San Francisco.

Subject matter: San Francisco business (including the Sutro Baths and the Cliff House), land development (including Sutro Heights), street railways, politics, and the Sutro Library, and mining in Nevada (including the Sutro Mill, the Sutro Tunnel and the Comstock Lode).

Significant persons: Carl Burgess GLASSCOCK (6), James Duval PHELAN (5), and Adolph Heinrich Joseph SUTRO (288).

Physical description: letters, manuscripts, documents, and maps.

Source: purchased from George D. Lyman, March, 1943, and W. P. Wreden, November, 1961.

SWEENY, THOMAS WILLIAM (1820–92)
1265 pieces, 1830–1944

Thomas W. Sweeny, U.S. military officer, came with his family to the U.S. in 1832 from Ireland. He served in the Mexican

War in 1846, losing his right arm in the battle of Churubusco. Sweeny fought in the Indian campaigns from Fort Yuma, California, against the Yumas in 1851–53, and from Fort Pierre, South Dakota, in the Sioux Expedition in 1855–56. He was sent in 1861 as brigadier general of the Missouri volunteers to southwest Missouri to oppose Confederate occupation. After recovering from a wound, he returned to service as a colonel in the 52nd Illinois Regiment, and fought in the battles of Shiloh and Corinth. Sweeny remained in the army until his retirement in 1870.

Subject matter: correspondence and military papers of Thomas W. Sweeny, chiefly for the years 1846–92, dealing with the Mexican War (1845–48), Fort Yuma (1851–53), the Sioux Expedition, the Nebraska Territory (Fort Pierre), South Dakota (1855–56), and the Civil War.

Physical description: letters, manuscripts (including 2 diaries), documents, drawings, and maps.

Source: purchased from Mrs. William M. Sweeny, 1956 and 1959.

T

TAPSCOTT, JOHN BAKER (ca.1830–ca.1906)
approximately 190 pieces, 1748; 1837–1943

John Baker Tapscott, Confederate soldier and engineer, was born in Virginia about 1830 and served during the Civil War as a lieutenant in the Confederate army engineer corps. By the end of the war he had settled in Clarksville, Tennessee, where he continued to work as an engineer. He died about 1906.

Subject matter: chiefly genealogical information about Tapscott, his two children, and the related families of Pegram, Baker, and Gilmer; some material relating to the Civil War (in particular, a scrapbook with information about the Confederate War Department and the Peninsular and Petersburg Campaigns).

Physical description: primarily letters, with a few manuscripts and documents (including 9 volumes of notebooks, diaries, etc.) and 4 family photographs.

Source: purchased from Mrs. Katherine T. Rohrbough, June, 1966.

TAYLOR, EDWARD DEWITT (1871–1962)
5108 pieces, 1885–1950

Edward DeWitt Taylor, San Francisco printer, was born in Sacramento, California, the son of Edward Robeson Taylor, physician, poet, lawyer and dean of the Hastings College of Law (University of California), and mayor of San Francisco (1907–09). Edward DeWitt Taylor became interested in printing as a young boy, and in 1896 established E. D. Taylor & Company, subsequently the printing firm of Taylor & Taylor of San Francisco. He also manufactured Taylor oil colors. Taylor was active in the printing firm until 1946, designed many works exhibited by the American Institute of Graphic Arts, and participated in organizations dedicated to etching and the graphic arts.

Subject matter: personal (1909–50) and business affairs (mainly concerning the printing business); a few manuscripts and poems by Edward DeWitt Taylor, his father, Edward Robeson Taylor, and others.

Physical description: letters, manuscripts, documents, and 4 photographs.

Source: gift of Edward DeWitt Taylor, 1951 and 1952.

TAYLOR, JOSEPH DANNER (1830–99)
68 pieces, 1863–81

Joseph Danner Taylor, lawyer, banker, and politician, was born in Ohio in 1830, studied law in Cincinnati, and was admitted to the bar in 1859. At the outbreak of the Civil War he joined the Ohio Volunteer Infantry, but was appointed judge advocate of the Department of Indiana for 1863 and 1864, and also served as prosecuting attorney for Guernsey County, Ohio, from 1863 to 1866. Taylor owned and published the *Guernsey Times* from 1861 to 1871, and was president of the Guernsey National Bank from 1872 until his death. Long active in Republican politics, he was elected to the House of Representatives in the 47th, 48th, 50th, 51st, and 52nd Congresses.

Subject matter: primarily personal and family matters, with a few references to Taylor's legal activities.

Physical description: letters.

Source: gift of Mrs. Gertrude Slaughter through the courtesy of Frederick J. Turner, 1929.

TAYLOR, ZACHARY (1784–1850)
41 pieces, 1846–48

Zachary Taylor, soldier and twelfth president of the United States, was born in Virginia, received his education from a tutor, then worked on his father's plantation in Kentucky. In 1808 he was appointed a first lieutenant in the infantry, and in 1810 he was placed in charge of Fort Knox by General William Henry Harrison. Taylor engaged in many Indian skirmishes on the frontier, and in 1846 he led troops into the Texas-Mexican border at the beginning of the Mexican War. Following successful battles there, he was made a brevet general by President Polk, led the attack on Monterrey, Mexico, and was later involved in other campaigns during the Mexican War. Taylor was nominated for president of the United States on the Whig ticket and was elected in 1848, serving until his death in office in 1850.

Subject matter: chiefly the Mexican War, as seen through letters from Zachary Taylor, mostly to Dr. Robert Crooke Wood, the U.S. Army surgeon who married Taylor's daughter.

Physical description: letters.

Source: purchased in 1918.

Bibliography: most of the letters have been published in *Letters of Zachary Taylor from the Battle-Fields of the Mexican War*, ed. William H. Samson (Rochester, N.Y.: The Genesee Press, 1908).

TERRY, DAVID SMITH (1823–89)
260 pieces, 1849–90; 1933

David Smith Terry, lawyer, politician, and California Supreme Court justice, was born in Kentucky and lived in Texas during the Revolution. Terry began the practice of law in Texas in 1845, joined the Texas Rangers during the Mexican War, then went to California to seek gold in 1849. He returned to Texas to marry Cornelia Runnels in 1852, then settled in California, where he became active in politics and was elected a judge of the Supreme Court in 1855. Political rivalry with David C. Broderick, U.S. Senator from California, culminated in the famous Terry-Broderick duel in 1859, in which Broderick was killed. Terry joined the Confederate army during the Civil War, returning afterward to California to resume his law practice. He met his death following the famous Hill-Sharon divorce case when he was shot after a personal feud with Justice Stephen J. Field.

Subject matter: Terry's family life and judicial and political career, the Terry-Broderick duel, and Texas frontier life and political events before and during the Civil War, as seen chiefly in the personal correspondence of Terry with his wife and family.

Significant persons: David Smith TERRY (55).

Physical description: letters and documents.

Source: purchased from Mrs. Cornelia Terry McClure, January, 1949.

Bibliography: much of the material has been published in A. Russell Buchanan, *David S. Terry of California* (San Marino: Huntington Library, 1956).

THOMAS FAMILY COLLECTION
1752 pieces, ca.1650–1933

The Thomas family and its relatives in the Otis, Stetson (or Stedson), Damon, Cushing, and Briggs families were prominent in Plymouth County, Massachusetts, in the eighteenth and nineteenth centuries.

Subject matter: modern copies of Massachusetts records relating to the above families, presumably collected for genealogical studies: muster and pay rolls, town rolls, bounty receipts, and church records of births, marriages, and deaths.

Physical description: documents.

Source: gift of Mr. Lloyd Vernon Briggs, ca.1950.

THOMPSON & WEST
150 pieces, 1828; 1874–91

Thomas Hinckley Thompson (1841–1915) and Albert Augustus West (1841–1918), both from Illinois, formed a partnership in Oakland, California, in 1875 to publish books patterned after the state and local histories which became popular in the United States in the latter half of the 19th century. These volumes were sold by subscription and were generally accompanied by biographies of the subscribers and prominent citizens. Thompson, a mapmaker, was responsible for the technical management of the operation, and West was the biographer and historian, directing the work of a group of interviewers, editors, and artists. The Thompson & West volumes are still considered worthy source material on California history.

Subject matter: material gathered for the publishing of local histories during the period 1875–90, mostly relating to California, mainly Yuba and Sutter Counties and the San Francisco Committee of Vigilance; also some information on Nevada, especially the Comstock Lode.

Physical description: letters, manuscripts, documents, 3 scrapbooks of clippings, 2 books of engraving specimens, and 12 pen and ink drawings.

Source: purchased from Dawson's Book Shop, July, 1956.

THRALL, WILLIAM HENRY (1873– ?)
approximately 3500 pieces, ca.1873–1962

William H. Thrall, conservationist and editor, came to California from Connecticut in 1888. As a boy of fifteen, he carried mail by stagecoach in Southern California. He worked in real estate (1923–33) and managed food stores (1933–38). Thrall loved to hike and became an authority on the trails and history of the San Gabriel Mountains of Southern California. From 1933 to 1938 he served as head of the Division of Mountain Education of the Los Angeles County Department of Recreation. He wrote many articles about the San Gabriel Mountains and was the publisher of *Trails* magazine from 1934 to 1939.

Subject matter: the San Gabriel Mountains and the publication of *Trails* magazine; secondary source material on Los Angeles County water supply, conservation, and recreation in the mountain areas.

Physical description: letters, manuscripts, and documents.

Source: purchased from Mrs. William H. Thrall, May, 1963.

TOWNSEND, EDWARD DAVIS (1817–1893)
163 pieces, 1761–1928

Edward D. Townsend, Union officer, was a grandson of Elbridge Gerry on the maternal side. He graduated from West Point in 1837, served in Florida, and entered the U.S. Adjutant General's Department in 1846, working on the Pacific coast and in Washington, D.C., for the next fifteen years. Joining Winfield Scott as an adjutant general in 1861, he rose to adjutant-general of the United States in 1862. After the war he supervised the compilation of the documents published in *The War of the Rebellion*. Townsend retired in 1880.

Subject matter: Elbridge Gerry's governorship of Massachusetts (1810–12) and also a little Revolutionary material, the Gerry family in the nineteenth century, Townsend's early life and his work in the Adjutant-General's Department, including his time in California and during the Civil War.

Significant persons: Elbridge GERRY (21), Edward Davis TOWNSEND (50), Mercy Otis WARREN (8).

Physical description: letters, documents, and manuscripts (including sketches of California and nine journals by Townsend and a sermon by Samuel Auchmuty).

Source: gift of Mr. and Mrs. C. David Herlihy, 1975.

Bibliography: one of Townsend's journals has been edited by Malcolm Edwards as *The California Diary of General E. D. Townsend* (Los Angeles: Ward Ritchie Press, 1970).

TRUXTON, THOMAS (1755–1822)
87 pieces, 1845–1903

Thomas Truxton, the naval officer best known for his successful service during the Revolution and in the naval war with

France in 1799–1800, was also involved less spectacularly in a shipping contract of 1795 with the French envoy, the violation of which by the latter resulted in substantial losses to Truxton. When, nearly a century later, the U.S. government assumed responsibility for such losses (known as French Spoliation Claims) by a Congressional Act of 1885, Truxton's heirs revived the case through the U.S. Court of Claims.

Subject matter: letters and papers exchanged between the various Truxton heirs, stating their case and attempting to trace all possible claimants to any monetary settlement. Included is genealogical data on the Truxton, Houston, Van Drieull, Eastman, and Talbot families, along with an abstract of Truxton's will and relevant biographical data.

Physical description: mostly letters, with some documents.

Source: acquired from Mrs. Helen Mangold, June, 1968.

TURNER, FREDERICK JACKSON (1861–1932)
approx. 20,000 pieces, 1862–1976

Frederick Jackson Turner, historian, became a leading scholar after he published, in 1893, his revolutionary thesis that American society owed its distinctive characteristics to experience with an undeveloped frontier. His scholarly work was first carried on at the University of Wisconsin at Madison, where he taught from 1891 to 1910. In the latter year he joined Harvard, retiring from there in 1924 and spending his last years as a research associate at the Huntington Library. Turner, president of the American Historical Association in 1909–1910, is also remembered for his work on the significance of sectionalism in American history.

Subject matter: Turner's education; family affairs; business affairs, particularly with his publisher Henry Holt and Co.; ideas about the frontier, sectionalism, historical scholarship, professional matters generally, and politics; relationship with Alice Forbes Perkins Hooper; teaching career; work with the Harvard Commission on Western History; work with the *Dictionary of American Biography* project; role in the American Historical Association, particularly the "Bancroft insurrection" of 1915. In his extensive research notes, maps, and graphs there is also a large body of data about American history.

Significant persons: Thomas Perkins ABERNATHY (14), Ephraim Douglas ADAMS (19), Clarence Walworth ALVORD (35), Herman Vandenburg AMES (6), Charles McLean ANDREWS (17), James Burill ANGELL (7), Frederic BANCROFT (8), Charles Austin BEARD (7), Carl Lotus BECKER (31), Herbert Eugene BOLTON (22), William Kenneth BOYD (9) Edward CHANNING (9), Edward Potts CHEYNEY (8), Archibald Cary COOLIDGE (22), Isaac Joslin COX (6), Avery Odelle CRAVEN (9), Wilbur Lucius CROSS (8), Alfred Lewis Pinneo DENNIS (6), William Edward DODD (25), William Archibald DUNNING (7), Max FARRAND (224), Carl Russell FISH (25), Worthington Chauncey FORD (19), Dixon Ryan FOX (7), Evarts Boutell GREENE (34), George Ellery HALE (8), Archibald HENDERSON (25), Alice Forbes (Perkins) HOOPER (300), Mark Anthony DeWolfe HOWE (16), Charles Henry HULL (19), Archer Butler HULBERT (39), John Franklin JAMESON (163), Allen JOHNSON (8), David Starr JORDAN (18), Lawrence Marcellus LARSON (11), Abbott Lawrence LOWELL (19), Andrew Cunningham McLAUGHLIN (65), Frederick MERK (32), Fulmer MOOD (11), Dana Carlton MUNRO (27), Herbert Levi OSGOOD (12), Frederick Logan PAXON (30), Ulrich Bonnell PHILLIPS (9), James Harvey ROBINSON (6), Joseph SCHAFER (108), Arthur Meir SCHLESINGER, Sr. (10), Albion Woodbury SMALL (12), Henry Morse STEPHENS (13), Reuben Gold THWAITES (26), Frederick Jackson TURNER, (2453)*, Charles Richard VAN HISE (46), Charles Halstead VAN TYNE (22).

Physical description: letters; documents, including maps, photographs, lantern slides, and research and lecture notes; manuscripts of speeches, essays, and books.

Source: gift of Frederick Jackson Turner, his family, correspondents, and other interested persons, 1928–76.

Bibliography: many of Turner's writings have been published. The following volumes contain useful anthologies: *"Dear Lady": The Letters of Frederick Jackson Turner and Alice Forbes Perkins Hooper, 1910–1932,* ed. Ray Allen Billington (San Marino: Huntington Library, 1970); idem, *Frontier and Section: Selected Essays of Frederick Jackson Turner* (Englewood Cliffs, N.J.: Prentice-Hall, 1961); idem, *The Genesis of the Frontier Thesis: A Study in Historical Creativity* (San Marino: Huntington Library, 1971); *Frederick Jackson Turner's Legacy: Unpublished Writings in American History,* ed. Wilbur Jacobs (San Marino: Huntington Library, 1965), reprinted in paperback as *America's Great Frontiers and Sections: Frederick Jackson Turner's Unpublished Essays* (Lincoln, Neb.: University of Nebraska Press, 1969); idem, *The Historical World of Frederick Jackson Turner. With Selections from His Correspondence* (New Haven: Yale University Press, 1968); F. J. Turner, *The Rise of the New West, 1819–1829* (New York: Harper and Bros., 1906); idem, *The United States, 1830–50: The Nation and Its Sections* (New York: Henry Holt and Co., 1935).

* mostly cataloged letters, excluding research notes, etc.

TURNER, JUSTIN GEORGE (1898–1976)
920 pieces, 1953–69

Justin George Turner, attorney, historian, and author, was born in Chicago in 1898. He was president emeritus of the University of Judaism, and was well known for his interest in the Civil War, his collection of Lincoln memorabilia, and for co-authoring the book, *Mary Todd Lincoln: Her Life and Letters*. In later years Mr. Turner lived in Los Angeles, California.

Subject matter: chiefly Turner's correspondence and other papers related to the Civil War Centennial Commission, particularly in California; papers relating to the Civil War Round Table, the Confederate Research Club, and the California Heritage Preservation Association. Strongest for the period from 1961 to 1965.

Physical description: primarily letters (most of which are carbon copies), with some manuscripts and documents. Also included are numerous printed form letters and announcements, along with other ephemera, including a few photographs.

Source: gift of Justin George Turner, December 10, 1969.

TURNER, ROBERT CHESTER (fl. 1887–1919)
1286 pieces, 1887–1921

Robert C. Turner, a mining engineer who lived in Berkeley, California, was vice-president of the Brunswick Consolidated Gold Mining Company with offices in New York and California.

Subject matter: the Brunswick Consolidated Gold Mining Company and mining enterprises in California and the West, as seen in the business correspondence and papers of Robert C. Turner.

Significant persons: Harvey Seeley MUDD (20), Seeley Wintersmith MUDD (113).

Physical description: letters, documents (including 5 volumes of accounts, by-laws, etc.), and 3 letterbooks.

Source: purchased from Grahame H. Hardy, July, 1953.

U

U.S. ARMY (CONTINENTAL). EASTERN DEPARTMENT
Journal of the Proceedings of Col. Rufus Putnam, Major Robert Boyd, and Lt. Col. William Hull . . . to Ascertain the Quantity of Forage Consumed by the Allied Army . . . in Westchester County, Last Campaign (1782)
MS. volume 61 leaves

Covers period from February 14 to July 2, 1782.

U.S. ARMY (CONTINENTAL). QUARTERMASTER FOR THE STATE OF NEW YORK
[Letterbook] (1780–82)
MS. volume 131 pp.

Consists of correspondence with officers of West Point and Generals Nathanael Greene, Alexander McDougall, and William Heath from New York Deputy Quartermaster Hugh Hughes.

[Letterbook] (1780–82)
MS. volume 33 pp.

Contains copies of the official correspondence from Hughes to his assistants.

U.S. ARMY. DEPARTMENT OF THE NORTHWEST. PAY-
MASTER (John Oscar Culver).
approximately 6000 pieces, 1861–1904

John Oscar Culver (b. ca.1830) of Sandy Hill, New York,
served during the Civil War as a major in the office of the paymaster for the Department of the Northwest. In later years
Culver was a post office inspector in San Francisco and Fresno,
California.

Subject matter: workings of the paymaster's office for the period 1861–65, including muster and payrolls, applications for
exemption, certificates of disability, affidavits of appointments
of attorneys to collect back pay, discharge applications, vouchers, and receipts. Although there are some vouchers or payrolls
for virtually all Union states, the documents are fullest for
regiments from Wisconsin, Illinois, and Missouri. A few papers
concern Culver's life and business affairs following the war,
particularly during the period (1880–1900) he lived in California.

Physical description: chiefly documents (including four ledgers
and ten receipt books), with a few letters and manuscripts.

Source: acquired from Miss Hazel Young, January, 1956, and
from Stanford University Library, March, 1964.

U.S. COMMISSIONERS UNDER THE SIXTH ARTICLE
OF THE BRITISH TREATY OF 1794
[Letterbooks] (1797–99)
MS. volumes 225 pp.

[Minutes of the Meetings of the Board] (1798–99)
MS. volumes 683 pp.

Receipts for Papers Returned (1800)
MS. volume 64 pp.

Register [of Claims Brought Before the Board] (1797–1800)
MS. volumes 179 pp.

U.S. DEPARTMENT OF STATE
[Letterbook] (1794–96)
MS. volume 167 leaves

Contains copies of official correspondence among the secretary
of state, the U.S. minister to France, and the French minister
to the U.S.

U.S. ENVOYS TO THE FRENCH REPUBLIC
[Elbridge Gerry's Copybook of Records of the Proceedings of
the XYZ Mission] (1797–98)
MS. volume 180 pp.

U.S. MINT, SAN FRANCISCO BRANCH
62 pieces, 1856–99

The U.S. Mint, San Francisco Branch, authorized by Congress
in July, 1852, began operation in April, 1854. The original ap-
propriation of $300,000 for the project was expended instead
on the U.S. assay office, but the mint was finally completed
with machinery built in Philadelphia which was installed in a
three-story brick structure situated on Commercial Street between Montgomery and Kearny Streets. The mint was capable

of coining $30,000,000 annually. It was moved to a new building on 5th Street in 1874.

Subject matter: instructions mainly for the period 1856–75, from Treasury Department officials in Washington, and employment recommendations from prominent persons.

Physical description: letters and documents.

Source: purchased from Edwin Grabhorn, January, 1945.

V

VALENTINE, ROBERT (1717–86)
305 pieces, ca.1712–>1919

Robert Valentine, Pennsylvania Quaker minister, was born in Ballybrumhill, Ireland, and came to Pennsylvania before 1746 when he married Rachel Edge. He traveled extensively as a "public Friend," in which capacity he made visits to Quaker families and groups in many areas, and came into contact with many leading Quakers. Valentine's longest trip was to England and Ireland from 1781 to 1784. His children married into the Sharpless and Ashbridge families.

Subject matter: the Society of Friends and daily life in Pennsylvania, England, and Ireland; the activities of a "public Friend," as revealed in the papers of Robert Valentine; included are addresses, minutes, etc., concerning Quaker meetings. Strongest for the years 1781–86.

Physical description: letters (including 1 copybook and 1 album), manuscripts (including 1 journal and 1 copybook), and documents (including 1 expense book).

Source: purchased from Dawson's Book Shop, 1958.

VALLE, REGINALDO FRANCISCO DEL (1854–1938)
371 pieces, 1835–1938

Reginaldo del Valle, California legislator and civic leader, was the son of Ignacio del Valle, who held office during the Mexican period and served as Alcalde of Los Angeles in 1850 and as state assemblyman in 1852. Reginaldo spent his youth in Los Angeles and at the family home, Camulos Ranch, in Ventura County. Following graduation from the University of Santa Clara in 1873, he studied law and was admitted to practice before the state Supreme Court and the U.S. Supreme Court. In 1879 he was elected to the state assembly and in 1882 to the state senate. Active in Democratic politics, he was a member of many public services commissions for the city of Los Angeles and was a director of the Metropolitan Water District of Southern California (1927–29). Del Valle was involved in public educational policy and local historical research groups.

Subject matter: California politics and government, water resources, the Owens Valley, the St. Francis Dam disaster, and the William Mulholland Memorial. Also includes land papers for the Camulos Ranch in Ventura County, California. Strongest for the period 1920–37.

Physical description: letters, manuscripts, documents (including 1 volume), and maps (in English and Spanish).

Source: gift of Lucretia Grady, June, 1940, and purchase from James Smalldon, March, 1965.

VALLEJO, MARIANO GUADALUPE (1808–90)
257 pieces, 1833–88

Mariano G. Vallejo, early California military leader, land owner, and legislator, was born in Monterey and was educated in civil, religious, and military schools. In 1831 he was elected a member of the provincial legislature and soon after was made the commandant of the Presidio of San Francisco. In 1835 he established a civil government for San Francisco and founded the town of Sonoma, which was the center of his extensive land holdings. He later also founded the towns of Vallejo and

Benicia (named after his wife). Following the change to an American administration in California, Vallejo served as a delegate to the first state constitutional convention and as a state senator in the first California legislature.

Subject matter: the defense of the northern frontier, relations with the missions, and the treatment of Indians by Father Jesús María Vásquez del Mercado. Strongest for the period 1840–50, when Vallejo corresponded with many prominent contemporary figures.

Significant persons: Juan Bautista ALVARADO (6), Jacob Primer LEESE (6), Manuel MICHELTORENA (6), John Augustus SUTTER (6), Mariano Guadalupe VALLEJO (41).

Physical description: letters and documents (in Spanish and English).

Source: purchased from Holmes Book Company, 1922.

Bibliography: the collection is described in the *Huntington Library Bulletin,* no. 7 (1935): 34.

VAN DEUSEN, DELOS (fl. 1861–65)
65 pieces, 1851–65

Delos Van Deusen, Union soldier, entered the 6th Missouri Volunteer Infantry as captain of Company H, and by the end of the war was promoted to lieutenant-colonel commanding the regiment. He participated in the siege of Vicksburg and in the Chickamauga and Atlanta campaigns.

Subject matter: Civil War, particularly the siege of Vicksburg and the Atlanta Campaign; soldier's life and troop movements; Van Deusen's personal affairs.

Physical description: letters and document.

Source: purchased from Miss Ann L. Finch (great-niece of Delos Van Deusen), 1937.

VANDEVORT, JOHN WESLEY (1837–ca.98)
794 pieces, ca.1865–98

John Wesley Vandevort, industrialist, was a native of Pittsburgh and an associate of Andrew Carnegie in the firm of Carnegie and Kloman. In 1885 he moved to Pasadena, California, for his health, and added participation in Pasadena social and civic affairs and San Diego real estate projects to his continuing interests in the steel and iron industries.

Subject matter: mainly Vandevort's Pittsburgh holdings; Vandevort's tours of Europe and a 1878–79 trip around the world with Carnegie; additional information about a European tour made by John Hallen Franks, about the Johnstown Flood of 1889, and about other aspects of the steel industry.

Significant persons: Andrew CARNEGIE (8), Henry PHIPPS (100).

Physical description: chiefly letters, with some manuscripts (including 8 volumes of diaries) and some documents.

Source: gift of D. V. Bell, 1949.

VAN SOELEN, THEODORE (1890–1964)
180 pieces, 1950–63

Theodore Van Soelen, Western artist, was born in Minnesota and studied art at St. Paul Institute from 1908 to 1911 and at the Pennsylvania Academy of Fine Arts from 1911 to 1915. He began his career as an artist in 1916 and was the recipient of numerous prizes. He went to New Mexico for his health, settled near Santa Fe, and specialized in the portrayal of Western life. His paintings and lithographic prints are in many important collections, including the Library of Congress.

Subject matter: Theodore Van Soelen's dealings with artists, writers, and prominent men in public life, concerning subjects such as art, New Mexican government, and politics.

Significant persons: Nicholas ROOSEVELT (8), Paul Starrett SAMPLE (97), John Field SIMMS (6), Edward STREETER (8), Paul Dudley WHITE (6).

Physical description: letters.

Source: gift of Theodore Van Soelen, 1963.

VINCENT, JOHN MARTIN (1857–1939)
4382 pieces, 1827–1940
John Martin Vincent, scholar and educator, was born in Ohio, where his father John Martin Vincent Sr. (1820–63) was a lawyer, state legislator, and editor of an anti-slavery journal. The younger Vincent studied at Amherst, Oberlin (where he received a B.A. in 1883), and Johns Hopkins (where he received a Ph.D. in 1890), joining the faculty of the latter in 1889 and specializing in the history and government of Switzerland. He remained at Johns Hopkins as professor of European History until his retirement in 1925. Vincent studied abroad, was a member of various international scholarly organizations, and was the author of, among other works, *State and Federal Government in Switzerland, Switzerland at the Beginning of the Sixteenth Century,* and *Municipal Problems in Medieval Switzerland.* He moved to Pasadena, California, for the last three years of his life to enjoy the offerings of the Huntington Library.

Subject matter: primarily family affairs and personal matters pertaining to John Martin Vincent and his wife, Ada Jane (Smith) Vincent; scattered comments on politics, religion, race, economics, and matters pertaining to the historical profession, such as plans for the Calvin Tercentennial Memorial; a few papers (1846–59) relating to John Martin Vincent Sr.

Significant persons: Herbert Baxter ADAMS (42), Charles McLean ANDREWS (13), Charles BEAUREGARD (24), Richard Theodore ELY (9), Herbert Darling FOSTER (23), Wendell Phillips GARRISON (11), Charles Ripley GILLETT (7), Daniel Coit GILMAN (8), Albert Bushnell HART (13), Charles Downer HAZEN (29), Joseph JASTROW (19), Samuel Macauley JACKSON (14), Chancellor MARTIN (92), Dana Carleton MUNRO (13), Moisei Yakovlevich OSTRO-GORSKI (6), Arthur Hubbell PALMER (17), James Harvey ROBINSON (5), Ida Minerva TARBELL (20), John Martin VINCENT, Sr. (96), John Martin VINCENT, Jr. (280), Woodrow WILSON (5).

Physical description: chiefly letters, with a few manuscripts (including four diaries and journals) and documents, and one Civil War ink-and-wash map.

Source: gift of John Martin Vincent, 1932–36.

W

WALKER, ELKANAH BARTLETT (1805–77)
84 pieces, 1837–71

Elkanah Walker, pioneer missionary in the old Oregon Territory, came from Maine and prepared himself for the ministry
at Kimball Union Academy in New Hampshire and at Bangor
Theological Seminary. His future wife, Mary (Richardson)
Walker, also a native of Maine, was educated at Maine Wesleyan Seminary and taught school from 1833 to 1834. Before
they met, both had applied to the American Board of Commissions for Foreign Missions and had considered posts outside
the United States but were persuaded to follow Marcus Whit-
man to the Oregon Territory. There was concern on the part
of the Board about a single person's taking a mission station,
so when Walker was told that a Miss Richardson had also applied, he made a sudden trip to visit her. They announced their
plans immediately and were married in 1838, just before leaving for the Oregon Territory. Together with Rev. and Mrs.
Cushing Eels, they established a mission at Tshimakain, near
Ft. Colville, Washington, where they lived from 1839 to 1848,
working with the Spokan Indians. Walker developed an alpha-
bet of the Spokan language and wrote a primer for the Indians.
The Walkers devoted nine years to their mission in Tshimakain, then moved to the Willamette Valley following the Whit-
man massacre.

Subject matter: the Walkers' trip across the plains from Maine
to Oregon Territory, the establishment of their mission, and

their work with the Spokan Indians; Indian Wars in Oregon history.

Physical description: manuscripts (including 29 diaries and 1 drawing), letters, and documents.

Source: purchased from A. S. W. Rosenbach, October, 1922.

Bibliography: Mary R. Walker's diary of June 10–December 31, 1838 has been published in *The Frontier*, 11, no. 3 (March, 1931). Elkanah Walker's diaries have been published in Clifford M. Drury, *Nine Years with the Spokane Indians* (Glendale, Calif.: Arthur H. Clark Co., 1976), and Mary Walker's diaries of September, 1838 to July, 1848 have been published in Clifford M. Drury, *First White Women Over the Rockies*, vol. 2 (Glendale, Calif.: Arthur H. Clark Co., 1963).

WALLER, HENRY (1810–93)
approximately 3000 pieces, 1830–85

Henry Waller, lawyer and land developer, was born in Kentucky and studied and practiced law in Maysville, but also began investing in land in and around Chicago. In 1837 he married Sarah Bell Langhorne and, sometime after 1855, moved to Chicago with his family. Waller continued his legal practice, as a master in chancery, but was also active in the development of the suburb of Austin. He moved to River Forest in 1886, and died seven years later.

Subject matter: chiefly life and family affairs of Henry and Sarah Bell (Langhorne) Waller, with some information about Waller's legal and financial activities; material concerning two of the Wallers' sons: Maurice, a minister and circuit preacher, and Edward, who developed the area known as North Woods in River Forest; Mrs. Waller's efforts to aid Confederate prisoners during the Civil War.

Physical description: chiefly letters, with a few documents and manuscripts, some newspaper clippings, and other ephemera.

Source: gift of Mrs. Norreys O'Conor, a descendant of the Waller family, August, 1964.

WALLING, ANNA (STRUNSKY) (1879–1964)
952 pieces, 1877–1958

Anna (Strunsky) Walling, socialist lecturer and writer, was a member of a family which had fled Czarist Russia to escape the persecution of the Jews and settled in San Francisco. While a student at Stanford, she excelled in debating and in 1897 became active in the socialist cause. She met Jack London at a Socialist Labor Party meeting in San Francisco in 1899, and collaborated with him in writing the *Kempton-Wace Letters*. Anna Strunsky married William English Walling, millionaire socialist poet and lecturer.

Subject matter: the socialist movement in the United States, William English Walling, Jack London, and literary subjects, as reflected in the personal correspondence of Anna (Strunsky) Walling.

Significant persons: Leonard Dalton ABBOTT (13), Melville Best ANDERSON (72), Frank Gelett BURGESS (7), Charmian (Kittredge) LONDON (67), Jack LONDON (110), Charles Edward RUSSELL (7), Irving STONE (7), Horace Logo TRAUBEL (24), William English WALLING (62).

Physical description: letters and manuscripts (including 1 diary).

Source: gift of Anna Strunsky Walling, 1953–62.

WALSWORTH, EDWARD BROWN (fl. 1840–89)
138 pieces, 1840–89

Edward B. Walsworth, Presbyterian minister and educator, was born in New York, graduated from Union Theological Seminary, and served as pastor of the Presbyterian Church in East Avon, New York, before sailing to California in 1852 as a representative of the American Home Missionary Society. He organized the First Presbyterian Church of Oakland in 1853 but soon left to become pastor of the Presbyterian Church in Marysville, also filling the post of Yuba County Superintendent of Schools. In 1861 Walsworth returned to the Oakland Presbyterian Church, then gave up his pastorate in 1865 to devote his time to the Pacific Female College, which he established in 1863. Because of financial problems the college was sold to the Pacific Theological Seminary in 1871, and Walsworth was put in charge of the Oakland Seminary before his return to New York in 1876.

Subject matter: the Presbyterian Church in New York State (1840–53), the Presbyterian Church in California (1852–83), and the Female College of the Pacific (1863–71).

Physical description: letters and documents.

Source: purchased from Edwin Grabhorn, January, 1945.

WARD, GEORGE CLINTON (1863–1933)
approximately 680 pieces, 1887–1936

George C. Ward, engineer and California utility company executive, received his engineering degree from Phillips Academy in Andover, Massachusetts. He was a native of New

York, where his first work was in the construction of iron bridges and in railroad engineering. He was chief engineer for the Racquette Lake Railroad in New York, owned by Collis P. Huntington. In 1902 Ward modernized a water supply system in Ohio for Henry E. Huntington, who in 1905 persuaded him to come to California. Here Ward became general manager first for the Huntington Land and Improvement Company and then for the Pacific Light and Power Company, where he was in charge of the Big Creek hydro-electric generating project. He was made vice-president of the Southern California Edison Company in 1917 and president in 1932. Ward was honored for his engineering work by the U.S. Chamber of Commerce and by the University of California, from which he received an honorary degree.

Subject matter: Ward's life in New York (1887–1900), two trips to the High Sierra in the area of Huntington Lake in 1922 and 1923, Ward's work with the Big Creek project.

Significant persons: Henry Edwards HUNTINGTON (10).

Physical description: letters, manuscripts (including 5 diaries), documents, photographs, and 1 scrapbook.

Source: gift of Louise Ward Watkins, 1946–54.

WARREN FAMILY COLLECTION
approximately 100 pieces, 1815–1960

The Warren collection contains the papers of four generations of the Horn and Warren families. Alexander Horn (? – 1817) was master of the ships "Hokar" and "Cato" from 1809 to 1812. His son Alexander (1814–1905) was a cabinet maker who lived in Ohio and Missouri before he emigrated overland to California in 1856, settling near Stockton. The second Alexander Horn's daughter, Minnie, married Charles Clifton Warren, and the couple moved to Cucamonga, California, in 1883.

Charles C. Warren became district agricultural inspector, ran a tree nursery, and helped organize the California Fruit Grower's Exchange in 1893. The Warrens moved to a fruit ranch in Glendora, California, in 1896. Their son, Leslie A. Warren, married Goldie V. Zumwalt, daughter of pioneer San Joaquin Valley resident, Daniel K. Zumwalt.

Subject matter: Alexander Horn's daily life as master of the ships "Hokar" and "Cato" sailing between New York, New Orleans, and the British Isles; family matters of his son, Alexander Horn, in the Midwest; daily life of Minnie (Horn) Warren in Glendora, California (1897–1955); three reminiscences of life in Southern California. There is also a description of a trip to Kings Canyon, California, in 1906 by Herbert C. Jones and Daniel Kindle Zumwalt.

Physical description: log book, letters, manuscripts (including 32 volumes of notebooks and diaries), documents, and photographs.

Source: gift of Mrs. Charles C. Warren, 1946, and Mrs. Leslie A. Warren, 1959–69.

WASHINGTON, GEORGE (1732–99)
551 pieces, 1714/15–1806

George Washington, soldier, statesman, and president, was surveyor of the Northern Neck in Virginia from 1748 to 1752. Inclined to soldiering, he made a reputation as a military leader during the Seven Years' War and then settled at Mt. Vernon as a gentleman planter. In the 1760s and early '70s he took an active part in Virginia politics. His military and political prominence earned him the command of the Continental Army. After the War for Independence he enjoyed a short interlude in private life (1784–87) before reentering public service as president of the Constitutional Convention and as the first president of the United States (1798–97). He then retired to Mt. Vernon, where he died in 1799.

Subject matter: the Seven Years' War; the War for Independence; the U.S. Army; the management and design of Mt. Vernon; surveying of the Northern Neck counties of Fairfax, Stafford, Spotsylvania, Culpeper, and Frederick, family affairs; U.S. politics and government.

Significant persons: Alexander McDOUGALL (39), George WASHINGTON (375), Martha (Dandridge) Custis WASHINGTON (12).

Physical description: letters; documents, including surveys of Mt. Vernon; manuscripts, including Washington's genealogy.

Source: purchased from George D. Smith, 1913 and 1915; William K. Bixby, 1918; A. S. W. Rosenbach, 1923; J. F. Meegan; and others.

Bibliography: the pieces by George Washington are largely published in *The Writings of George Washington,* ed. John C. Fitzpatrick, 39 vols. (Washington: Government Printing Office, 1931–44), and *The George Washington Atlas,* ed. Lawrence Martin (Washington: George Washington Bicentennial Commission, 1932). Pieces from this collection also appear in *The Papers of George Washington,* ed. Donald D. Jackson (Charlottesville: University of Virginia Press, 1976–).

WATKINS, LOUISE (WARD) (1890–1974)
approximately 7500 pieces, 1871–1974

Louise Whipple (Ward) Watkins, leader in women's rights, California politics, and Los Angeles organizations, came to California from New York with her family when she was fifteen years old. Her father, George Clinton Ward (q.v.), was a prominent civil engineer and became president of the Southern California Edison Company. Louise studied dramatics in New York and law at the University of Southern California. In 1915 she married Edward Francis Watkins, the son of Edward Lancaster Watkins, early Southern California pioneer. Mrs. Watkins was active in the cause of woman suffrage, women's clubs, the Japan American Society, and Republican politics. She served on several state commissions, founded the Southern California Republican Women (1935), and ran for the U.S. Senate in 1938.

Subject matter: Louise (Ward) Watkins; George Clinton Ward; California politics; Japan; Watkins family. Includes an unpublished autobiography of Louise (Ward) Watkins.

Significant persons: John Steven McGROARTY (10).

Physical description: letters, manuscripts (including 23 diaries, 1915–74), documents, 17 scrapbooks, and photographs.

Source: gift of John F. Watkins, February, 1975, and purchase from Dawson's Book Shop, April, 1953.

WATSON, JOHN FANNING (1779–1860)
165 pieces, 1803–45

John Fanning Watson, antiquarian, publisher, and financier, was born in New Jersey, and after some early education there, worked in a countinghouse in Philadelphia where he stayed until 1798. He held a clerkship with the United States War Department until 1804, and later was appointed to an army post in Louisiana. After the death of his father, he returned to Philadelphia, opening a bookshop in 1809 and entering the publishing business. He published a literary journal which he sold in 1812, and retired from the book business in 1814 to become cashier of the Bank of Germantown. Watson engaged in gathering historical material and did research, publishing the *Annals of Philadelphia* in 1830 and other books on historical subjects. His interests brought about the establishment of the Historical Society of Pennsylvania in 1824. In 1847 Watson resigned from the bank to become an officer of the Philadelphia and Morristown Railroad, from which he retired three years prior to his death.

Subject matter: life in New York and Pennsylvania in the first half of the nineteenth century as seen in the personal correspondence of John Fanning Watson with the Fanning family, the children of Azel Backus (Congregational clergyman and first president of Hamilton College), and other prominent persons of the period; Watson's acquisition of historical material; matters concerning the United States Navy, including letters of sea-captain and explorer Edmund Fanning, relating to the United States Exploring Expedition of 1838–42 in the Pacific Ocean.

Significant persons: James BARRON (8), Edmund FANNING (9).

Physical description: letters.

Source: purchased from the Book Den, December, 1965.

WEBB, RICHARD THOMPSON, SR. (1887–1974)
20,740 pieces, 1798–1974

R. Thompson Webb, Sr., California educator, was born in Tennessee, the son of educator and U.S. Senator William R. ("Sawney") Webb. The younger Webb graduated from the University of North Carolina in 1911 and came to Southern California in 1913, where he engaged in ranching until 1918. He returned to Tennessee, where he taught in the Webb School (founded by his father), then came back with his family to California in 1922, founding the Webb School in Claremont. He served as headmaster of the school until his retirement in 1962. Webb was active in community and educational affairs, and retained his interest in ranching, taking part in agricultural projects.

He lived in semiretirement in Claremont until his death in 1974.

Subject matter: personal, professional, and business affairs of Richard Thompson Webb, Sr., concerning education (especially the Webb School in Claremont, California), agriculture in the Coachella Valley and Riverside, the town of Claremont, and religious organizations. Strongest for the period after 1905.

Significant persons: Marshall STIMSON (5), Horace Jerry VOORHIS (49), William Robert WEBB (24).

Physical description: letters, manuscripts, and documents.

Source: gift of Richard Thompson Webb, Jr., January, 1975.

WEINBERG, FRANK (? –>1933)
56 pieces, 1901–12

Frank Weinberg, nurseryman, specialized in cacti, orchids, and rare plants. He was proprietor of a nursery business in Long Island, New York, until 1911, when he came to Hollywood, California, to work as horticulturalist on the Holmby Hills estate of Arthur Letts, Sr.

Subject matter: mainly botanical information, especially on cacti, orchids, and rare plants. There are numerous letters from Joseph Nelson Rose, associate curator of the U.S. National Museum at the Smithsonian Institution.

Significant persons: Joseph Nelson ROSE (40).

Physical description: letters.

Source: gift of William Hertrich.

WEINLAND, WILLIAM HENRY (fl. 1884–1920)
approximately 2100 pieces, 1853–1946

William H. Weinland, Moravian church missionary, was a native of Pennsylvania, who graduated from the Moravian Col-

lege and Theological Seminary in Bethlehem in 1884. The next
year he and his wife went to Bethel, Alaska, to serve as missionaries to the Eskimos. When ill health in the family forced
them to return to the United States, Weinland became pastor
of the Moravian Church at Gracehill, Ohio (1887–89), until
he was assigned to work among the Indians of Southern California. The Weinlands devoted nearly forty years to missionary
work among the Indians, especially at the Morongo Indian
Reservation near Banning, California.

Subject matter: the missionary work of Mr. and Mrs. William
H. Weinland (1885–1932) and of the Moravian Church in
Alaska and on the Morongo Indian Reservation near Banning,
California. There are two sub-collections, the Rock family let-
ters (1911–16), written from an Alaskan Mission, and the
Gilman family papers (1853–1946), containing correspond-
ence, land papers, and historical notes on the Banning area.

Physical description: letters, manuscripts (including 39 diaries), documents, and 6 drawings.

Source: gift of Clarence E. Weinland, 1946 and 1951, and of
Jean Weinland and Maria G. Hunt, 1970.

WELLES, GIDEON (1802–78)
approximately 600 pieces, 1846–1902

Gideon Welles, secretary of the navy during the Civil War,
was born in 1802 in Glastonbury, Connecticut. He studied law,
became editor of the *Hartford Times* in 1826, and served in
the state legislature from 1827 to 1835. In 1846 Welles was
appointed chief of the Bureau of Provisions and Clothing for
the Navy, and lived in Washington until the fall of 1849. Lincoln appointed him secretary of the navy in 1861, and he
served throughout the war years, improving the organization
and efficiency of the service. After retiring from the post in

1869 Welles left Washington, but continued his interest in public affairs and wrote numerous articles about the Lincoln and Johnson presidencies, the direction of the war, and plans for Reconstruction. He died in Hartford in 1878.

Subject matter: naval affairs during the Civil War (including blockades, letters of marque, the capture of New Orleans in April, 1862, and requests for appointments); Civil War and Reconstruction politics; Lincoln; Andrew Johnson; the Bureau of Provisions and Clothing for the Navy (1846–49); criticism of Welles's successor, George Maxwell Robeson, and Robeson's assistant David Dixon Porter (q.v.); Welles's trip to New York and Pennsylvania in 1822. Strongest for the years 1861–70.

Significant persons: Samuel Sullivan COX (7), Andrew Hull FOOTE (7), Gustavus Vasa FOX (17), William Buel FRANK-LIN (13), Ira HARRIS (6), Joseph Roswell HAWLEY (6), Thornton Alexander JENKINS (10), James Edward JOUETT (21), Hiram PAULDING (8), Samuel Jackson RANDALL (34), Alexander Hamilton RICE (5).

Physical description: letters, manuscripts (including diaries), documents and ephemera.

Source: purchased from Stan V. Henkels, 1924.

WELLS, FARGO AND COMPANY
approximately 2200 pieces, 1839–1911

Wells, Fargo and Company, express and banking firm, was founded in New York in 1852. Henry Wells (1805–78) and William George Fargo (1818–81), who had been involved both as partners and as competitors in various express enterprises for several years, joined their independent concerns in 1850 with another competitor, John Butterfield, to form the American Express Company. In 1852 Wells, Fargo, and others, after careful scrutiny of developments following the Gold

Rush, decided to enter the field in the West and formed Wells, Fargo and Company, mainly to capture business from their successful rivals, Adams and Company. Conservative management policies enabled Wells, Fargo to survive the financial crisis of 1855, which caused the failure of Adams and Company and other express firms, and by 1859 Wells, Fargo and Company was the largest business in the West. In 1863 the company extended operations to Mexico and also prospered as a result of the Comstock mining boom in Nevada. After completion of the transcontinental railroad, the Pacific Union Express Company was formed by the railroad interests in order to compete with Wells, Fargo and Company, but Wells, Fargo subsequently absorbed the new company, and Lloyd Tevis, one of its stockholders, became Wells, Fargo president in 1872. He was followed by John J. Valentine in 1892. Wells, Fargo and Company continued during this period to operate and expand by gaining control of express rights on railroads. In 1876 the banking and express departments of the firm had been separated, and in 1905 the banking portion of Wells, Fargo merged with Isaias W. Hellman's Nevada National Bank. By 1909 the Southern Pacific Railroad, headed by Edward H. Harriman, became the largest stockholder in Wells, Fargo and Company.

Subject matter: business matters, chiefly within the 1870–1900 period, of Wells, Fargo and Company, mainly of Hosmer Benjamin Parsons (1846–1908), who joined the company in 1867 and successively held the positions of cashier, assistant secretary, vice-president, and president of its bank in New York; financial matters, especially express rights and rates on railroads.

Significant persons: George HEARST (9), Lloyd TEVIS (122), John J. VALENTINE (953).

Physical description: letters (including 11 volumes of letter-books) and documents.

Source: purchased from William P. Wreden, May, 1961.

WILLARD, ABIJAH (fl. 1755–59)
Abijah Willard's Orderly Book [and] A Journal on the Intended Expedition to Nova Scotia (1755–59)
Autograph MS. volume 299 pp.

The orderly book covers April 28, 1755 to July 17, 1759; the journal covers April 9, 1755 to January 5, 1756. The volume concerns the British capture of Ft. Beauséjour, Nova Scotia. The journal was published as *Journal of Abijah Willard, 1755,* ed. John C. Webster (St. John, N.B., 1930?).

WILLARD, CHARLES DWIGHT (1860–1914)
749 pieces, 1853–1913

Charles D. Willard, newspaperman, author, and publicity director, was born in Illinois and graduated from the University of Michigan in 1883. He later moved to California for his health, working as a reporter for the *Los Angeles Times* and the *Herald* newspapers. In 1891 he became secretary of the Los Angeles Chamber of Commerce, and in the next several years was active in municipal affairs, leading the fight for a free harbor at San Pedro. In 1894 Willard started the magazine, *The Land of Sunshine* (taken over soon afterward by Charles F. Lummis [q.v.]), and in 1897 he was made manager of the *Los Angeles Express* newspaper. He wrote several books, including the *History of Los Angeles* and *The Free Harbor Contest.*

Subject matter: mainly family matters, especially Willard's college career (1879–83); the *Los Angeles Herald* (ca.1889–90), and the Los Angeles Chamber of Commerce (ca.1891–95).

Significant persons: Theodore ROOSEVELT (12).

Physical description: letters, manuscripts (including 1 diary), documents, and photographs.

Source: gift of Mr. and Mrs. Colin Clements, 1943 and 1969.

WILLIS, BAILEY (1857–1949)
approximately 10,000 pieces, 1861–1949

Bailey Willis, professor of geology, was born in New York, studied in Germany from 1870 to 1874, and graduated from Columbia University in civil engineering in 1879. Willis served in various positions as a geologist with the U.S. Geological Survey from 1880 to 1916. His geological work took him to many parts of the world, such as the expedition he led for the Carnegie Institution to Northern China in 1903–04, and included studies of Patagonia and the Nahuel Huapí lake district made in Argentina. He served as head of the Geology Department at Stanford University from 1915 to 1922 and was renowned for his seismological research.

Subject matter: Bailey Willis, his works, travels, and family; geology, especially earthquakes; scientists and scientific institutions; Raphael Pumpelly (q.v.). Includes early photographs of China (1903–04) and Argentina (1911–13).

Significant persons: Albrecht PENCK (8), Raphael PUMPELLY (19).

Physical description: letters, manuscripts (including diaries and scientific reports), documents, and photographs.

Source: gift of Mrs. Margaret Willis Smith, Cornelius Grinnell Willis, and Robin Willis, June, 1962, and October, 1969.

WILSON, BENJAMIN DAVIS (1811–78)
approximately 3500 pieces, 1847–1920

Benjamin D. Wilson, pioneer California rancher and business-man, was a native of Tennessee who came to California from New Mexico in 1841 as a member of the Rowland-Workman party. He bought the Jurupa Rancho (Riverside, California) in 1843 and in 1844 married Ramona Yorba, daughter of Bernardo Yorba, well-known land owner during the Mexican period. After Ramona's death, Wilson in 1853 married Margaret S. Hereford, a widow from St. Louis related to the Sublette family of the Rocky Mountain Fur Company. She had gone with her husband to Santa Fe, then to Chihuahua, Mexico, making her way to California by steamer via Mazatlan, while her husband (who died a year later) came overland. Wilson became prominent as California changed from Mexican to American rule. In 1851–52, he was elected the second mayor of Los Angeles, in 1852 he served as U.S. Indian Agent under Superintendent Edward F. Beale, and in 1855–57 and 1869–72 he served as state senator. He purchased Rancho de Cuati and adjacent land to develop his Lake Vineyard Ranch (now a large part of the city of San Marino), and with John S. Griffin (q.v.) purchased Rancho San Pascual, which has become the city of Pasadena. Wilson planted vineyards and citrus groves, and became active in business circles. He was the father of one son and three daughters, one of whom married James DeBarth Shorb (q.v.), who became business manager of the ranch. Another married George Smith Patton (1856–1927) and became the mother of General George S. Patton, Jr., of World War II fame.

Subject matter: business and social life in California (1850–90); Indian affairs in Southern California (1852–56); the wine industry; early history of Pasadena, San Marino, and Wilmington, California; the estate settlement of Solomon Sublette; and the Santa Fe trade.

Significant persons: Phineas BANNING (52), Edward Fitzgerald BEALE (16), Joseph Lancaster BRENT (12), Cave Johnson COUTS (5), Stephen Clark FOSTER (6), John Charles FRÉMONT (5), John Strother GRIFFIN (24), William McKendree GWIN (10), Benjamin Ignatius HAYES (7), Henry Edwards HUNTINGTON (7), George Smith PATTON, SR. (114), Jonathan Trumbull WARNER (5), and Benjamin Davis WILSON (182).

Physical description: letters, manuscripts, documents, and maps.

Source: purchased from Mrs. C. J. McClung, 1933, and gift of Miss Anne W. Patton, 1959.

Bibliography: the collection has been described in John Walton Caughey, "Don Benito Wilson: An Average Southern Californian," *Huntington Library Quarterly,* 2 (1938–39): 285–300.

WINTER, UNA (RICHARDSON) COLLECTION
440 pieces, 1895–1954

Una R. Winter, director of the Susan B. Anthony Memorial Committee of California, collected material about woman suffrage leader Susan (Brownell) Anthony and her family (q.v.).

Subject matter: Una Winter's efforts in gathering material for the Susan B. Anthony Memorial Library Committee.

Significant persons: Mary (Ritter) BEARD (21), Carrie (Lane) Chapman CATT (9), Alma LUTZ (50).

Physical description: letters and manuscripts.

Source: acquired as a part of the Susan B. Anthony Memorial Collections, donated from 1945–56.

WOLFSKILL, LEWIS (1848–84)
1622 pieces, 1830–92; 1904–46

Lewis Wolfskill, Southern California rancher and businessman, was the son of the pioneer landowner, William Wolfskill, who had come to California from New Mexico in 1831 and married the daughter of early Californian José Ygnacio Lugo. Lewis Wolfskill married Luisa Dalton, daughter of Henry Dalton, another prominent early ranch owner in the Los Angeles area. He held extensive interests in ranching, mining, real estate, and other business ventures. In 1866 he inherited Rancho Santa Anita but sold it soon after. He conducted the affairs of Henry Dalton from 1873 to 1875 and managed the Centinela Orchard from 1873 to 1879.

Subject matter: many California ranchos; mining in California (mainly San Bernardino) from 1864 to 1881, the Centinela Orchard, and legal papers pertaining to the litigation of Henry Dalton concerning squatters' claims; also the papers of Wolfskill's son Herbert (1906–46) and of the Francisca (Wolfskill) Shepherd Estate (1904–46).

Significant persons: Henry DALTON (52), William WOLF-SKILL (20).

Physical description: letters, manuscripts, documents, and maps.

Source: gift of Frank A. Wolfskill, February, 1949, and purchased from Mrs. Robert H. Dart, January, 1959.

WOLTER, CHARLES (1792–1856)
448 pieces, 1792; 1827–1970

Charles Wolter, ship captain and pioneer California land owner, was a native of Germany, who went to sea at the age of eighteen. He sought his fortune in the coastal shipping trade off the coast of South America and settled at Lima, Peru, for two years. He extended his business to Mazatlan, Mexico, and, as master of the ship "Lenore," came to Monterey, California, in about 1833. There he married Josefa Antonia (daughter of José Mariano Estrada), the widow of Rafael Gómez, the first attorney general sent from Mexico City to California. Wolter adopted her five children, and they had five more of their own. He served as pilot for Commodore Stockton and the American forces during the Mexican War. Wolter invested in property in the city of Monterey and in Rancho Lupyomi in partnership with the artist Edward Vischer.

Subject matter: land and business matters in early Monterey, California, Rancho Los Tularcitos, and Rancho El Toro; genealogical notes on the Wolter family and memorabilia of the grandson of Charles Wolter, Harry Meiggs Wolter (1884–1940), who became a professional baseball player and Stanford University coach.

Significant persons: Edward VISCHER (9), Charles WOLTER (14).

Physical descriptions: letters (including 5 letterbooks), documents (including 2 account books), 11 scrapbooks, and photographs.

Source: gift of Mrs. Harry Meiggs Wolter, 1971 and 1976.

WOOD, CHARLES ERSKINE SCOTT (1852–1944)
Approximately 30,000 pieces, 1846–1974

C. E. S. Wood, army officer, lawyer, and author, was born in Pennsylvania and graduated from the U.S. Military Academy in 1874. He became an aide to General Oliver O. Howard in 1877, serving with him in the Pacific Northwest during the Bannock and Paiute and Nez Percé Indian wars, where he became a friend of Chief Joseph. After returning to Washington, D.C., Wood continued with General Howard at West Point and then became adjutant at the Military Academy. In 1882 and 1883 he took leave from the Academy to attend Columbia University, where he obtained his law degrees. He resigned from the army in 1884, and established a practice of maritime and corporation law in Portland, Oregon. In addition to his successful law practice, he painted, wrote, and was a champion of social justice, defending Emma Goldman, the I.W.W., and others he felt needed his help. Wood and Sara Bard Field (1882–1974), the poet and suffrage advocate, whom he later married, were active supporters of liberal causes and became the center of an artistic and literary circle in the San Francisco area. Wood wrote *The Poet in the Desert* (1915), *Heavenly Discourse* (1927) and many other books as well as articles for the *Pacific Monthly* and *Century* magazines. Sara Bard Field [Wood] is known for *The Pale Woman, Barabbas,* and her many poems published in literary magazines. After Wood died at his home in Los Gatos at the age of 92, his wife moved to Berkeley where she continued her extensive correspondence with literary figures until her death in 1974.

Subject matter: William Maxwell Wood and his part in the acquisition of California during the Mexican War; Indian campaigns (including the Nez Percé, Bannock and Paiute); Chief Joseph; the *Los Angeles Times* bombing case (1911); woman suffrage; Emma Goldman; the defense of Leon Trotsky; manuscripts of the poetry, drama and prose works of C. E. S. Wood and S. B. F. Wood including Wood's autobiography and Sara Bard Field's partial biography of Alva E. Belmont; and correspondence with other writers, critics, publishers, social reformers, artists, sculptors, theatrical figures, musicians, etc.

Significant persons: Alva Ertskin (Smith) Vanderbilt BELMONT (10), William Rose BENÉT (85), Alfred Laurens BRENNAN (53), Beniamino Benvenuto BUFANO (15), Witter BYNNER (10), Bennett Alfred CERF (26), Clarence DARROW (13), Alexander Wilson DRAKE (30), Max EASTMAN

(13), Zona GALE (5), Gilson GARDNER (11), Frederick Childe HASSAM (20), Francis Clarence Westenra Plantagenet HASTINGS, 16th Earl of Huntingdon (9), Oliver Otis HOWARD (19), Langston HUGHES (5), Robinson JEFFERS (10), Alexander MEIKLEJOHN (14), Harriet MONROE (12), Frederick O'BRIEN (15), Fremont OLDER (13), Alice PAUL (34), George Foster PEABODY (6), Louis Freeland POST (13), John Cowper POWYS (67), Alexander Phimister PROCTOR (12), William Marion REEDY (8), Corinne (Roosevelt) ROBINSON (17), William Edwin RUDGE (16), Albert Pinkham RYDER (5), Upton SINCLAIR (5), Theodore B. SPIERING (42), Joseph Lincoln STEFFENS (39), Doris STEVENS (30), Genevieve TAGGARD (15), Louis UNTERMEYER (5), Mark VAN DOREN (42), William Cornelius VAN HORNE (7), Clinton WAGNER (16), Olin Levi WARNER (14), Julian Alden WEIR (10), William Allen WHITE (5)

Physical description: letters, manuscripts, documents, diaries, sketches, photographs, and scrapbooks.

Source: gift of Mrs. Sara Bard Field Wood, family members, and friends, 1947–78.

WOOD, HENRY ELLSWORTH (1855–1932)
537 pieces, 1854–1932

Henry E. Wood, mining engineer, was born in Illinois and at the age of thirteen went with his father to Colorado with Major John Wesley Powell in 1868 on an expedition to cover the headwaters of the Colorado River preliminary to his exploration of the Grand Canyon. Wood graduated from Yale University in 1876 and went immediately to Colorado to work in the mines in Boulder County. In 1878 he opened an assay office and laboratory in Leadville, in 1889 he established the same business in Denver, and in 1898 he added the Henry E. Wood Ore Testing Works, which became internationally known.

Subject matter: reminiscences regarding mining in Colorado, and a copy of "Colorado in 1868" (taken from a notebook of his father William Cowper Wood, on the expedition to Colorado with Major John W. Powell), some business affairs.

Physical description: letters, manuscripts, documents (including 1 account book, 1873–78), and photographs.

Source: purchased from Joseph W. Jones, April, 1955.

WOODWORTH, SELIM E. (1815–71)
approximately 1600 pieces, 1834–1947

Selim E. Woodworth, Sr., United States naval officer and son of poet Samuel Woodworth, was born in New York City. In 1834, he sailed on a three-year cruise to the South Seas, and from 1838 to 1845 served in the United States Navy. He was sent across the continent in 1846 with an official message of the declaration of war with Mexico. Shortly after his arrival in San Francisco in the winter of 1847, he led the rescue of the Donner Party. Woodworth was elected to the California State Senate from Monterey in 1849, and soon after entered the commission business in San Francisco and became president of the First Vigilance Committee in 1851. Woodworth later reentered the navy (from 1862 to 1867), serving as an officer in the United States fleet on the Mississippi River during the Civil War.

Subject matter: Woodworth's service at sea (including journal kept aboard the ship "Margaret Oakley" from New York to South Pacific [1834–35], log of ship "Ohio" in the Mediterranean [1838–39], and naval orders for the Civil War period); Selim Woodworth, Jr. (including commissions, orders [1871–99], and journal of a voyage to Mexico and Peru [1878–79]); San Francisco business papers of Selim and his brother Frederick A. Woodworth; a few letters of his father, the poet Samuel Woodworth; and mining papers for the Blue Wing Quartz Mine in Calaveras County, California, (1860–64).

Physical description: letters, manuscripts, documents (including 3 volumes), and photographs.

Source: gift of Captain Selim E. Woodworth III, July, 1955.

WOOLWINE, THOMAS LEE (1874–1925)
approximately 600 pieces, 1914–22

Thomas L. Woolwine, Los Angeles attorney, was a native of Tennessee. He received law degrees from Cumberland University in Tennessee in 1903 and from George Washington University in 1904. Woolwine, who came to California in 1896, was married to Alma Foy, the daughter of Samuel C. Foy (q.v.), early Los Angeles businessman. Woolwine served in several capacities in Los Angeles city, county, and federal justice departments from 1897 to 1908. He was elected district attorney of Los Angeles for the years 1915–23.

Subject matter: mainly Thomas L. Woolwine's term as Los Angeles city attorney; Los Angeles politics and Woolwine's campaign for governor of California in 1922.

Subject matter: letters, 1 manuscript, and documents.

Source: gift of Alma Foy Woolwine Gravel, October, 1944.

WORDEN, JAMES PERRY (1866–1945)
approximately 500 pieces, 1821–1936

James Perry Worden, historian and newspaperman, was born in New York and graduated from Columbia University in 1895. He continued his studies in Europe, receiving his Ph.D. in

Germany in 1900. He was a special correspondent for the *New York Sun* and *New York Tribune,* and contributed to the *Pasadena Star News.* Worden wrote California history and book reviews and was the advisory editor for Harris Newmark's *Sixty Years in Southern California.*

Subject matter: Section 1: correspondence and documents of the Thomas Chilton (1798–1854) family of Kentucky and Alabama, and of Franklin W. Bowdon (1817–57), United States congressman from Alabama, with references to national politics; 18 letters regarding the 32nd Massachusetts Infantry Volunteers during the Civil War; and a few pieces relating to Texas. Section 2: secondary source material gathered by Worden relating to California history.

Physical description: letters, manuscripts, documents, and photographs.

Source: purchased from Mrs. James Perry Worden, June, 1948.

INDEX

Index

Bainbridge, William, 151
Bagg, John Sherman, 21
Baird, E. T., 48
Baird, Spencer Fullerton, 307
Baja California. *See* California (Baja)
Bakeless, John Edwin, 260
Baker, Ada (Nutting), 89
Baker, Frederick, 279
Baker, Obadiah Ethelbert, 22
Baker, Robert Symington, 22–23
Baker family, 357
Baldwin, Abraham, 25
Baldwin, Anita May, 23–24
Baldwin, Elias Jackson, 23
Baldwin, Frank Dwight, 24
Baldwin, Henry, 25
Baldwin, Simeon, 290
Baldwin family, 24–25
Bancroft, Frederic, 365
Bandini, Juan, 343
Bank of the United States (1816–36), 231
Banking industry: California, 5, 20, 64–65, 67–68, 135; New York, 134, 287; Virginia, 47
Banks, Nathaniel Prentiss, 112
Banning, Phineas, 25–26, 327, 394
Banning Co., 25–26
Banning (Calif.), 388
Bannock War, 397
Baptist Church: in New England, 333; Trinity Baptist Church (Los Angeles), 56
Barbary Wars. *See* Tripolitan War
Barclay, Henry Augustus, 26–27
Bard, Thomas Robert, 27, 114, 223, 327
Barker, Jacob, 28
Barnard, Frederick Augustus Peter, 307
Barnett, T. J., 30
Bargrave, John, 28
Barker, Jacob, 28
Barlow, Joel, 25
Barlow, Samuel Latham Mitchell, 20, 28–31
Barney, Hiram, 31–32

Barrington, William Wildman, 2nd Viscount Barrington, 217
Barron, James, 386
Barron, Samuel, 103
Barry, John Stewart, 21
Bartlett, Julia S., 32
Bartman, George, 217
Barton, Clara Harlowe, 32–33
Barton family, 33
Baseball, 396
Bates, Edward, 207
Bates, Henry Moore, 127
Bates, James Allen, 48
Bauer, John Leopold Jurgens, 272
Bayard, James Asheton, 30
Beale, Edward Fitzgerald, 23, 394
Beale, James, 266
Beard, Charles Austin, 252, 365
Beard, Mary (Ritter), 320, 394
Beattie, George William, 33
Beattie, Helen (Pruitt), 33–34
Beauregard, Charles, 377
Beauregard, Pierre Gustave Toutant, 69, 181, 221
Bechdolt, Frederick Ritchie, 211
Becker, Carl Lotus, 365
Bedford, 4th Duke of. *See* Russell, John
Beeson, John, 51
Behymer, Lynden Ellsworth, 34
Belcher, Jonathan, 217
Belgium, 94
Bell, Horace, 34–35, 60
Bell, James Alvin, 35
Bellomont, Earl of. *See* Coote, Richard
Belmont, Alva E. S. V., 397
Belmont, August, 30
Benedict, Russell, 36
Benét, William Rose, 397
Benjamin, Judah P., 30, 181, 221
Berkeley, Sir William, 40
Berry, Daniel Marsh, 107–08
Beverly (Mass.), 268
Bidamon, Emma (Hale) Smith, 36–37
Bidamon, Lewis Crum, 36–37
Bidwell, John, 130

Index

Brown, James, 47
Brown, John, 106, 315–16
Brown, Olympia, 75
Brown, William, 48
Brown, William A., 52
Brown family, 47
Browne, William Montague, 30
Bruff, Joseph Goldsborough, 52–53
Brundage, Avery, 265
Brunswick Consolidated Gold Mining Co., 367
Bryant, William Cullen, 31
Brydges, James, 1st Duke of Chandos, 350
Bucareli y Ursúa, Antonio María, 125
Buck, Americus D., 321
Buck family, 320
Buckner, Aylett Hartswell, 54
Buckner, Simon Bolivar, 53–54
Bufano, Beniamino Benvenuto, 397
Bull, Joseph, 136
Bullock, Rufus Brown, 54–55
Burdette, Clara (Bradley), 55–56
Burdette, Robert Jones, 56
Burgess, Frank Gelett, 380
Burnett, Wellington Cleveland, 57
Burnett family, 57
Burr, Aaron, 57, 58
Burriel, Andrés Marcos, 58
Bursum, Holm Olaf, 111
Burton, Lewis T., 343
Burton, Ralph, 217
Business. See banking industry, cattle industry, citrus industry, commerce and manufacturing, construction industry, insurance industry, lumber industry, mining industry, motion picture industry, ostrich industry, petroleum industry, railroads, real estate (by place), shipping industry, steel industry, whaling industry, wine industry, wool industry. See also specific states; United States: business in

Business Women's Legislative Council of California, 59
Butler, Benjamin Franklin, 30, 69
Butler, Pierce Mason, 9
Butler, William Allen, 31
Butterfield, Daniel, 164, 266
Butterfield, Lyman Henry, 4
Butterfield Overland Mail Co. See Overland Mail Co.
Bynner, Witter, 397
Byrd, William, 49

Cabell family, 47
Cable railways: in San Francisco, 355; Los Angeles Cable Railway Co., 84, 214
Cactus, 313–14, 387
Calcraft, John, 217
California: See also specific cities and counties; Voyages to the Pacific Coast
—Afro-Americans in, 172, 253
—agriculture in, 64, 131, 159, 185, 229–30, 330, 386
—arts, crafts, and costumes of, 172
—banking industry, 5, 20, 65, 67–68, 135
—Bear Flag Revolt, 120
—botany, 64, 212, 275, 313–14, 387
—business opportunities for women in, 59, 122
—cattle industry in, 82, 88, 319, 342
—citrus industry in, 18–19, 20, 84, 98, 283, 327, 337, 383
—commerce and manufacturing in, 25–26, 51–52, 93, 122, 203, 299, 342
—gold rush, 16, 38, 51, 52, 52–53, 60, 70, 89, 90, 93, 102, 105, 126, 132, 177–78, 185, 193, 222, 232, 237, 241, 247, 253, 264, 297, 347–48, 348–49, 351
—higher education, 64
—history, writing of: (1542–1822) 73, 125; (1823–47) 73,

Index

419

and Western, 29; Northern Pacific, 353; Northern Railway, 302; Ohio and Mississippi, 20, 29; Oregon Central, 80; Pacific Railway Co., 84; Pennsylvania Railway, 190; Placerville and Sacramento, 38; Southern Pacific, 230, 302; Texas, Topolobampo & Pacific Railway and Telegraph Company, 277; Union Pacific, 190; Virginia and Truckee, 259; Western Pacific, 159, 302

Randall, Henry Stephens, 163, 303
Randall, Samuel Jackson, 389
Randolph, Edmund, 192
Randolph, Edward, 40
Randolph family, 47
Rawdon, John, 1st Earl of Moira, 155
Rawdon-Hastings, Francis, 1st Marquis of Hastings, 155–56
Ray, Charles Henry, 303–04
Raymond, Rossiter Worthington, 144
Raymond Hotel (Pasadena, Calif.), 20
Read, Conyers, 92
Real estate. *See names of specific cities and states*
Redfield, Isaac Fletcher, 100
Redfield, Leonard G., 304–05
Reedy, William Marion, 398
Reeve, Sidney B., 336
Reid, Perfecto Hugo, 343
Reform movements. *See* capital punishment, conservation of natural resources, peace movement, temperance movement, Townsend Plan, utopian colonies, and women
Reinhardt, Aurelia (Henry), 56
Religion: 134, 186, 270, 376, 379. *See also* Andover Theological Seminary; Baptist; Christian Science; Civil War Chaplains; Congregational; Episcopal; Freemasonry; Judaism; Methodist;

Methodist Episcopal; Missions and Missionaries; Moravian; Mormon; Presbyterian; Unitarian
Remington, Frederic, 178
Reorganized Church of Jesus Christ of Latter Day Saints. *See* Mormons and Mormonism
Republican Party: in California, 56, 347, 385; Convention of 1860, 99; Georgia, 55; Illinois, 304; Kansas, 162; New York (state), 195
Requa, Isaac Lawrence, 305–06
Requa, Mark Lawrence, 306
Revere, Joseph Warren, 121
Revilla Gigedo, Conde de. *See* Güemes Pacheco, Juan Vicente de
Reynolds, John, 218
Reynolds, John Fulton, 164
Reynolds, Thomas Caute, 106
Rhees, William Jones, 306–08
Rhodes, Eugene Manlove, 85, 199
Rhodes, May Louise (Davison) Purple, 85, 191, 199
Rice, Alexander Hamilton, 389
Richardson, Augustus G., 5, 309
Richardson, Israel Bush, 70
Richardson, William H., 48
Richmond (Va.), 49
Riddle, Albert Galatin, 174
Riesenberg, Felix (1879–1939), 309–10
Riesenberg, Felix (1913–65), 310
Rigaud, Pierre, Marquis de Vaudreuil-Cavagnal, 219–20
Riley, James Whitcomb, 56
Rio de Janeiro (Brazil), 184
Ripley, Roswell Sabine, 70, 221
Rising Sun and Los Angeles Vineyards, 188
Ritch, William Gillet, 310–11
Riverside (Calif.), 268, 387
Roads in California, 222
Robbins, Caroline, 92
Robertson, James, 218

433